Banking 4.0

Mohan Bhatia

Banking 4.0

The Industrialised Bank of Tomorrow

🐎 Springer

Mohan Bhatia
Wipro Ltd.
Mumbai, Maharashtra, India

ISBN 978-981-16-6071-9   ISBN 978-981-16-6069-6   (eBook)
https://doi.org/10.1007/978-981-16-6069-6

This Springer imprint is published by the registered company Springer Nature Singapore Pte Ltd.
The registered company address is: 152 Beach Road, #21-01/04 Gateway East, Singapore 189721, Singapore

Foreword by Sashidhar Jagdishan

I am delighted to write this foreword, not only because Mohan Bhatia has been a friend and an occasional sounding board for me on banking processes and technology, but also because I believe that it is time for banks to reimagine financial services keeping the customer at the centre and leveraging technologies of today. Technology is no longer an enabler but a differentiator!

How do we make banking more *intuitive* and *contextual*? How do we provide access to financial services to every citizen in the country especially in semi-urban and rural areas at a sustainable price point? How do we make banking *easy, safe*, and *secure* leveraging the technologies of cloud, AI/ML, data science, blockchain, open source, etc. How do large, successful, and long-standing banks with legacy systems modernise safely and with agility? How do they move from legacy monolith architecture to loosely coupled cloud-native systems with microservices? How do we build resilient banking systems that are always available and ever changing? How do we push the envelope of innovation and yet be compliant to the regulatory framework? How do we leverage applications, APIs, and analytics to build a sustainable bank that can compete with Fintech and Bigtech?

Those who can do this better and faster will be the leaders of tomorrow.

Mohan shares his view on building a bank of tomorrow based on his rich experience of regulatory frameworks (ex-RBI) and technology (ex-Infosys, Oracle, and Wipro). He has also been a practitioner as the Technology Risk Officer of Shinsei Bank, Japan, thereby making his approach lot more acceptable to the community of technology and digital practitioners. This will be a good read for people who are preparing to align their organisation competencies for the world of tomorrow.

I wish him and the readers the very best!

Sashidhar Jagdishan
CEO, HDFC Bank
Mumbai, India

Foreword by Hans Tesselaar

The financial services industry (FSI) is undergoing major changes. Not only in the so-called open banking spaces but, even more inside the bank.

For decades financial service companies primarily focused on automation, new systems, and new channels to serve their customers better.

To deal with the increased competition from challenger banks and Fintechs, banks are being forced to move from automation to industrialisation. This industrialisation will not only lead to cost reduction but even more to higher quality and an increased speed in services.

When this industrialisation is done well, using standard building blocks and aligning industry standards, it will also make organisations extremely agile and adaptable to new customer needs.

This book will provide you with an insight into all the factors that lead to this change, the path towards industrialisation, as well as how to gain the benefits in a limited period of time.

I wish you much pleasure reading this book and I'm also convinced it will open your eyes in discovering unknown opportunities.

Hans Tesselaar
Executive Director
Banking Industry Architecture Network (BIAN)
Frankfurt am Main, Germany

Preface

During the past decade, I was fortunate enough to encounter several opportunities to implement technology solutions for business use cases at financial services firms of varying size and type, across geographical and regulatory regimes. The most important lesson learnt from all these engagements is that financial services firms are experiencing diminishing returns from several of their technology initiatives.

The question is why are technology initiatives increasingly face diminishing returns? It is a well-known fact that returns are a function of cost and revenue.

On the cost side, the reason for diminished returns is the accumulated technical debt that must be cleared off to generate returns. The quantum of technical debt varies substantially across underlying technologies. The rate of accumulation of technical debt and its quantum benchmarks may provide an indicative measure to better manage the impact on cost.

The most difficult part is managing the revenue. Business and revenue models in the financial services industry are undergoing a tectonic shift and technology development will further accelerate this shift. The foundational shift being experienced by the banks is so profound that the existing technology and its practices are inadequate to cope.

Since 2015, most banks have failed to realise the promised and planned returns from investments in transformation initiatives such as robotic process automation (RPA), infrastructure as a service to migrate hardware to the cloud and data visualisation, migration, and quality to enhance decision-making, front office digitisation through mobile and omnichannel platforms, and back office digitisation through workflow automation and case management.

The primary reason for the banking industry's inability to generate the promised returns is attributed to their approach, whereby banks have used technology as an automation tool rather than a tool to deliver a new business model. The banking business may not have completely shifted to the marketplace as not all customers are using smart devices and applications to conduct their banking transactions. However, a shift in that direction is imminent. This means it is imperative for banks to enhance technology and processes to engage machines and applications in a standardised, consistent, re-usable, agile, resilient, self-corrective, and self-sustainable manner and, in real time, service a very high volume of complex business. This enhanced and new way of working is called industrialisation.

Transformation or industrialisation of a fully functional bank is like replacing an aircraft engine mid-air, especially since the new business and revenue model is evolving and changing direction with every new development and adoption of technology. This makes industrialisation a long and iterative process. To make transformation sustainable, leading banks have developed the best practices for industrialisation.

To understand the industrialisation practices developed over the past six years I have studied and analysed more than 50 banks, financial services technology product companies, system integrators, strategy consulting firms, and financial services regulators through:

1. Secondary research: extensive study of annual reports, analysts' reports, accolades and industry recognition, published interviews and presentations, patents filed, products and offerings.
2. Primary research: interviews and discussions with key decision-makers; CEOs, CTO, C-level executives at BFSI firms, regulators, technology firms, big tech, and SI firms.
3. Hands-on experience delivering transformation projects in: cognitive technologies, machine learning, analytics and visualisation, API and marketplace, and cloud adoption.

This book is about helping banks to leverage best practices in the industry to build a structured and coordinated approach for industrialisation of banking processes. The book provides a roadmap and template to industrialise financial services firms over iterative cycles.

Calibrated and Coordinated Delivery of the Digital Experience

To achieve the planned business and revenue outcomes at optimum costs, digital experience transformation must be calibrated and coordinated across front and back office, and scaled and timed against external innovation benchmarks and Fintechs. For sustenance, data industrialisation must be ingrained, banking AI embedded, and data and banking AI engines harmonised on an iterative basis with digital experience delivery engines.

Spread over several chapters, the book provides a calibration and coordination framework for the delivery of digital experience.

Scaling and Timing of the Technology Design and Business Model Benchmarked to External Innovation

The bank needs to continuously benchmark technology design and business models with innovation benchmarks created by the competition, bigtech, Fintech and the marketplace. The bank needs to create BAU processes with the requisite urgency to scale the technology and business model on time to remain ahead of the innovation curve.

This book provides an approach to build innovation in a BAU mode.

Developing and Embedding Banking AI

Banking AI is still in the nascent stage and learning is captured manually by experts. Every bank must create a corpus and develop learning algorithms to establish banking AI. The maturation of banking AI is the foundation from which to spread the digital experience, hyper-personalisation, and machine interface and self-service. Banking AI maturity is an iterative process aided by mature data. All processes need to be aligned over a long period for its development. This book provides a BIAN framework-based roadmap to build banking AI leveraging cloud AI platforms.

Industrialise Data

Industrialise data to process a huge volume of data in real time, including unstructured human communication data. Industrialisation of data pipes, storage and processing, analytics, and data visualisation, along with adoption of machine learning is a long and iterative process. It requires continuous alignment of engines to deliver redefined business and technology architecture, people skills and technology implementation or, in other words, the entire target-operating model of the bank. This book provides a roadmap of continuous alignment of data industrialisation engines at banks.

Capital Allocation as a Measure to Align the Entire Bank on Industrialisation Initiatives

Calibration, coordination, harmonisation, and investing for a leadership position in the revenue and business model requires long-term investments to be ahead of the curve technology design. It is very difficult to align initiatives and priorities unless all decision-making criteria are denominated in a single measure. Capital allocation is the most important decision-making measure at banks. A capital allocation denominated planning and assessment framework brings consistency to the alignment of technology design and initiatives across business units and time. The book provides an approach to extend the strategy risk evaluation framework to industrialisation initiatives.

Banking 4.0 practices aim to build, continuously align, and sustain engines of industrialisation and innovation to deliver business and revenue outcomes. The aim is to deliver innovation in the BAU mode and allocate the capital to keep the engines running. Here, engines of industrialisation and innovation along with an approach to build a business case to invest in alignment and sustenance are identified.

It is my fervent hope that this book will provide a refreshing approach from which to view emerging banking business models. Let me know your feedback: bhatia1000@yahoo.com

Mumbai, India   Mohan Bhatia

Acknowledgements

While I was working on this book for the past six years, I received lot of encouragement, support, guidance, and feedback from my colleagues, clients, partners, friends, senior professionals, and mentors, in the field of banking and information technology, and I would like to place on record my sincere gratitude and appreciation towards each one of them.

I am thankful to Sashi Jagdishan, the CEO of HDFC Bank, for writing a Foreword for the book. I also had an opportunity of exchanging ideas in this book with him, and our discussions helped me in getting more clarity on how the entire bank, the CEO, and the Board needs to be aligned towards the industrialisation initiative and creation of the business case.

Being a member of the Certification Working Group at BIAN, I had an opportunity to understand the BIAN framework closely. I could sense that this is the framework to reduce application and data duplicity. BIAN provides templates to develop banking AI services. My special thanks to Hans Tesselaar, the ED of BIAN, for listening to my hypothesis and asking very logical and pointed questions and writing a Foreword for the book on behalf of BIAN. Thanks are also to him for organising a review of two chapters by BIAN architects and providing constructive feedback.

I am thankful to my batch-mate and Executive Director, Reserve Bank of India, Jayant Dash for providing insights on fintech regulation across the regimes.

I also had an opportunity of a very long discussion and debate with Arundhati Bhattacharya, the ex-CEO of the State Bank of India and then Independent Director of Wipro Ltd., on how non-retail banks will industrialise and the possible impact industrialisation will have on corporate and investment banking structures. We agreed that industrialisation will converge and consolidate business units within industrialised banks. Probably banks will be reorganised on the lines of platforms and marketplaces and not on the lines of customer types as is the case at present. The division between the business units will start fading as banks deal with third-party products and services. Ultimately, banks that do not industrialise, need to white label the products, services, and technology platforms of industrialised banks.

My thanks are also due to my guru and mentor G. Gopalakrishna, ex-Executive Director RBI, and ex-Director CAFRAL, for providing insights into regulatory aspects of digitisation, information security, and fraud prevention across the regimes.

I come from the risk, finance, and compliance function. So, it was but natural to create forward-looking frameworks in these areas. I call it RFC 3.0. It is necessary to deliver Bank 4.0—the industrialised bank of the future, a bank that needs to industrialise the RFC function. I had an opportunity of presenting my forward-looking framework for risk, finance, and compliance to several CXOs globally. Let me thank a few of them, with whom I had hours of discussion.

- Anthony Gill, Head of Credit Risk IT at Credit Suisse, who gave input on the Credit Risk Management 3.0 Framework and tremendous insight into building early warning signals for credit risk.
- Simon Barkla, Vice President, Head of Risk and Finance Technology Solutions at TD Bank, for his input on Finance 3.0 and his insight into the impact of building accounting as a service at a bank.
- Scott Mescall, Senior Director Data Engineering Data Science, at Capital One, for his insights into the ORM 3.0 framework and managing operational risk on a real-time basis.
- Jason Wynne, Head of Risk Technology ANZ Bank, on Conduct Risk 3.0, incorporating the recommendations of the Royal Commission in the Misconduct in Banking, Superannuation and Financial Services Industry and the KPI to be measured and monitored as a part of sales and performance analytics to manage the conduct risk in a forward-looking mode.
- Kay Labare, SVP, and Financial Crimes Management Head, US Bank for her input on the future of fraud risk management and building the real-time fraud detection engines with multiple scenarios relevant for real-time fraud detection and managing all financial crimes cases through a single case manager.
- Several CXOs, at JP Morgan, Citi Bank, and HSBC, for their input on the implementation of RPA in the Customer Onboarding, KYC Risk Rating and Ultimate Beneficial Owner, and AML 3.0 Framework.
- Mrutyunjay Mahapatra, the Chief Digital Officer of SBI, who was involved with building a digital native SBI YONO platform.

Several people don't appear by name in this book but their ideas were critical in shaping its content. I am thankful to each of them. I had an opportunity to engage with several architects at AWS, Google, Azure, Oracle, IBM, Salesforce, and SAS on Cloud, AI/ML platforms, and visualisation products and capabilities.

Being a Fellow, Distinguished Member of Technical Staff, I had an opportunity to participate and build the AI/ML platform HOLMES and had an opportunity to work closely with CTO, K. R. Sanjiv and BFSI Global Consulting Head Santhosh G. Nair. I am thankful to both for all their guidance and insight.

I had an opportunity of discussing a technology strategy for industrialisation and received insight into different strategies being pursued by banks globally from BFSI America CEO, Angan Guha, BFSI Consulting Head Harpreet Arora, and Keyur

Maniar, Country Head India. Thanks to all of them for sharing their knowledge and insight.

Last but not the least, I would like to thank my colleagues Sunil Pai and Pradeep Godbole, who worked as a sounding board for me. Both listened to my logical and illogical hypothesis patiently, helped me straighten my thinking by asking very logical and pointed questions. Both have patiently reviewed every chapter of the book, multiple times, and have provided amazingly detailed and insightful commentary and annotations. Without them, this book would not have been possible.

I need to thank both Sunil Bhatia and Chandni Bhatia, who are Data Scientists, Digital Technicians, and AI Architects, who provided a forward-looking and fresh view on AI/ML, digitisation, and implementing conversational banking at a scale.

For the last two years, I had a great time debating and discussing with experts all the ideas that went in to this book. Needless to say, I learnt a lot about the industrialisation at banks from hundreds of interactions I had with experts from the financial services industry and technology industry. For all the insights provided in the book, each one has contributed. For any or all the shortcomings of the book, only I am responsible.

I owe special thanks to the editorial team lead by Ralf Gerstner for their guidance and hard work in completing the book.

Contents

Chapter 1
Industrialise and Innovate to Deliver Banking 4.0 Services

1.1 Introduction: Evolution of Banking

Technology has been the prime mover and enabler of banking business model evolution for the past four decades. Banks are replacing, upgrading, automating, and industrialising their information technology to build a profitable, systemic risk resilient, and cyber-secure business franchise. The banking business model has evolved with the development of technology.

1.1.1 Banking 1.0: System of Record on Mainframe-Enabled Business Model

Banks in North America, Australia, Japan, Europe, and some parts of Asia started adopting information technology and automation some four decades ago, starting with the implementation of mainframe as a system of record for transactions. The banking business model enabled by a system of record on mainframe can be referred to as Banking 1.0.

1.1.2 Banking 2.0: System of Record on 4GL Technology-Enabled Business Model

The development of interoperable open systems in the 1990s led banks across the globe including Asia, Africa, and the Middle East to implement their system of records on 4GL technologies included Core Banking Solution (CBS), Product Processor (PP), Loan Management System (LMS), Treasury Management System (TMS), and Accounting.

© Springer Nature Singapore Pte Ltd. 2022
M. Bhatia, *Banking 4.0*,
https://doi.org/10.1007/978-981-16-6069-6_1

| 1980-2000 System of Record on Mainframe | 1995-2005 Treasury Management System | 1996-2005 Core Banking, Product Processor and Accounting | 1998-2010 Loan Management System |

| Bank 1.0 - era of a system of record on Mainframe | Bank 2.0 - era of a system of record on 4GL Programming Language |

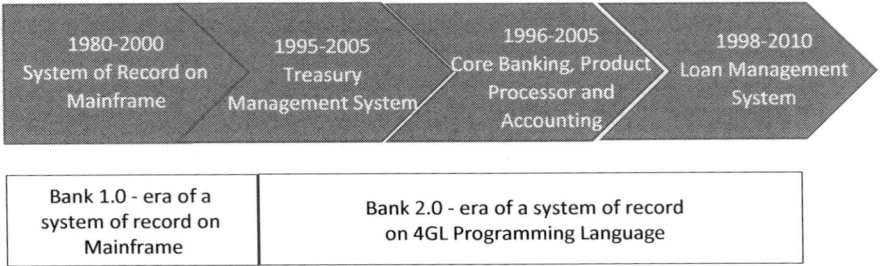

The banking business model enabled by a system of record on fourth-generation language (4GL) technology can be referred to as Banking 2.0.

1.1.3   Banking 3.0: Self-Service for Payments-Enabled Business Model

The advent of the Internet and mobile technologies and the rapid adoption of these technologies led to industry-wide electronification of payments. Banks expanded and strengthened self-service payments and transactions.

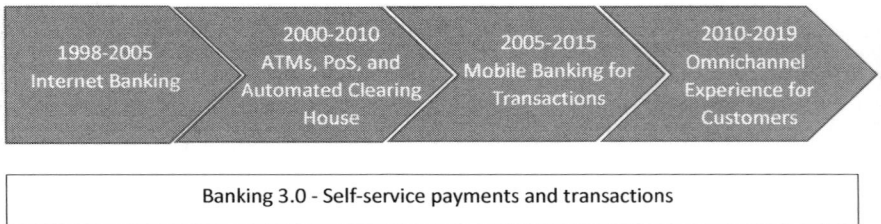

| 1998-2005 Internet Banking | 2000-2010 ATMs, PoS, and Automated Clearing House | 2005-2015 Mobile Banking for Transactions | 2010-2019 Omnichannel Experience for Customers |

| Banking 3.0 - Self-service payments and transactions |

The implementation of internet banking started in 1998 in several countries and was ubiquitous by 2005. ATMs, PoS, and ACH electronic payments started in the early 2000s and are now a global norm. Whilst electronic payments started with batch mode, as of 2020 more than 90% of payment transactions worldwide are now executed in real time. More than 60% of payment transactions are on omnichannel. To top it all, mobile banking started in 2005 and within a decade most banks with $ 5 Bn+ in assets were offering mobile banking services.

This variety in channels raised the demands for a uniform experience across channels and from 2008 onwards most banks had a roadmap for implementing omnichannel self-service.

The banking business model enabled by the provision of a consistent customer experience across the channels for self-serviced payments on omnichannel is known as Banking 3.0.

1.1.3.1 Banking 3.0 Manages the Low Complexity, High Volume Processes in the Bank

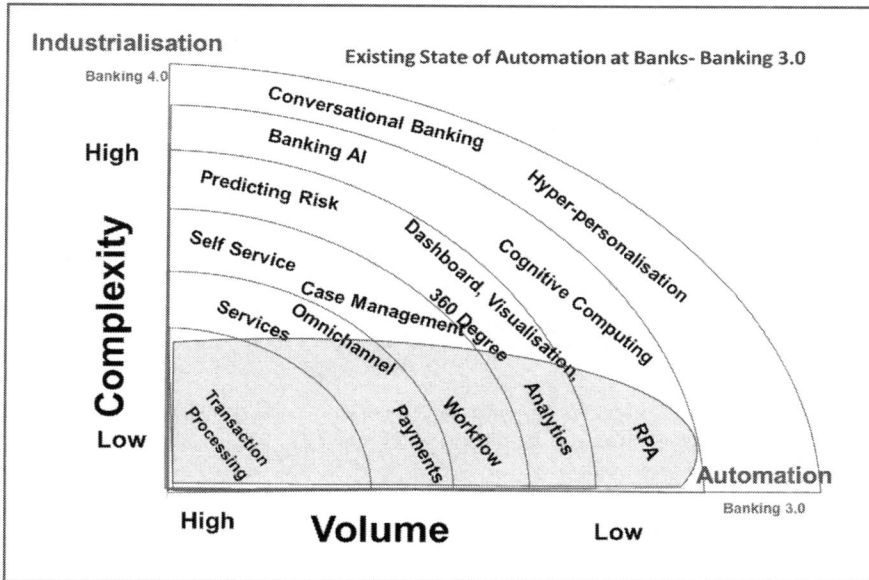

The third-generation systems, further automated the medium volume process, leaving behind the low volume manual tasks of capturing data into the system by reading documents, screens, mails, and emails.

1.2 Major Shortcomings of Banking 3.0

Ever since banks started implementing channels, technology investments have been concentrated in front office systems. This has helped banks to move forward and keep up with smart devices and real-time payment assent amongst customers.

1.2.1 Third-Generation Banks Invested in Self-service Rather Than Delivering Digital Experience

The focus of third-generation banks on the faster time to market and costs optimisation led most banks to implement self-service tactically. Many firms added channels 'without' digitising them or making channels flexible, configurable, and straight through. At many banks, the payment system integration is point to point, manual, or at best semi-automated.

1.2.2   Third-generation Banks Are Under-invested in the Back Office and Mid Office

Third-generation banks operate with processes that require manual interventions, reconciliation, and significant maintenance. Consequently, banks struggle to add newer services to the customer engagement portfolio.

1.2.3   Third-generation Banks Are All-pervasive With Data and Application Duplication

Over the past two decades, third-generation banks invested in monolithic front and back office applications for:

1. Credit underwriting and approvals
2. Customer management system
3. Private banking
4. ATM, Internet banking, mobile banking, omnichannel
5. Integration with payment networks
6. Corporate, commercial, trade finance, and factoring
7. Risk, finance, performance management, and reporting
8. Trading and broker
9. Cash management and trade finance.

Due to being monolithic and technology limitations, each application is built on a standalone basis, which has resulted in more than 90% duplication in data definition, more than 80% in data, and more than 50% redundancy in applications.

1.2.3.1   Inability to Capitalise on Emerging Business Opportunities

Due to limitations in their existing technological capabilities, third-generation banks are unable to upgrade their business model swiftly to capitalise on any new business opportunities.

- **Servicing and engaging digital natives:** In emerging countries, 65% of the population is below 35 years of age and 50% of the population is below 19 years of age. The younger generation are technology savvy, digital natives who use personal smart devices for commercial and financial transactions. To engage and deliver services to digital natives, banks need to deliver a digital experience in front office operations and industrialise back office.

- **Real-time back office and mid office**: In the past five years or so, Europe and the US have established real-time payment networks. With faster payment and real-time payments in Europe and the US, more than 90% of the transactions and payments in the front office are being delivered in real-time globally. To support the front office, the bank needs to industrialise back office assembly line processes to deliver in real time the internal and external integration with payment systems, clearing and settlement processes, channels, accounting, and reporting systems, risk measurement, financial crimes management, and regulatory reporting.
- **Delivering marketplace banking:** Marketplaces are evolving with newer structures and redefining the business model. In a marketplace, banks are trusted institutions providing fund transfers and transaction funding, and establish banking platforms that are capable of embedding banking services within the marketplace value chain. Participation in the marketplace is a substantial value-generating opportunity for banks with a compound business model in terms of participation, ownership, and management.
- **Delivering a Fintech business model:** Fintechs have become benchmarks in delivering a digital experience and innovative financial products and services, industrialising processes for better, faster and cheaper, and real-time service delivery. Following is an illustrative list of products and services where the market share of Fintechs is growing:

  - Retail payments
  - Money transfer services
  - Digital lending
  - ID services
  - Digital KYC
  - Financial advisory services
  - Wealth management services
  - Services to SME customers
  - Conversation banking
  - Blockchain, smart contract
  - Trade Financing
  - Financial inclusion
  - Cyber security analytics.

1.2.4   Inability to Create a Business Case for Technology Investment

Inability to create a business case for technology investment needs to address the shortcomings.

To capitalise on the existing business opportunities, banks have invested in industrialisation. Banks need to address the shortcomings of third-generation banking technology as migrating a third-generation bank to the fourth generation is a generational shift.

The existing project-based funding structures cannot create and deliver a generational shift business case. A generational shift needs very large investment in technology without the immediate linking of business benefits in the short term. This investment is termed a 'Technical Debt'.

Existing banks are operating under revenue and margin pressures and finding it extremely difficult to pay the technology debt due to the current low interest rate regimes, the globally constrained business environment, and a relentless onslaught on the banking business model from neo-banks.

1.3   Banking 4.0: Services Delivered by Tomorrow's Industrialised Bank

1.3.1   The Banking 4.0 Vision Statement

Banking 4.0 industrialises the banking process to deliver agile, scalable, and resilient business outcomes. It delivers a digital experience to customers, partners, and employees by industrialising its front and back offices which are then integrated.

To process a very high volume of structured and unstructured data in real-time, the industrialised bank industrialises the data platform. The industrialised data platform leveraging cloud technologies delivers a very high level of agility, scalability, and resiliency.

- Integrated model development, training, and deployment
- Industrialised data platform AI as a service
- Integration with industry utilities, and subscribed and public data
- Loosely coupled intelligent integration with internal data sources.

Banking 4.0 industrialises Financial Crimes Management Process 3.0 to deliver real-time financial crimes management in the emerging business models and this includes.

- Financial crime risk model development, training, and deployment on a low-latency Compliance data infrastructure.
- Risk-based financial crime model building public and shared data for cyber, AML, and fraud.
- Omnichannel cyber resilience.
- Omnichannel financial crime intelligence.

Banking 4.0 embeds the industrialised Risk Management 3.0 to process for real-time risk measurement and management in the front office.

- Integrated compliance and finance—model development, training, and deployment
- Risk measurement APIs
- Integrated fraud detection
- Engaging customers in collection and complaints and fraud investigation
- Risk as a service integrated with front office.

Banking 4.0 aims to deliver the bank as a provider, distributor, and enabler of financial and non- financial services.

Banking 4.0 industrialises banks by building APIs as an integration framework to integrate applications and data and deliver both API banking and marketplace banking. The industrialised bank has the following capabilities:

- Cognitive reading of documents and data sources
- Machine learning and enterprise decision engines
- Intelligent Finance 3.0
- Intelligent Regulatory Reporting 3.0
- Marketplace and industry platforms
- Digital IDs
- Hyper-personalisation
- Digital customer
- Onboarding
- Conversational banking
- API banking
- Stronger and contactless authentication.

To embed it into every customer journey, the industrialised bank delivers banking as a service to customers, partners, and the marketplace. Industrialised banks build platforms to provide risk, compliance, regulatory reporting, and financial management as services for regulators and the management of the bank. The industrialised bank leverages AI platform to deliver banking AI as a service. This also helps in delivering conversational banking.

Deliver Banking 4.0 – Digital Experience in Front Office and Back Office				
Deliver Digital Experience in Back Office	Industrialised Back Office	Banking 4.0	Industrialised Front Office	Deliver Digital Experience in Front Office
Cognitive reading of documents and data sources Machine Learning and Enterprise Decision Engines	Intelligent Finance 3.0 Intelligent Regulatory Reporting 3.0	Provider, Distributor and of Financial and Non- Financial Services- API Banking and Marketplace Banking	Marketplace and Industry Platforms Digital IDs	Hyper-personalisation Digital Customer Onboarding Conversational Banking API banking Stronger and Contactless Authentication
Integrated risk, compliance and finance- Model development, training and deployment	Risk Measurement APIs	Industrialised Risk Management – Risk 3.0	Integrated Fraud Detection. Engaging customers in collection and complaints and fraud investigation. Risk Measurement Embedded in Front Office	Risk as a Service integrated with Front Office
Financial crime risk model development, training and deployment Low-latency Compliance Data Infrastructure	Risk Based Financial Crime Model Building Public and Shared Data for Cyber, AML and Fraud	Industrialised Financial Crimes Management (FCM 3.0)	Omnichannel cyber resilience	Omnichannel Financial Crime Intelligence
Integrated model development, training and deployment	Industrialised Data Platform AI as a Service	Industrialised Data	Integration with industry utilities, subscribed and public data	Loosely coupled intelligent integration with internal data sources

Deliver Banking 4.0 by integrating industrialised Front Office with Industrialised Back Office

The industrialised bank builds an intelligent machine interface to provide self-service to customers and partners, and straight-through processing for employees. The industrialised bank is embedded in every customer journey, delivers personalised service to individuals, machines, devices, and applications. The industrialised bank's technologies are intelligent to engage and deliver services to machines and devices. Industrialised banks deliver conversational banking at a scale and the intelligence level of a bank's machine is not very different from humans.

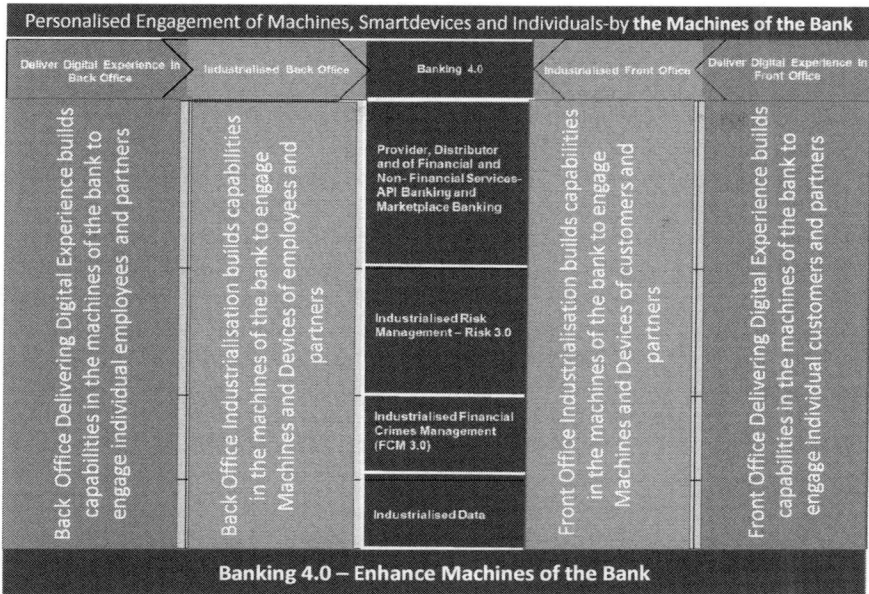

The industrialised bank with enhanced and intelligent machines manages external changes better by adopting innovation in a BAU mode.

1.3.2 The Industrialised Bank of Tomorrow

1.3.2.1 Banking 4.0 Is Not a Hyper-automated Banking 3.0

Third-generation banks have hardly left any area without automation. Banks have been implementing automation at a process, sub-process, and task level to tactically manage and extract value out of legacy technology.

Automation is the application of technology that allows employees in a company to configure computer software or a 'robot' to interpret and process a transaction, transform data, trigger a response to business events or communicate with other digital systems.

Eventually, banks experience diminishing returns on automation due to the prevalence of huge technical debt and lack of banking intelligence in the technology. This makes automation non-sustainable.

1.3.2.2   Industrialisation Is Not More Automation

Until banks are industrialised, automation is a short-term tactical approach to automate manual tasks, implement point solutions, and desktop solutions. Automation is a stopgap arrangement to deliver straight-through processing at a task level. Banks are leveraging RPAs as a non-invasive means to integrate systems and processes by automating tasks.

The purpose of industrialisation is to build banking intelligence into technology. It is based on standardisation, consistency, re-use, agility, resiliency, self-correction and self-sustenance, real-time, and high volume. Industrialisation is enhancing the capabilities and capacity of the bank's machines to engage machines, smart devices, and human beings in a personalised way, thus making machines intelligent. by enabling them to deliver highly complex and unstructured processes.

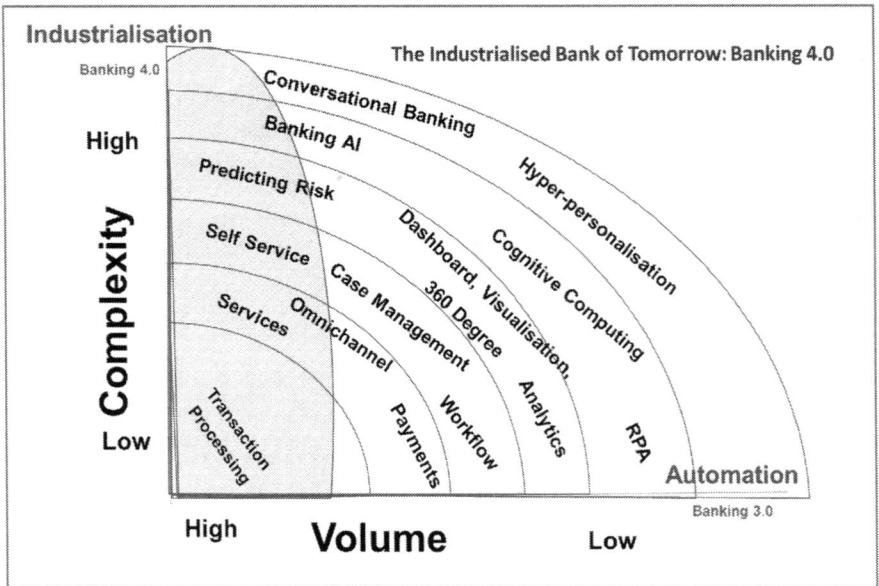

1.3.2.3   Industrialisation Is the Capability of the Bank's Machines to Manage the High Volume of Extremely Complex Processes

Machines at industrialised banks manage highly complex and high volume processes and this includes engaging individuals on human communication channels as well as engaging both individuals and machines using banking AI. Industrialisation thus means capabilities of machines to manage complex tasks.

Industrialisation is delivered through a self-service facility where risks are managed by machines through a predictive risk shield that is embedded in every banking process. Unstructured data like text, document and voice, and video are managed by machines and individuals are engaged by machines on human communication channels of chat and voice communications. The industrialised bank delivers a digital experience to customers, partners, and employees through hyper-personalisation engines.

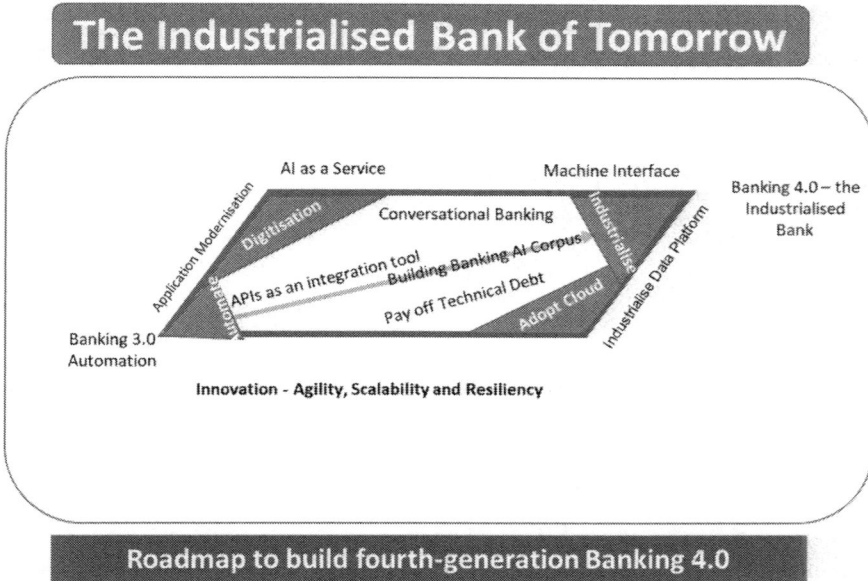

1.3.3 Delivering Digital Experience to Customers, Partners, and Employees

Delivering digital experience transforms the bank from front to back. This makes it nimble and reduces latency in the data flow across the bank, bringing services to market in less time. The basic principle underlying the digital experience is to provide the customer with a very similar experience whether are using a paper document or electronic data.

1.3.3.1 Banking AI As a Service

Building banking AI is a long journey. The bank needs to consistently invest for many years to build a banking AI corpus and algorithms to deliver the Banking 4.0 vision.

The three most important areas where banking AI can make a major impact are:

- Conversational banking at scale
- Personalisation at scale
- Industrialisation of document management.

The bank may plan the development of banking AI according to its contribution to the Banking 4.0 vision.

1.3.3.2 Paying Off Technical Debt

Technical debt is the additional costs or expenses or the investment the bank has to incur to attain the freedom to innovate their business model to its full potential. When the bank is managing the future through technology projects and not via the Banking 4.0 vision, technical debt is either managed in a sub-optimal way or not at all. The debt is created when the scope of the project is curtailed or completely missed due to funding, design, architecture, implementation, or technology selection. Its creation is not only the result of short funding, but can be due to the design, architecture, implementation, or technology selection. Technical debt is the investment required to correct the shortage in funding or defects in the above-mentioned aspects.

1.3.3.3 Conversational Banking at Scale

This means to hyper-personalise every customer experience to replace client-facing staff, advisers, and branches with conversational banking, including textual chat and voice chat.

1.3.3.4 Application Modernisation

Application modernisation means implementing microservices and API based application design to deliver agility, scalability, and resiliency of business model. The purpose of application modernisation and industrialisation is to eliminate technology complexity to deliver real-time banking services through self-service and a personalised digital experience. Application modernisation is a basic building block of a bank's industrialisation.

Industrialised banks build microservices (MS) based applications where each service delivering a business capability is developed and deployed independently of the other. Microservice focuses on delivering the business process or tasks very well. Each service should be autonomous and consisting of dedicated technology processes, communications, and database. MS-based architecture helps to overcome the challenges of a monolithic model.

From a business perspective, services should adapt to customer needs and business practices. However, a bank with monolithic applications is slow in adapting to business changes due to the large codebase, longer testing, and code promotion cycles and duplication.

Microservice architecture is highly flexible, resilient, and quickly adjustable to customer and market realities. From a development perspective too, it has lower operational overheads, minimal coordination between teams, and is adaptable to automation. Microservices also enable ways to deliver scalability and continuous integration and deployment.

1.3.3.5 API Wrappers to Repurpose, Re-factor, and Re-architect the Legacy Applications

Currently, the functionalities embedded in the product processors, channels, GL, risk, and financial crimes management systems built as a part of Banking 2.0 and Banking 3.0 are not easily accessible from the processing or experience layers of smart devices, marketplaces, and third-party applications. This renders the bank unable to capitalise on the available opportunities.

The embedded functionalities required by the processing and experience layers can be made accessible by building a system layer API around the legacy applications. The system layer API wrappers hide the complexity of the Legacy Applications. The API wrappers are managed as a centralised layer to deliver the vision of Banking 4.0 vision for the bank.

Legacy application is re-factored and re-architected using cloud-native principles to produce a distributed MS-based stateless application. Banks generally re-factor monolithic legacy application over a period of time. They initially start with wrapping legacy application and exposing certain functionality as microservices or APIs and continue wrapping additional functionality so that application data and functionality is accessible to cloud-native applications. In the process, the bank starts breaking the monolithic legacy application and keep building microservices and APIs. However, it should be noted that the required level of granularity of the wrapped back office application is quite coarse. Repurposing of legacy applications is an iterative process. Based on Banking 4.0, the bank keeps updating the API wrappers.

1.3.3.6 Agility, Scalability, and Resiliency by Cloud Enablement and Cloud Adoption

For better alignment of the technology environment to business outcomes, banks are cloud-enabling legacy applications. The provision of Software as a Service (Saas) empowers business managers, customers, and partners to deliver business outcomes better.

Managing the cost of technology (storage, computing, database, services) resources through cloud adoption is a small part of the strategy. The impact created by the infrastructure as a service is very small on the overall Banking 4.0 scheme.

The real benefit of the cloud is SaaS and banking AI as a service. Cloud adoption helps to orchestrate SaaS as per the bank's specific requirements. Software as a Service is capable of creating a real impact on achieving the Banking 4.0 vision as it eliminates uncertainty about the technology infrastructure and enables software to enforce policies to ensure business outcomes.

The cloud enables API/microservices/software-based integration of applications, data, and infrastructure to build agility, which determines the capability to manage a dynamic business environment.

Matured ability to implement the technology processes of continuous integration and deployment makes the entire bank agile which is much more than software agility. A matured CI/CD capability in the bank helps improve the time to production of changes thus managing the environment better and faster.

1.3.3.7   Industrialised Data Platform

The industrialised data platform enables standardisation, consistency, re-use, and self-service. It provides AI platforms to build banking AI to deliver as a service.

Banks are adopting cloud data capabilities to deliver an industrialised data platform. The cloud data platform capabilities help in industrialising data management processes.

The industrialised data platform provides industrialised capabilities to manage:

- Data integration, preparation, and transformation using process orchestration and pipeline capabilities.
- Data exploration and transformation through machine learning models and visualisation.
- Embedding data engineering, data transformation, computation, modelling, and model and analytics deployment on smart devices and in applications using microservices and API.
- Structured data, documents, voice, and textual chats using a strong NoSQL.
- Managing both transaction and analytical data.
- Managing metadata across data platform modules, across clouds, and on-premise technology assets.

  - Metadata management at the technical and business level along with data search capabilities helps in controlling the data duplication to the minimum.
  - Reduction in duplication drastically reduces technology resource requirements, the complexity of managing systems, enables straight-through processing and self-service, and reusability of technology assets.

1.4   The Six Engines of Industrialisation and Innovation

The bank's Banking 4.0 vision helps identify changes in the engines of industrialisation and innovation.

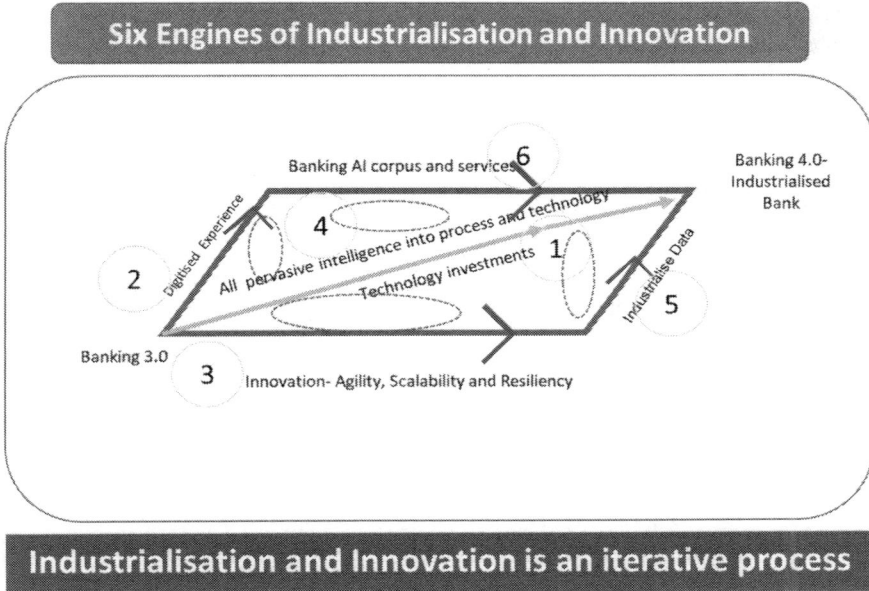

1.4.1   Technology Investments

(1)   Align the bank to make investments into the other five engines of innovation. Capital allocation to pay off the technical debt so that all other five engines are synchronised at all times and every engine is supporting other engines to deliver. To cope with internal and external changes, banks monitor and manage risks and capital daily. Similarly, to cope with the internal and external changes and innovations, fourth-generation banks build and align engines of industrialisation to innovation.

1.4.2   Deliver Digital Experience

(2)   Deliver digital experience in front and back office to customers, partners, and employees. The bank must align the delivery of the digital experience (Engine

2) to customers, partners, and employees (Engine2) with upgrades planned for the other engines. This may include using enterprise-level analytical and visualisation applications, NoSQL DB to manage unstructured data, straight-through processing for data quality, reconciliation, and near real-time data processing. A major realignment is also required in the target operating model. An implementation of such a project may be a multi-cycle (years) project.

1.4.3 Embedded Innovation

(3) Embedding innovation through agility, scalability, and resiliency into the business model through cloud enablement and cloud adoption.

- The bank must align agility, scalability and resiliency of applications, and infrastructure design and architecture to support and exploit capabilities built by other engines to deliver the Banking 4.0 vision.
- It must build and assess the design and architecture for a hybrid cloud (all infrastructure and applications will be migrated) with an on-premises or multi-cloud.
- The bank must plan to align agility, scalability, and resiliency at the bank level.

1.4.4 Intelligent Process and Technology

(4) Create engines to build all-pervasive intelligence into process and technology. To deliver a digital experience, the bank has to embed risk, compliance, and financial crime intelligence into processes and technology (Engine 4).

1.4.5 Industrialised Data

(5) Industrialised data infrastructure to process an enormous volume of data including unstructured human communication data in real-time.

- Third-generation banks are upgrading their data infrastructure to cloud-based data infrastructure.
- To derive the optimum benefits from the industrialisation of data infrastructure, without leaving behind technical debt, the bank must align the five other engines at the enterprise level and should not embed the technology investment or components or design of cloud adoption, digital experience, intelligence, and banking AI into the data infrastructure project.

- The Banking 4.0 vision must drive the alignment of investment, design, and plan for other engines and not burden the objectives or budget of the data infrastructure project.

1.4.6 Banking AI As a Service

(6) Banking AI corpus and services to deliver machine interfaces to engage machines, applications, and individuals with equal ease. To deliver the Banking 4.0 vision, the bank must align banking AI as a service (Engine 6) to deliver digital experience (Engine 2). Banking AI as a service (Engine 6) is enabled by the industrialised data infrastructure engine (Engine 5) and agility and scalability (Engine 3) and it also helps to deliver embedded intelligence (Engine 4)

We have discussed the building and alignment of each of the engines in this book in detail and how to manage a very high volume of processing in near real time (Engine 5).

1.5 Conclusion—Banking 4.0 Is an Iterative Process

Fourth-generation banks are decoupling business outcomes from technology limitations by providing more certainty in technology services. They are designing process and controls for data quality, coverage, timeliness, completeness, lineage, and availability.

Banking 4.0 means modernising and modularising technical estates, leveraging new technologies such as public cloud, adopting microservices and APIs for front-to-back integration, and industrialisation of the front office, mid, and back offices. This will provide intelligent technology for self-service and straight-through processing using a machine interface.

Banking 4.0 is an iterative journey. Multiple initiatives are taken up simultaneously. These are application modernisation, wrapping of legacy technology, building APIs as an integration layer, building agility into technology through cloud enablement, adopting cloud-native technology, building AI into the technology, building intelligent conversational systems, building platform banking. These parallel and iterative initiatives will merge and undergo manifold iterations to ultimately build a truly industrialised bank.

In this book, these issues are addressed in separate chapters. We have discussed learning from the convergence of these initiatives and iterations.

Chapter 2
Tactical Approach to the Industrialisation

2.1 Introduction—Manual Tasks in Banking Processes

All banking processes are co-mingled with manual tasks of uneven size, type, and complexity. Second- and third-generation legacy applications at banks need numerous human interventions to complete a banking process. When legacy applications were built, technology was not sufficiently mature for end-to-end management of documents and unstructured data. Documents were extracted and captured manually. The numerous tasks of reading and capturing information from documents, managing complex data, processes, and decisions were left out for manual processing outside the applications.

In the chapter 'Aligning Engines of Industrialisation and Innovation to Deliver Banking 4.0 Services' we explain the primary aim of industrialisation: to build and strengthen the machine interface within banking processes. Industrialisation aims to transform manual tasks into machine delivered processes, experiences, and outcomes.

2.1.1 The Genesis of Manual Processes

Legacy applications were not built to be flexible and change cycles have been very long and time consuming. To manage longer change cycles, all complex computations, processes, and tasks needing frequent changes were set aside as manual tasks and processes outside the legacy application.

© Springer Nature Singapore Pte Ltd. 2022
M. Bhatia, *Banking 4.0*,
https://doi.org/10.1007/978-981-16-6069-6_2

2.1.2   Legacy Applications Use GUI for Data Capture

Graphical user interface for human agents was and is a widely used data capture
mechanism for legacy applications.

2.1.2.1   40% of Employees at Banks Deliver Manual Tasks

Banks have been managing data and process complexity manually. According to
one back of envelope estimate, more than 40% of bank employees are deployed on
manual processes to manage data complexity and documents.

As the adoption of technology has increased at banks, there have been several
iterations to reduce manual processes.

2.1.3   15–20% of Employees at Banks Manage Data and Documents for Credit Management

Credit management manual process volumetric benchmarks for banks with $100 Bn– $1 Tn asset size		
Annual credit rating and credit Approval Volume	Corporate + Commercial	Retail + SME
	0.1–1 M	5–50 M
Legacy systems for credit approvals	**Corporate**	**Retail**
Source systems	10–50	
Document management system	10–50	
Document type with version	10–50	
Annual credit analysis document Processing Volume	10–100 M	50–125 M
Areas of automation	**RPA Based Task Automation 2021**	**Industrialisation 2030**
Credit administration	10–20%	70–80%
Collateral management	10–20%	70–80%
Margins	10–20%	70–80%
Credit risk provisioning	20–50 models	500–1000 models
Scenario management	100–300	1000–2000
Model management	4–8K	20–40K

2.1.4 15–20% of Employees at Banks Manage Financial Crimes Prevention Data

KYC and AML Manual Process Volumetric Benchmarks for Banks with 8 M-50 M Customers			
Distribution of customers	High Risk	Med Risk	Low Risk
Re-rating required (high risk 6 months, med risk 2 years, and low risk 5 years)	3%	20%	77%
	0.24–1.5 M	1.5–10 M	6.5–40 M
KYC customers and cases		8 M Customers	50 M Customers
KYC data sources		10+	50+
Document management systems		10+	50+
Document types and versions		10+	50+
KYC volume in page search/year		500 M	3 Bn
KYC volume incremental cases/Year		3 M	20 M
Real-time KYC cases/year		0.08 M	0.5 M
Transaction monitoring			
Transaction systems		10 +	125+
Transactions volume/year		700 M	9000 M
Alerts investigated/year		7 M	90 M
SAR filed/year		0.07 M	0.9 M
Client list screening			
CLS lists		40–100	400+
Refresh screening/year		200 M	1.3 Bn
Level 2 alerts investigated		0.2 M	1.3 M
Level 2 investigation (document pages)		4 M	25 M
SAR Filed/Year		0.002 M	0.013 M
Payment screening			
Payment volume (international 20%)		140 M	1.8 Bn
Level 2 alerts		0.14 M	1.8 M
Level 2 investigation (doc scans)		4 M	25 M
SAR filed/year		0.014 M	0.18 M

2.1.5 5–10% of Employees at Banks Manage Data for Financial Risk and Regulatory Reporting

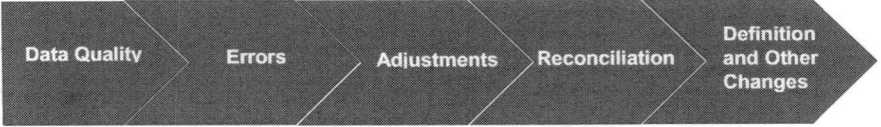

2.2 Automation of Manual Tasks Versus Industrialisation of the Bank

2.2.1 Third-Generation Technology Automates High Volume, Low Complexity Manual Tasks

Since the implementation of second-generation legacy applications, banks have been focusing on the automation of manual tasks in both the front and back office processes. Banks prioritised high volume, low complexity tasks, while low volume, and highly complex tasks continued to be manual.

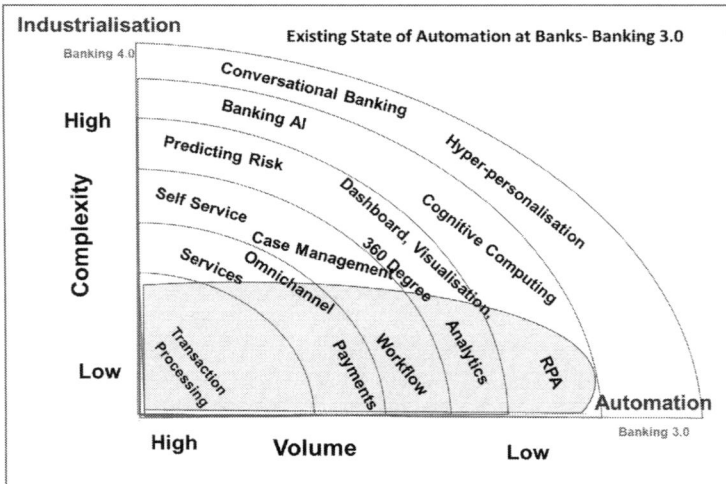

In the quest to automate high volume low complex tasks, banks have built transaction processing systems as third-generation legacy systems and automated payments across omnichannels through self-service in the front office. Banks have automated manual processes dealing with documents through workflow and reconciliation and managing data through analytics.

The third-generation systems further automated the medium volume process, leaving behind the low volume manual tasks of capturing data into the system by reading documents, screens, mails, and emails.

2.2.2 Robotic Process Automation (RPA) Automates Low Volume Low Complexity Manual Tasks

For the past five years, banks have started leveraging RPA to automate low complexity, low volume, and rule-based manual tasks.

Some six years ago, when banks started using RPA, some experts were of the view that RPA would evolve to provide capabilities to manage complex tasks in terms of cognitive computing, hyper-personalisation, conversational banking, and banking AI. However, RPA technology has not been able to evolve sufficiently to manage complex processes and unstructured data and human communication.

In a nutshell, automation is for high volume, low complexity processes primarily used for handling structured data.

2.2.3 Machines at Industrialised Bank Manage High Volume High Complexity Processes

Machines at industrialised banks manage highly complex and high volume processes and this includes engaging individuals on human communication channels as well as engaging both individuals and machines using banking AI. Industrialisation means capabilities of machines to manage complex tasks.

Industrialisation is delivered through a self-service facility where risks are managed by machines through a predictive risk shield that is embedded in every banking process. Unstructured data like text, document, and voice and video are managed by machines and individuals are engaged by machines through human communication channels of chat and voice communications. The industrialised bank delivers a digital experience to customers, partners, and employees through hyper-personalisation engines.

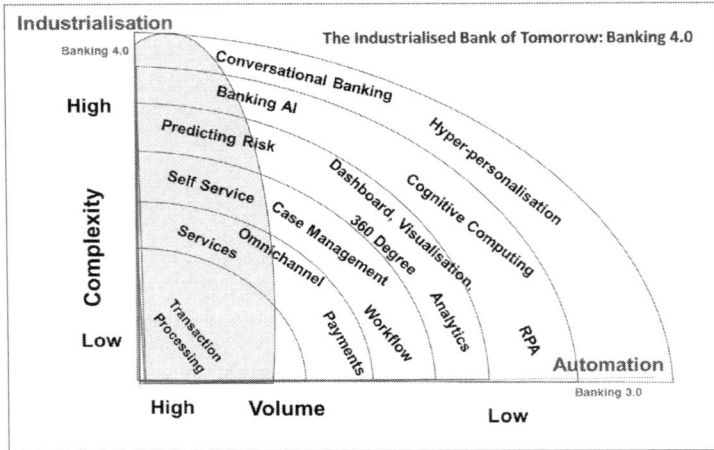

2.2.4   To Industrialise the Bank—Across the Valley of Investment, Innovation, and Alignment

The chapter 'Aligning Engines of Industrialisation and Innovation to Deliver Banking 4.0 Services' has identified six engines of industrialisation and innovation.

The purpose of industrialisation is to build capabilities in the bank's machines to manage high volume, highly complex processes.

Some examples of high volume, highly complex process are:

- Managing conversational banking at scale.
- Managing various types of risks, when the bank is servicing its customers through third-party APIs and in a self-service mode through its machines.
- Delivering a digital experience to customers, partners, and employees leveraging hyper-personalisation engines and banking AI, specifically built by the bank for its machines.

There is a huge gap in terms of investment, industrialisation, innovation, and alignment of the six engines of industrialisation.

In investment terms, for each bank, the investment gap may be running into billions of dollars.

This gap can be called the 'Valley of investment, industrialisation, and innovation'.

This entire book is an approach to cross the valley from automation to industrialisation.

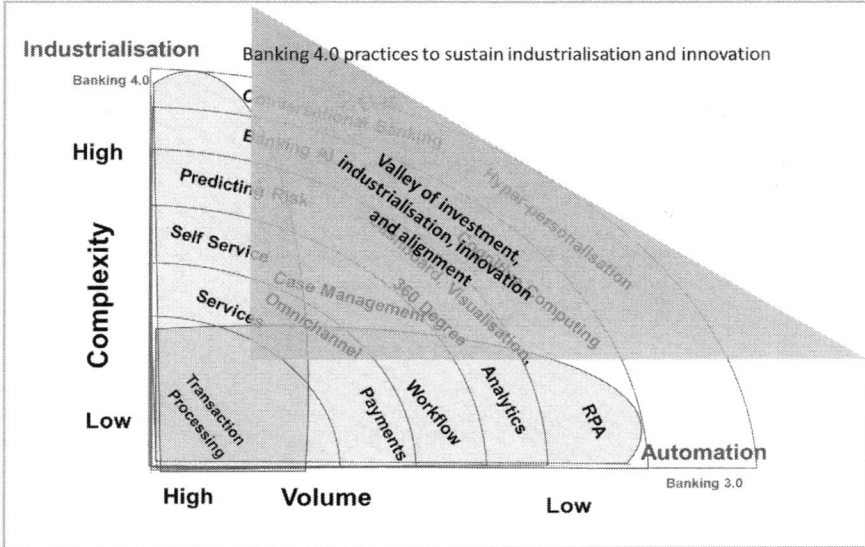

2.2.4.1 Integrate Automation into Legacy Modernisation Strategy

Legacy applications will continue to be in use at banks for the foreseeable future. The digitisation of a bank is a continuous process and complete transformation could take another five to ten more years. Until then, legacy applications will co-exist with microservices based cloud-native applications.

Manual tasks are a part of every legacy application. To manage a legacy application until it is retired and replaced with digital applications, third-generation banks are automating manual tasks embedded within processes that are supported by legacy applications. The purpose of automating such processes is to decouple the manual tasks from the legacy application. Doing so presents an optimised roadmap to extend and retire legacy application through repackaging, re-platforming, and re-factoring.

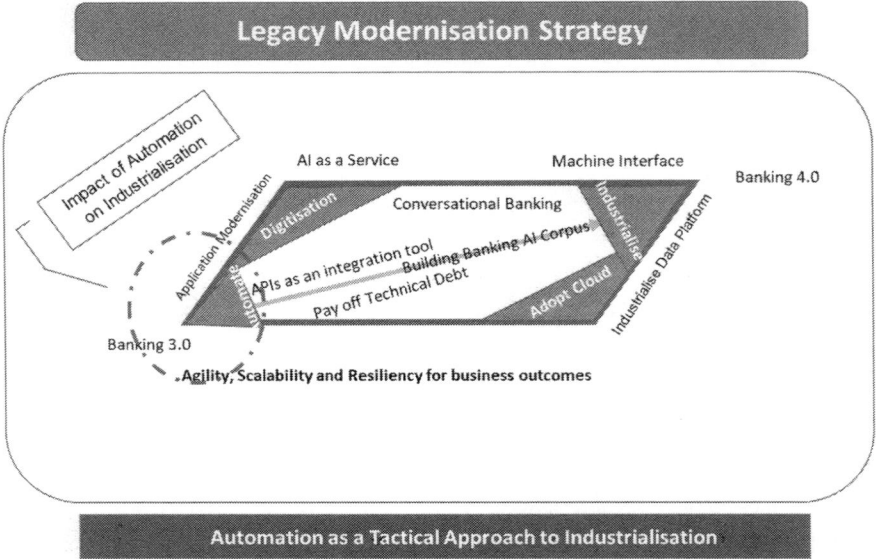

There are two approaches to legacy application management: preliminary and tactical.

2.2.5 Preliminary Approach to Legacy Application Management Through RPA

Banks automate manual tasks through RPA. This is discussed in detail in the next section.

2.2.6 Tactical Approach to Legacy Application Modernisation

Using a tactical approach, the bank delivers its short-term vision of industrialisation. It delivers a part of digital experience—either to a particular segment or for a set of products or a part of experience—and embeds cognitive capabilities in its legacy application as a part of the modernisation programme to automate and industrialise manual tasks.

We discuss the tactical approach in detail through a case study in the next section.

2.3 Robotic Process Automation (RPA) Automates Manual Tasks

Robotic process automation (RPA) provides a non-invasive way to integrate systems and processes. It is also called a (ro)bot. The International Robotic Process Automation Association (IRPA) defines RPA as 'The application of technology that allows employees in a company to configure computer software or a 'robot' to capture and interpret existing applications for processing a transaction, manipulating data, triggering responses, and communicating with other digital systems'.

Robotic process automation works similarly to human analysts and uses the same desktop configuration and applications as human analysts. It can be deployed on a desktop, a server, a private cloud, a public cloud, or hybrid environment. Robotic process automation is generally used as a short-term measure to extract maximum value out of existing applications when a bank does not have a clear business case for industrialisation, when technology has not yet matured, and when human intervention is required. It is most suitable for repetitive, manually intensive, and rule-based tasks. The ultimate purpose of RPA adoption is better management of operational risk and error rates, generating efficiencies, and accelerating the cycle time.

2.3.1 RPA Tool Automates Granular Tasks

Robotic process automation mechanises tasks at a granular level that requires multiple handoffs between system and human analysts. Multiple tasks are combined to build a sub-process.

Features of RPA technology	
Non-invasive Ways	Very similar to human analysts. Uses same desktop configuration and applications
Lightweight IT	Does not add much to performance or hardware requirements and extracts value out of legacy IT. It is a business tool, not an IT tool
Audit Trail and Security	RPA tools have an inbuilt capability to capture audit trail, enforce security, and access control
GUI-based for Business	Can be trained by process or business experts. No need for programming or code writing

2.3.2   Case Study: Survey of Commercially Available RPA Tools for Capabilities to Automate a Banking Process

Robotic process automation may also have basic cognitive process automation capabilities. The level of cognitive capabilities drives the level of granularity which is automated. An RPA with no cognitive capability automates tasks whereas RPAs with good cognitive capabilities automate processes with a higher level of intelligence that would otherwise be performed by humans.

Case Study: Seven Categories of Tasks Automated by RPA Tools
An illustrative list of seven categories of tasks executed by top RPA tools as of the end of 2020 follows:

1. *Managing System*

    - Log into web/enterprise applications
    - Connect and interact with the system via a user application interface
    - Toggle between screens
    - Toggle between applications
    - Move folder
    - Move file
    - Download file.

2. *Screen Scrapping*

    - Read database
    - Gather data from a screen
    - Store data in a database
    - Retrieve data from the database
    - Retrieve data from a screen.

3. *Managing Mouse and Keyboard Activities*

    - Record keystrokes
    - Orchestrate multiple bots.

4. *Desktop Activities*

    - Capture data in virtual/Citrix desktop
    - Desktop automation
        a.   Copying and pasting data between applications
        b.   Filing online forms
    - OCR document conversion.

5. *Managing Emails*

   - Open email
   - Open email attachment
   - Read email
   - Draft email
   - Send email.

6. *Managing Document Templates*

   - Preparing document using template
   - Comparing contents between two files
   - Screen scraping and tabulating data
     a. Read screens visually using basic screen-scraping techniques and image recognition technology. Screen scraping includes dynamic mappings to an application's controls.
   - Web Automation
     a. Collecting social media data
   - GUI automation
   - Desktop automation.

7. *Applying Business Rules*

   - Applying business rules
     a. Verifying and validating data
     b. Adjudication
     c. Applying formulas
     d. Computation
   - Excel Automation
     a. Extracting and reformatting data into Excel.

2.3.2.1   Illustrative List of Manual Tasks Automated by RPA

Banks are leveraging RPA capabilities to automate the aforementioned seven categories of tasks, and consequently fixing gaps in the existing monolithic transaction processing, workflow, and analytical applications.

RPA automates manual tasks in Transaction Processing, Payments, Workflow and Analytics
Industrialisation

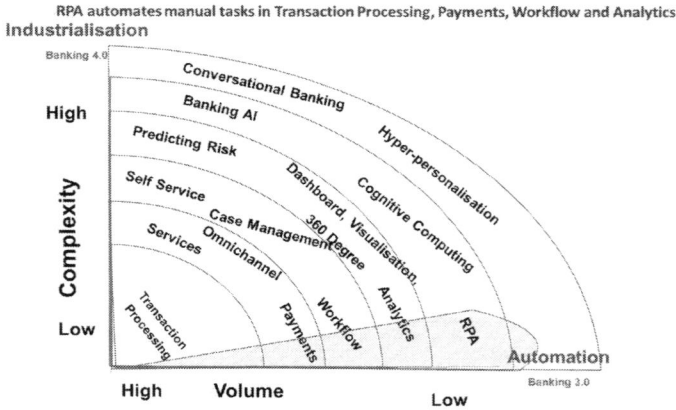

Banks are leveraging the RPA tool to deliver human tasks, for example, tasks within the banking process like Know Your Customer, customer onboarding, credit management, insurance underwriting, financial crimes investigations, help desk, call centre, finance, and accounting, General Ledger, regulatory reporting, etc.

Leverage RPA's capabilities to automate seven task categories—managing systems, screen scrapping, managing mouse, keyboard activities, desktop, emails, and document templates, and applying business rules to automate tasks within the banking sub-process.

- **Customer Onboarding**

  - Fill KYC details
  - Fill in Sanction screening details.

- **AML/Fraud/Cyber Risk/Sanction/Payment Screening Alert investigation**

  - Match L1 alert details
  - Match L2 alert details
  - Verify L3 alert details.

- **Credit Application**

  - Fill the template with collateral data
  - Fill the template with property value data
  - Fill financial statements template.

- **Credit Administration**

  - Fill template for loan repayment
  - Fill authority for cancellation

  - Fill pre-payment penalties
  - Fill creation of trust orders
  - Fill follow-up schedule
  - Fill checklist
  - Verify signature
  - Fill exemption order.

- **Fill Credit Servicing**

  - Name change
  - Fill address change
  - Fill PA registration.

- **Finance, Risk, and Regulatory Reporting**

  - Match data quality checks for finance, risk, and regulatory reporting
  - Match data capture checks
  - Automate reconciliation
  - Fill planning template
  - Fill variance reports
  - Fill regulatory report templates
  - Verify computer-based pre-established rules.

2.3.2.2 Robotic Process Automation Delivers Limited Benefits

Rather than being a tool to industrialise banking processes, RPA is a tool to automate tasks. The return on investment from RPA may not be very high as it is a low-cost extension of existing technology.

The benefits of RPA at banks are suboptimal due to its dependence on human intervention. Whilst RPA speeds up and improves the accuracy of the process, handoff between humans and machines diminishes the benefits. The benefit from automation is inversely proportional to the number of machine–analyst handoffs. Unless augmented with cognitive capabilities, the RPA tool cannot support a banking function beyond a very granular task. At present, granular tasks are integrated by human intervention. In addition to the limitation of automating granular level tasks, RPA tools also can cover only around 20% of tasks at banks.

2.3.3 Case Study: RPA Delivers Suboptimal Benefits

Take an example. Assume a sub-process at a bank is divided into six tasks of equal effort size, each requiring ten minutes of human effort. The total human effort required to complete the sub-process is 60 min.

Assume step numbers 1, 2, and 4 use bots. Assume the set up time for each bot task is 10% or 1 min. The total time t_{tot} required to accomplish the sub-process theoretically should be equal to t_{bot} (bot assisted time) + t_{man} (manual) where.

$$t_{bot} = 0.1 * \sum_{1}^{n} (t_1 \ldots t_n)$$

$$t_{man} = \sum_{1}^{n} (t_1 \ldots t_n)$$

(in the above example $t_{tot} = t_{bot} + t_{man} = 33$ min). However, this does not assure that the agent will be able to deliver productivity of 27 min on other tasks. He may deliver productivity equivalent of 15 min or less on other sub-processes because the bot-assisted processes cannot be left completely unsupervised and thus some effort will be spent on supervision. Whilst bots improve productivity the ROI might be limited.

With only RPA capabilities full benefits of automation are not realized.

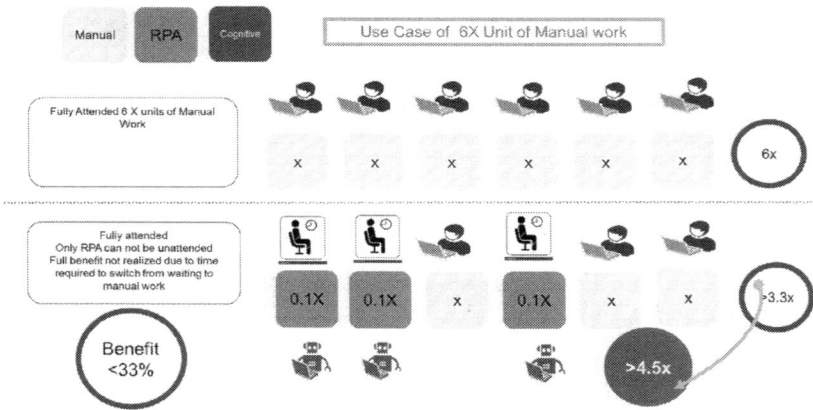

2.3.4 Case Study: Automate the Process and Not the Tasks

Process automation means a series of a larger number of manual tasks are automated with no intermediate human interventions.

To achieve automation of the banking process, instead of automating manual tasks, all human interventions should be front- or back-loaded. Let robots execute unattended and wait for the human intervention after completion of all automated tasks, or let a robot take all human intervention upfront instead of the human waiting for the robot to complete the task. It may not be possible to automate all intermediate steps only with RPA capabilities and cognitive capabilities might be needed in many scenarios.

For better benefits intersperse RPA with Cognitive Process Automation(CPA) and back-load error correction

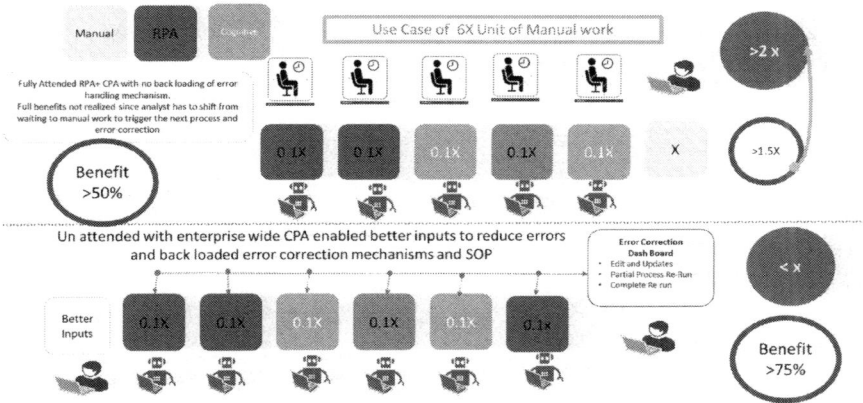

Therefore, RPA has a very small role to play in industrialisation.

2.3.4.1 Cognitive Process Automation is Beyond Automation of Manual Tasks

The capabilities of RPA need to be supplemented with cognitive capabilities to handle either complex data or unstructured data.

We know that RPA vendors have not improved their platforms with CPA capabilities to the extent that is required for building the banking process. Of late, cloud platform providers have started providing machine learning and AI libraries as cognitive bots to automate complex and unstructured data for customer engagement and front office industrialisation.

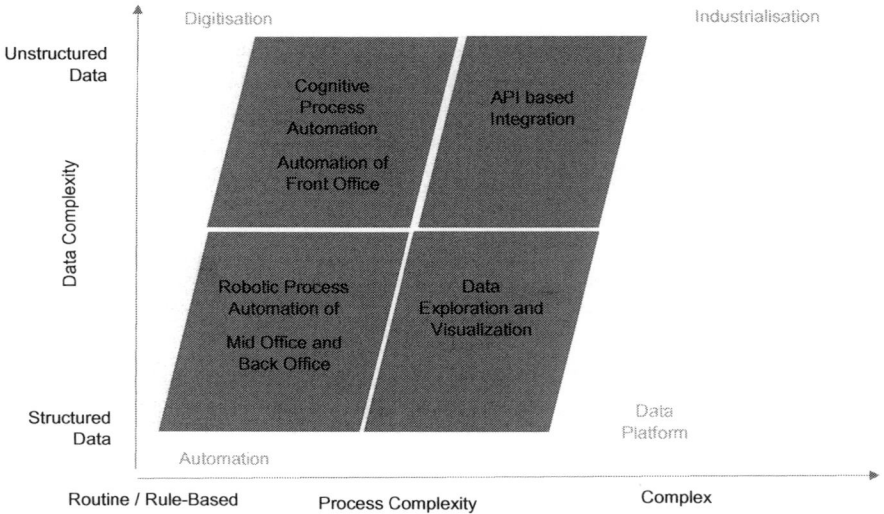

2.3.5 Automation in Handling Unstructured Data Needs Cognitive Capabilities

To deliver business outcomes the bank needs to adopt cognitive process automation. In the case where a bank has widely implemented a third-party RPA tool, it must explore leveraging the Cognitive Process Auatomation(CPA) libraries so that the tool can integrate with the CPA libraries provided by RPA tools.

Vendors	Enhancements to their RPA platform in the past 2 years
Automation Anywhere	AI-powered document extraction and process orchestration to integrate bots
UiPath	Extracting information about document through a document understanding module; process orchestrator to integrate bots and AI fabric to deploy, manage, and improve ML models
Blue Prism	Digital Exchange (DX)—Online marketplace for cognitive bots
WorkFusion	Built-in intelligence—Automate and analyse documents with intelligent bots and advanced analytics
Others	Similar capabilities—however, up until 2020 no one had so far built banking process-specific cognitive capabilities

Third-party CPA libraries might be insufficient and banks might have to build cognitive and AI capabilities on their own.

2.3.6 Cognitive Process Automation Is Contextual to the Banking Process

- Deep learning and assembling techniques
- Banking, capital markets, and insurance tasks and sub-process dictionary, knowledge, and regular expression
- Input character reading
- Digital camera OCR, digital camera for ICR, mobile scanning application, window scanner application, barcode reader
- Structured, semi-structured, and unstructured document pages.

2.3.7 Case Study: Dictionary and Domain Covered

For example, ABBYY has built an industry-specific solution for education, retail, and government. However, no commercial solution is available for banking services. Some fintech firms supplement existing OCR with domain dictionaries and training to enhance accuracy and context. Banks need to build their domain libraries.

2.3.8 Cognitive Computing Bots Available on Cloud Platforms

- A bot is provided as a web application, using APIs to send and receive messages.
- The most important differentiator between a bot and other web applications is the bot allows people to interact with bot services intelligently. The bot provides an experience of dealing with a person and not a computer application.
- Bots vary widely depending on the level of complex experiences.
- A bot provides user interaction between text and GUI. A more intelligent bot also enables speech interaction.
- Bots provide an experience that feels less like using a computer and more like dealing with a person – or at least an intelligent robot.

2.3.9 Case Study: Cloud-Provided Bots

Cloud-provided bots integrate environments to build, connect, test, deploy, and manage intelligent bots. Cloud providers also provide integration with additional libraries.

- Natural language processing
- Natural conversational
- Text analytics with machine learning
- Spell check
- Knowledge extraction
- Entity resolution
- Entity linking
- Knowledge graph
- Conversational
- Web search APIs
- Extract information about images
- Processes text in images
- Analyse human face across eight emotion categories
- Detects video motion
- Track faces
- Motion thumbnail summary
- Human face comparison
- Virtual assistance
- Channel integration
- User input types
- Input devices
- Pre-built task level bots.

2.3.10   Case Study: Pre-built Integration and Connector Services

For example, Azure Bot Service provided pre-built integration with Facebook, Messenger, Kik, Skype, Slack, Microsoft Teams, Telegram, text/SMS, Twilio, Cortana, and Skype.

2.3.11   Industrialisation of Bots Through Orchestration on Cloud

Orchestration and integration of intelligent bots create business processes instead of automating tasks. With inbuilt cognitive and AI capabilities, the digital process becomes predictive as well as enabling.

- Integration and orchestration of tasks to minimise manual intervention and inputs.
- Manual intervention may reduce the overall efficiency achieved by preceding and successive bots by 10–90%.
- What is required to reduce manual intervention?

- Integrate and orchestrate multiple tasks before the system pauses for manual intervention.
- Three much-needed capabilities are:

  The system should be easy to build and deploy and use the bot's orchestration framework.
  Cognitive capabilities to take decisions which otherwise would have needed manual input/intervention.
  Intelligence and architecture to front-load all inputs and back-load all error handling. Bots should not pause or wait for input or managing errors.

2.3.11.1 Industrialisation Originates in Banking AI and not in RPA

With the major regulatory focus on KYC and AML, and simultaneous availability of RPA platforms since 2015, some of the leading banks have invested in RPA platforms. The banking industry was hoping that some of these platforms would drastically expand their capabilities to help banks in their automation journeys. However, RPA platforms have failed to fulfil the expectations as none of them has a banking industry focus.

Since 2019, we are seeing renewed interest by banks in cloud technology—both public as well as private clouds. The good news is that cloud technology providers have embraced open-source technologies with both hands, and each comes with generic AI capabilities. This means that cloud technologies provide a configurable and modular architecture to use generic AI capabilities. At present none of the cloud technologies has a banking focus. However, the need for banking industry taxonomies, data models, and definitions for API banking bolsters the case for banks and cloud providers to invest in banking industry-specific AI. It means some of the banks may jump-start industrialisation without taking the RPA path.

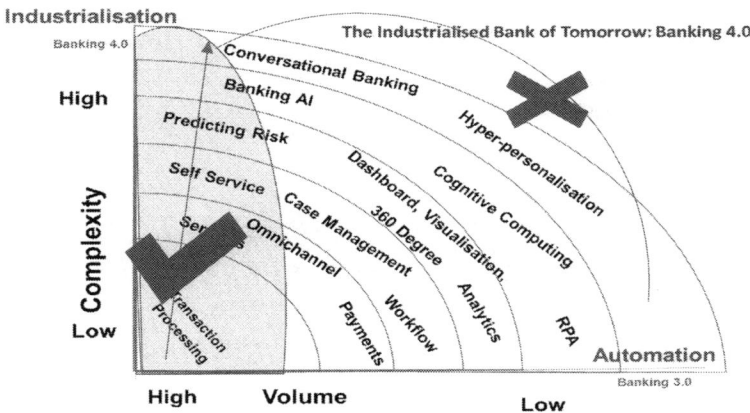

2.3.11.2   Tactical Approach to Industrialisation

Repurpose existing legacy applications through a modernisation programme while also leveraging industrialisation engines.

- A tactical approach to industrialisation is to build a new application in the front office to deliver an intermediate level digital customer experience.
- Build agility, scalability, and resiliency through wrapping and modernising legacy application.
- Leverage and industrialise data infrastructure to automate decision-making, and implement AI platform.
- Build banking AI and embed intelligence into technology and process.

Please note that, since this is a tactical approach, it may end up leaving behind technical debt, losses, and investment write-offs. The tactical approach has to be evaluated based on the timelines required for industrialisation and the business benefits of the tactical implementation.

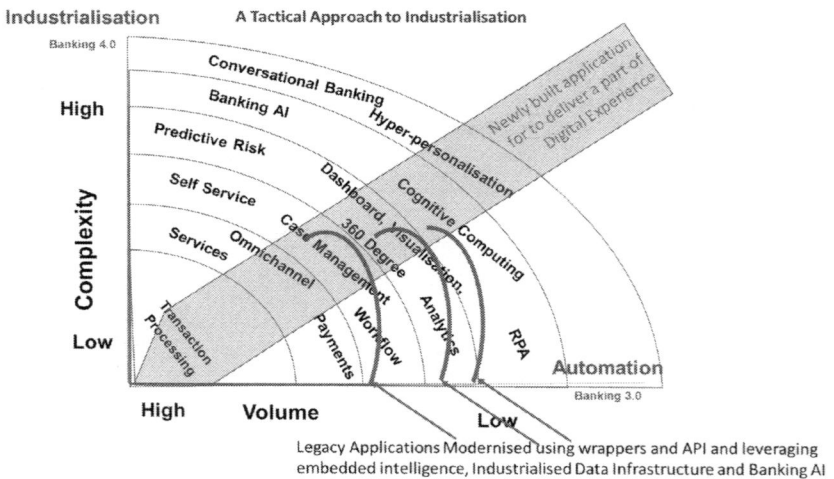

Legacy Applications Modernised using wrappers and API and leveraging embedded intelligence, Industrialised Data Infrastructure and Banking AI

2.3.12   *State Bank of India YONO Case Study—Digital Retail Banking Platform Embedding Automation into the Repurposed Legacy Applications*

Transformation of the entire bank is an enormous task. Some of the banks like the State Bank of India (SBI) opted to build an intermediate digital platform with a design and architecture to roll out digital experience over a few cycles.

The net impact may be that the new platform was made available to digitally native customers with simple retail products and simpler product features.

The SBI is delivering digital customer experience through an intermediary industrialised retail banking platform called YONO. The platform is built on repurposed workflow and analytics augmented by cognitive, banking AI, and industrialised data infrastructure capabilities on the repurposed core banking system wrapped through APIs.

A platform for the younger population co-existing with traditional core banking and channels. YONO is the flagship customer-facing digital customer experience platform of SBI, catering to various banking, financial services, and lifestyle requirements. It aims to deliver a world-class customer experience through distinctive omnichannel and seamless customer journeys.

The SBI has designed and implemented 100 + customer journeys. It has implemented a two-pronged approach, first, to repurpose the existing core banking solution through wrapper APIs, and second, to repurpose the existing workflow and analytics to deliver the planned customer journey and customer experience.

For employee-facing tasks, the bank has robotised the banking processes and automated routine tasks. The bank has deployed robots to extract information to service paperless loan applications. It has created templates for receiving service requests from branches for further processing and centralised the servicing and has supplemented the existing workflow with RPA.

The net result is the bank has transformed the retail banking landscape for the younger customer population by leveraging automation and API wrappers.

In the chapter on AI as a service, we discuss in detail the implementation of the AI platform, while the chapter on digital banking provides customer journeys in detail.

2.4   Conclusion–Leverage Industrialisation Engines for Tactical Realisation of Automation Benefits

As a tool RPA is a very preliminary approach of automation suitable only for repetitive manual tasks, and without CPA capabilities its value proposition is very small. Banks leverage RPA only up until when legacy applications are not modernised or until the time a more tactical approach for managing legacy applications is implemented.

Automation as a tactical approach can help banks realise much better benefits when a legacy application modernisation programme leverages industrialisation engines.

- For the next decade, banks will continue implementation of first-, second-, and third-generation legacy application modernisation programmes. Each legacy application has hundreds of manual tasks.
- With Banking 4.0 vision, banks are also implementing industrialisation engines.
- Powering legacy modernisation and manual task automation programmes with industrialisation engines can enhance the benefits multifold for the bank.

Chapter 3
Investing in Alignment of Industrialisation and Innovation Engines

3.1 Introduction—By Default Industrialisation and Innovation Engines Are Never Aligned

External competition, technology, banking products and services, customer preferences, and customer demands are changing at such a fast pace that banks need to keep their industrialisation and innovation engines running constantly. In the hyper-changing environment, banks need to consume innovation dose daily.

The chapter 'Industrialisation and Innovation Engines to Deliver Banking 4.0 Services' identified six engines of industrialisation and innovation.

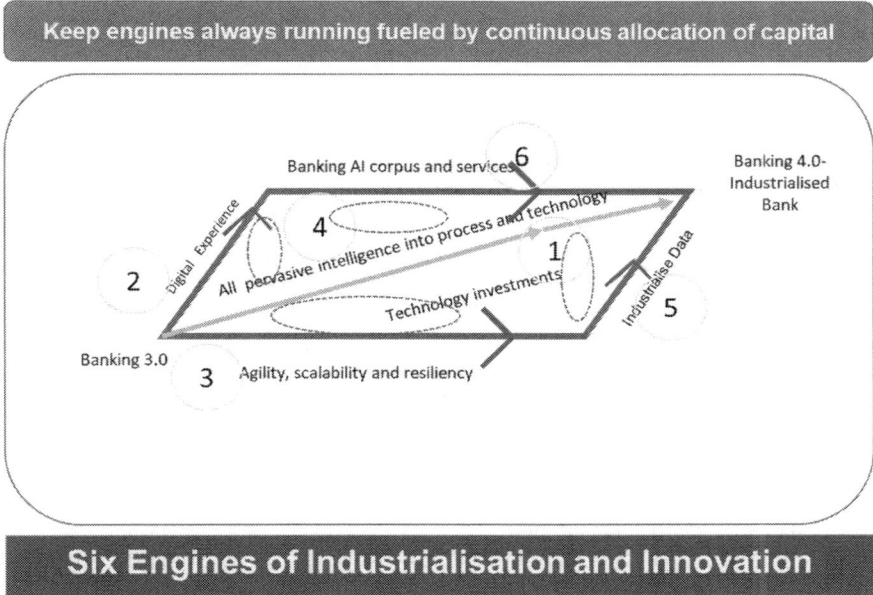

© Springer Nature Singapore Pte Ltd. 2022
M. Bhatia, *Banking 4.0*,
https://doi.org/10.1007/978-981-16-6069-6_3

Technology investment kick-starts and keeps other engines running to deliver industrialisation and innovation. Technology investment is thus the first engine of industrialisation and innovation. The benefits from industrialisation and innovation accrue in the future, therefore, the investment includes both revenue expenditure and capital allocation for the investment made in this cycle.

1. Delivering digital experience (DDE) to customers, partners, and employees is the primary aim of industrialisation and innovation at most banks. It is the second engine of industrialisation and innovation and is dependent on other engines. It needs an intelligent front office and a matured banking AI which need industrialised data, which in turn needs agile, scalable, and resilient technology.
2. Delivering agility, scalability, and resiliency in the business model through cloud adoption is the third engine of industrialisation and innovation.
3. Embedding intelligence into the front and back office processes and technology is the fourth engine to industrialisation and innovation at a bank.
4. Industrialised data infrastructure, processing a very high volume of data in real time is the fifth engine.
5. The sixth engine is to deliver banking AI as a service for the bank's machines to engage in real time its customers and their machines including via human communication. It has a dependency on industrialised data and agile, scalable, and resilient technology.

3.1.1 Misaligned Engines Start Accumulating Technical Debt

By default, at any point in time, engines will never be aligned with each other. The bank must invest, plan, design, and implement strategies to align them in future. Investment in the alignment of engines is called technical debt.

Technical debt is the additional cost or expenses or the investment the bank has to incur in order to align the industrialisation engines in future. Technical debt is the cost of misaligned engines and, if not paid off, keeps accumulating.

Technical debt accumulates at a much sharper rate in the fast-changing businesses of the bank. To attain the freedom to innovate their business model as far as possible banks need to repay their technical debt.

Align Industrialisation Engines to Manage Technical Debt
The bank must allocate capital based on its assessment of how to achieve the vision of Banking 4.0 and make ahead-of-the-curve investments to align the six aforementioned engines.

An integrated approach to alignment is necessary because of the inherent dependency of one engine on the other five. As a foundation to the integrated approach, the end state of each engine must be derived out of the vision of Banking 4.0 at the end of each cycle and subsequent cycles.

Industrialisation is inherently an iterative process. After every cycle of investment and implementation, the Banking 4.0 vision and plan for engine alignment of the next set of cycles must be rediscovered and benchmarked to create a virtuous cycle of innovation sustenance.

Technical debt starts accumulating if industrialisation engines are not continuously aligned and it does so exponentially if misalignment continues over a long period. Engines remain misaligned for a longer period if the bank does not identify and recognise innovations.

Over a longer period, technology generations change, leaving behind a larger number of applications and technology for upgrading and replacement. Technical debt does not disappear if the debtor chooses not to repay it, and many banks are currently in a technical debt trap! This means either that banks are accumulating more debt than they are clearing or they do not have the capital to sustain investment into future technology and business models or innovation.

Discover Innovation in a BAU Mode
The bank must continuously adopt innovation to ensure there is alignment of the future vision of the bank with market reality. Innovation that is not discovered or implemented for a longer time leaves behind a massive technical debt.

3.2 Build-Up of Technical Debt

Technical debt managed sub-optimally results in an accumulation over the period.

3.2.1 Technical Debt Built up Due to Factors Beyond the Control of the Bank

As hypothesised by Moore's Law, over the past three decades technology evolved at a very fast pace, with each change drastically disrupting banking technology. For example mainframe, client–server, internet, and now serverless (cloud).

Each technology disrupts the cost curves. Migration to the next-generation technology is driven by economics rather than by technology spend, thus migration has an impact on RTB (running the bank) and CTB (change the bank). Unless the next generation drastically disrupts cost and revenue curves, the bank continues with the existing technology and manages additional spend at diminishing returns. However, continued use of old technology may create technical debt for surrounding systems. Unfortunately, at present, the technical debt created for surrounding systems is not considered in the technology replacement decision.

(a)   *Uneven Diminishment in Technology Returns*

For some technologies, returns diminish faster than others. Therefore, each technology accumulates technology debt at a very different rate. Technology advancement and adoption has largely been a parallel process. Full migration to next-generation technology has not been completed at most banks; some technologies are one generation behind and some two or three generations behind. It is also very difficult to predict the rate of diminishment in the returns. Banks do not collect data, have not implemented activity-based costing, and may not have technology cost allocation policies.

(b)   *Banks Accumulate Technical Debt Due to Uneven Technology Maturity Rates*

Banking 1.0 to Banking 3.0 technologies laid the foundation for bank industrialisation very well, but did not industrialise banks. Industrialisation at a scale has only become possible with the advent of public and private cloud, big data, and wider adoption of API and microservices, availability of NoSQL platforms for at-scale implementation, at commercially viable rates over the last three to five years.

3.2.2   Technical Debt Built up Due to the Decisions and Choices Made by the Bank

Internal decisions of a bank include but are not limited to technology selection, architecture, design, and investment to deliver the vision of the bank.

Decisions vary significantly across the banks, even within a bank across different business units and even within the same business unit across time. The reason for a significant variation in decisions is the absence of a bank-wide vision with regard to industrialisation and innovation.

At present, assessment, planning, design, architecture, and implementation are driven by project objectives. Few banks have built Banking 4.0 vision for the entire bank, and few have developed on a very limited scale mechanism to benchmark project objectives, designs, architecture, and vision. Banks have not developed any mechanisms for bank-wide aggregation of project vision and objectives.

Due to these limitations, in most cases in the past banks have implemented fragmented point solutions which were not industrialised.

Industrialisation by definition means standardisation, mass-scale production, and re-usability. Fourth-generation industrialisation necessarily means intelligent or cognitive automation and real-time response, none of which can be achieved by siloed systems. It necessarily means extracting the industrialisation engines from the project and implementing them at bank-wide level to deliver standardisation, mass-scale production, re-usable components, and real-time systems with cognitive intelligence. Industrialisation and innovation engines/components hidden within the projects need to be aggregated and designed, architected, managed, and governed at the bank level.

a. *Project-level Decisions and Choices Make the Technical Debt Management Sub-optimal*

Technical debt is either not managed or managed in a sub-optimal way when the bank is managing the future through technology projects rather than Banking 4.0 vision.

Technical debt is created when the scope of the project is s curtailed or completely missed due to funding, design, architecture, implementation, or technology selection.

Technical debt creation is not only the outcome of short funding but it can also be as a result of design, architecture, implementation, or technology selection.

Technical debt is the investment that will be required to set the right shortage in funding or defects in design, architecture, implementation, or technical selection.

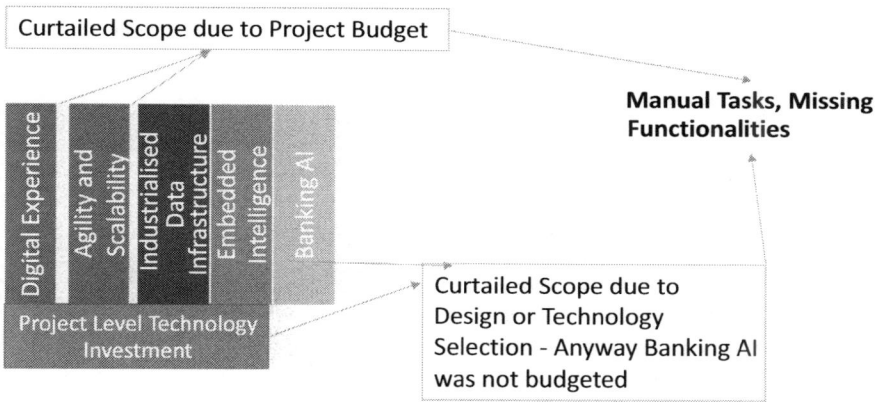

b. *Case Study: Technical Debt at a Project Level*

Technical debt is the changes that must be made in other engines for one engine to deliver. For example, to deliver a digital experience, the bank may not have implemented an online fraud monitoring system (gap in Engine 4, however, the bank does not leverage industrialisation and the innovation engines framework). So at a project level, the bank has the following three options:

(a) Implement online fraud monitoring at a much smaller scale as part of the digital experience—leaving behind the additional investment required to manage the smaller solution manually and additional investment required for integrating case management solution with the embedded solution.
(b) Reschedule implementation of digital experience until online fraud monitoring is implemented (Engine 4) bank-wide 'all-pervasive intelligence into process and technology' and lose the revenue stream to be generated from digital experience during the intervening period.
(c) Change the future vision of the bank and do not pursue DDE, thus losing all the planned revenue and savings, all the costs and, in the process, all the profits.

3.2.3   Technical Debt Build-Up Creates Existential Level Questions for the Bank

Banks have accumulated huge technical debt as a result of decisions taken over the years and many are in a debt trap! The technical debt trap means banks are not able to raise sufficient capital to undertake a plan to deliver the long-term Banking 4.0 vision of the bank.

High Latency Everywhere
Existing technology infrastructure at most banks is slow and not geared for low latency. In the past five years or so, banks have built faster payments. While banks have achieved low latency in payments, their processes in services, financial closures, risk management, mis and dashboards, regulatory reporting, customer onboarding, and document processing is abysmally slow.

Technology processes for deployment of changes in production, model development, training, and deployment are also very slow making it extremely difficult to deliver the digital experience.

a.   *No Business Case for Investment in Technology!*

This is a paradoxical situation: because the bank did not invest in technology in the past, there is no business case for investment in future!!

Banks need to modernise legacy and monolithic applications, completely replace existing control and integration design to deliver the marketplace business model and digital experience to compete with Fintechs. A very high technology cost of changes in the peripheral system makes a business proposal for these new opportunities non-viable from the beginning and over a period competitive advantage and market share is lost to competition and Fintech, that is, players with lower technical debt or Fintech forge ahead.

b.   *Impact on Service Quality*

Unless the existing technical debt is paid off substantially, service quality and delivery, types of services, and cost structure of the bank differ and are unable to provide the digital experience in real time or offer products and services as offered by Fintechs or banks with low technical debt.

c.   *Restrained Innovation*

Short-term, tactical, and cost-cutting, short-sighted decisions, project-level technology design, architecture, and implementation restrain banks from innovation at a future date.

d.   *Case Study: Nubank Has Emerged as a Challenger Bank in Brazil*

With over 25 million customers in the seven years since inception, Nubank is valued at over $10 Bn. The Brazilian banking market is dominated by four or five traditional players. Nubank emerged as a challenger bank with no brick and mortar stores and providing all of its services through digital channels, making it one of the largest digital banks in the world.

3.3 Managing Technical Debt

3.3.1 Case Study: UBS Has Budgeted to Spend 10% of Revenue on Technology

We spent more than 10% of our revenues (around USD 3.5 billion) on technology in 2019, including amounts spent on regulatory change programmes and innovative solutions for our businesses and clients.

UBS Annual Report 2020

3.3.2 Empirical Study of Managing Technical Debt at 12 Banks

Researching through over 200 annual reports, investor presentations, regulatory filings, and interviews published in the public domain of 12 banks for the past 3–10 years across product offerings, geographies, and customer focus across regulatory jurisdictions, technology, and business strategies, investment planned to indicate that the banks have largely completed their first round of investment in mobile banking and omnichannel and banks have started investing in:

- Delivering digital experience to customers, partners, and employees
- Establishing a Banking 4.0 vision of the industrialised bank of tomorrow
- Aligning industrialisation and innovation engines.

Methodology of an Empirical Quantitative Study over Three Years (2016–2018): Annual Reports of 12 Banks
Banks communicate short- and medium-term technology strategy objectives, investment, and achievements in annual reports.

We counted the number of times a bank used the word 'technology' and 'digital' in its annual report as a proxy to third-generation technology vs strategy for industrialisation of the bank.

Measure	As the proxy for
Count of the word 'digital' in the annual report (with all variations and including cloud, AI, machine learning, intelligence)	Banking 4.0 vision of the industrialised bank to deliver digital experience, business agility, and marketplace banking, with a focus on industrialised data and AI investment

(continued)

(continued)

Measure	As the proxy for
Count of the word 'technology' in the annual Report (with all variations)	The legacy technology projects and strategy
Ratio of the word count of digital/technology	An alignment ratio of >100% is an empirical indicator of the alignment of technology strategy and investment to the Banking 4.0 vision Across the years a ratio of >100% is an empirical indicator of bank-wide consistency in the Banking 4.0 vision

Bank	Count and ratio measures	2018	2017	2016
DBS Singapore	Digital word count	193	264	136
	Technology word count	75	56	69
	Alignment ratio (%)	257	471	197
OCBC Singapore	Digital word count	145	21	24
	Technology word count	49	48	51
	Alignment ratio (%)	296	44	47
PNC bank USA	Digital word count	25	19	9
	Technology word count	44	42	34
	Alignment ratio (%)	57	45	26
Capital One USA	Digital word count	47	41	42
	Technology word count	102	69	63
	Alignment ratio (%)	46	59	67
Rabo Bank (Europe)	Digital word count	72	94	52
	Technology word count	15	34	32
	Alignment ratio (%)	480	276	163
State Bank of India	Digital word count	117	86	67
	Technology word count	63	81	75
	Alignment ratio (%)	186	106	89
HDFC Bank (India)	Digital word count	57	27	24
	Technology word count	39	28	36
	Alignment ratio (%)	146	96	67
Lloyds Bank (UK)	Digital word count	119	89	85
	Technology word count	49	40	27
	Alignment ratio (%)	243	220	315
Barclays Bank (UK)	Digital word count	58	51	38
	Technology word count	85	58	65
	Alignment ratio (%)	61	88	58

(continued)

(continued)

Bank	Count and ratio measures	2018	2017	2016
Nedbank (South Africa)	Digital word count	89	106	30
	Technology word count	26	23	12
	Alignment ratio (%)	342	461	250
HSBC (UK)	Digital word count	38	14	14
	Technology word count	43	26	16
	Alignment ratio (%)	88	54	88
Citi Bank (USA)	Digital word count	40	45	18
	Technology word count	39	33	23
	Alignment ratio (%)	103	136	78

Interpreting the Alignment Ratio

The alignment ratio of >100% is a proxy indicator of the alignment of technology strategy and investment to the Banking 4.0 vision. The ratio is thus also a proxy indicator for delivering the bank's Banking 4.0 vision.

An alignment ratio of >100% is a proxy indicator that the bank has started reaping the benefits of lowering its technical debt. The bank can consistently allocate capital year after year to implement its Banking 4.0 vision. It is an indicator that the bank is aligning its industrialisation and innovation engines for its digital and industrialisation journey.

For a medium-sized bank, the ratio of digital/ technology term keeps growing. This also means that the industrialisation and innovation strategy starts maturing across the cycles. The Banking 4.0 vision across the cycles also changes based on benchmarking exercises conducted by the bank.

Across the years the alignment ratio of >100% is a proxy indicator of bank-wide consistency in the Banking 4.0 vision. For large banks, the ratio fluctuates across the years from <100% to >100%. The variation across the years at large banks is an indicator that the bank is implementing a BU-wise Banking 4.0 strategy. After achieving a certain level of maturity in one BU, it starts investing in another.

3.4 Adopting Industrialisation and Innovation Engine Alignment Framework to Manage Technical Debt

Technical debt means the bank has made an enormous investment to kick-start the industrialisation and innovation at the bank, both of which are iterative processes. The secret to keeping the bank free of technical debt is to ensure that the industrialisation and innovation engine is running and self-sustaining and that friction in the process is minimised.

In the previous section as well as in the chapter 'Aligning Engines of Industrial-isation and Innovation to Deliver Banking 4.0 Services', we identified six engines of industrialisation and innovation. Keeping these engines running continuously and self-sustaining will reduce the friction and the technical debt drastically.

3.4.1 The Project-Based Approach to Managing Technology Debt

A project-based approach to technology design, architecture, and delivery is not suitable to keep industrialisation and innovation running and churning out business outcomes.

Third-generation banks work on a project-based structure to deliver change in the technology and process. In this approach, each of the engine components will be built as part of the project delivery.

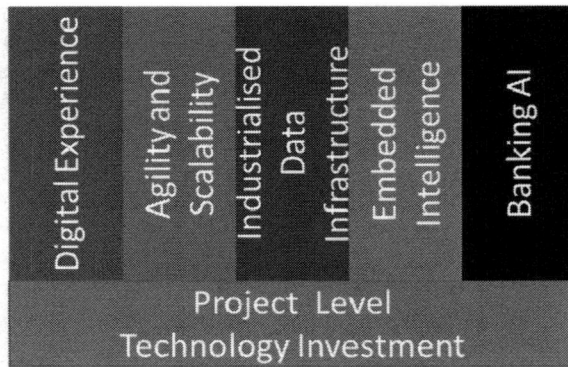

In an ideal situation, let us assume the project gets the full required budget of technology investments approved, and all the required engines as planned, designed, and architected at the project level are implemented and delivered. In this scenario, the project team feels that the project has not left behind any technical debt.

However,

1. All components are designed, architected, built, and financed from a project budget with project timelines. To optimise or minimise involvement from other teams, the project duplicates many sub-modules or functionalities and duplicates the data required for processing. A log of duplication is built by the project. The entire project design is driven by the project goals, so the next time another project requires interfaces with the application or data covered by the project, it needs to build those interfaces as a part of the other project and from another projected budget. Both of these add to huge technical debt for the bank.

2. The project builds sub-modules and functionality within the project. With the project approach, the design and architecture do not consider the re-usability of these components by other applications or projects. The same components are built by other projects. Examples are banking AI and embedded intelligence. For example, if a fraud monitoring solution is built within the solution, it cannot be used by other products. The same is true for workflow, case management, etc.

3. A part of the functionality is built within the project application. With functionality fragmented across the projects, with no centralised vision, re-usability, design, or architectural framework aligning them with the Banking 4.0 vision or the innovation benchmarks centrally, it is very difficult to map fragmented engines to the industrialisation vision of the bank. With fragmented budgets and assumptions, it is challenging to even estimate capital requirements and allocation. This makes it increasingly difficult to engage the bank's Board of Directors on innovation, Banking 4.0 vision, competition or market share, or business strategy.

3.4.2 Establish a Bank-Wide Vision for Industrialisation and Innovation

After reading about the project approach to manage technical debt, please do not conclude that the project approach to building technology is bad or that banks do not take up or deliver centralised, bank-wide initiatives.

Establish Industrialisation Engines

The purpose of the Banking 4.0 vision and framework must be to deliver bank-wide industrialisation and innovation. The purpose is to identify and document a bank-wide vision of the industrialisation and innovation vision about the future at the end of every cycle of the selected period. As the bank implements the projects, the bank can start by:

- Making the assets, design, and architecture built by each project visible for designing industrialisation and innovation engines centrally.
- Standardise to make everything re-usable at the project level—be it process, technology, design, interfaces, architecture, intelligence, applications, APIs, etc.
- Identify, define, and document the industrialisation and innovation engines at a bank level.

Establish Innovation in a BAU Mode

The purpose is to establish a mechanism to continuously benchmark the bank's vision about the future with external benchmarks in order to build and strengthen a feedback loop on innovation. The aim of this framework is to identify, articulate,

and document the industrialisation and innovation vision about Banking 4.0 periodically—at least once a year. Identify the alignment required in each engine to realise
the industrialisation vision of the bank.

Identify the Innovation Benchmarks Relevant for the Bank
The bank must continuously update its vision about industrialisation by benchmarking the bank's vision against Fintech, Bigtech, marketplace, digitally native
and cloud-native customers, and competing banks and financial services institutions.
The bank should establish a BAU and IT governance processes to receive external
benchmarks and assess the bank's vision continuously (but at least once per cycle to
plan for the next cycle).

Innovation leader banks invest ahead of the cycle to ensure that all engines are
aligned for the next two or more cycles of industrialisation and innovation.

Banks must identify all misalignment that will remain at the end of the next cycle.
Leader banks identify misalignment that is likely to happen in the next two or three
or more cycles.

Benchmarking misalignment against the innovations likely to be brought to the
market by Fintechs help to prioritise and secure capital allocation for the next cycle(s).
The chapter on Fintech discusses its new role as an innovation benchmark.

Non-alignment of industrialisation of innovation engine for one or more cycles
can result in a loss of revenue, market position, growth (loss of capital accretion), or
other financial losses.

Proactively Discover, Manage, and Pay Off Technical Debt
Proactively identify the alignment requirements and invest in the alignment of
engines, so that industrialisation and innovation never stops and technical debt never
starts accumulating. Earlier alignment drastically reduces technical debt accumulation. Spread the future vision of the bank across all business units to get the board's
backing, by allocating capital for industrialisation and innovation engines.

3.4.3 Mapping the Project-Based Approach to Industrialisation and Innovation Engine Framework

Banks manage technology through projects and each bank may prefer to continue
managing technology through projects. Managing a smaller chunk of the work as
a project enhances the success rate of delivering the project. Building the Banking
4.0 framework does not aim to increase the average size of the project. The framework aims to grow the design, architecture, standardisation, re-usability, and benefit
coverage to ensure each project has a bank-wide impact.

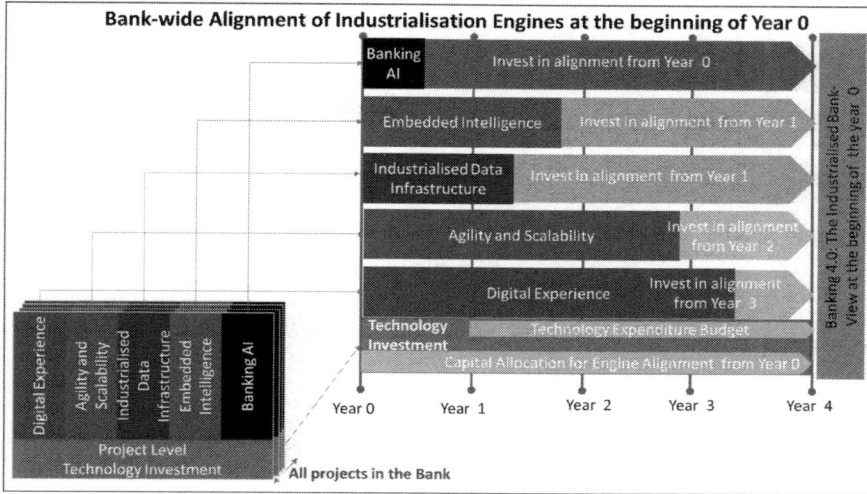

Bank-wide Alignment of Industrialisation Engines at the beginning of Year 0

Allocate Capital for Industrialisation and Innovation Engine Alignment

The banks will have to engage the Board of Directors and investors by presenting the economic capital required at each step of the Banking 4.0 roadmap. ICAAP methodology to compute capital for strategy risk can be used to estimate the capital required to operationalise the bank's vision of Banking 4.0.

The banks will have to start proactively paying off technical debt by investing in the alignment of the engines of the industrialisation of the bank. Paying off technical debt is a long and tortuous journey. Financial services firms have to make a focused investment for many years without getting immediate business results.

The banks also have to invest in the current cycle to upgrade an industrialisation engine to create the capabilities needed by other engines in future cycles. This also means not embedding proactive investment made into the project budget. Investment in the alignment should be allocated and charged to the user of the system. It is an investment in the future.

After every cycle, the bank will have to assess and allocate capital to invest in engines so that all engines continue to be completely aligned for the next cycle.

Alignment of Industrialisation and Innovation Engines Can Be Used as a Template to Compute Capital Allocation

Technology strategy is an important pillar of a bank's business strategy. As part of the Banking 4.0 vision, to implement a multi-year technology strategy, banks allocate capital towards a business and technology strategy. However, banks are not required to separately disclose investment or capital allocation for the latter.

In 2020, the European Central Bank (ECB) mandated the public disclosure of overall Pillar II capital requirements (covering the capital requirement for business strategy). However, the ECB has not mandated a split in the Pillar II capital. For the year 2021, ECB has highlighted 'Disruptive digital innovation and non-bank competition' as one of the key risk drivers for Pillar II capital.

Alignment of industrialisation and innovation engines can be used as a template to compute capital allocation for technology strategy consistently across the years and the business units.

Keep Aligning the Industrialisation and Innovation Engines at Least Once a Year. More Frequent Alignment Is Recommended
Compared to technology platforms (Google, Facebook, etc.), banks have not been able to industrialise technology. For banks, migrating out of technical debt is not a simple decision as it requires a long-term roadmap to pay off the technical debt amid its iterative process. This book itself presents a roadmap to redeem technical debt.

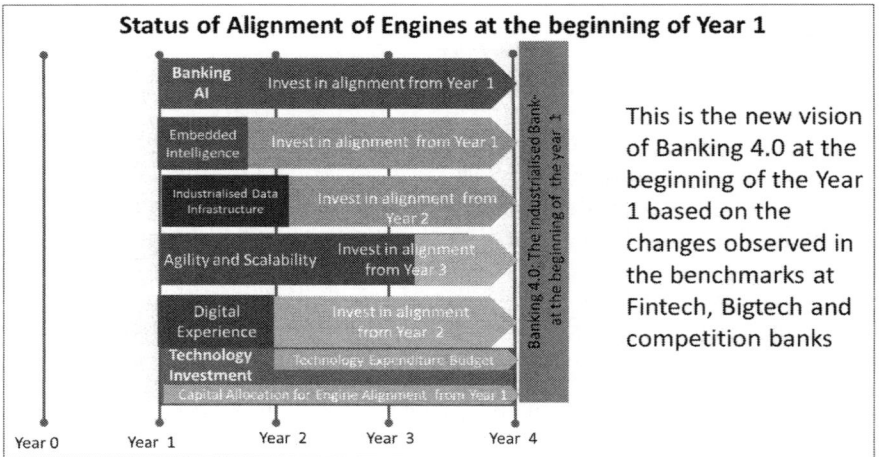

3.5   Managing the Alignment Process

3.5.1   Continuously Rediscover Banking 4.0 Vision

Continuously acquiring investment and capital allocated for alignment of industrialisation and innovation engines may be difficult unless Banking 4.0 vision starts delivering business outcomes. An illustrative list of Banking 4.0 functionalities to deliver desired business outcomes in terms of revenue growth and cost reduction is outlined below.

Uplift Revenue		Additional Revenue Stream	Automate to Reduce Costs and Losses		
Prospect Marketing	Customer Sales	Low Capital Intensive services	Automation BOTs, and Workflow	Self Service	Predictive Risk Shield
Customer Similarity Segment	Auto approved products and limits	API Banking	Auto data collection	Customer channel affinity	Collection Dashboard
Feedback and Social Network Funnel – Sentiments	Customer Product affinity	Promote and participate in Marketplace	Data extraction	Hyper personalisation for services	Early Warning for Credit
Customer counterparty's affinity	Customer Portfolio dashboard	Third-party financial and non financial product distribution	Auto fill of application	Differentiated pricing	Fraud Prevention
Recommendation Engine	360 degree view of customer	Promote and participate in Blockchain based platforms	Auto verify and reconcile	Digital Onboarding	Customer counterparty Delinquency Signals
Lead Generation	Hyper personalisation for sales	Digital ID and authentication service	Process analysis	Digital non financial transactions	Customer Delinquency Signals
Prospect segmentation	Recommendation Engine	Value added services for fees based products	NLG to complete report	Digital Lending	Better Underwriting
API Banking	Low capital intensive product dashboard	Tax and Accounting Services	Conversational BOTs	Digital Trade Finance	Monitoring Correspondent Banks
Third party product distribution	Daily Relationship performance dashboard	Data services for customers	Chatbots	Digital Deposit	Account Activities and Fund Diversion
Campaign Management	Simulation for RMs	Risk measurement services for customers	Q&A BOTs	Digital Collection and Fraud investigation	Capital Simulator
	Relationship pricing inputs	Office and Document Management Services	Automated Underwriting	Digital self service	RAROC Dashboard
	Customer Persona	GST and Payroll services	Extract and Write Narration	Conversational banking	Liquidity Monitoring
	Revenue Leakages	Inventory Management for customer	Partner / Vendor Fees paid / services consumed dashboard	Digital experience	

3.5.2 Promote and Adopt Banking Technology Standards

There is a significant opportunity and business case to standardise data, their definitions, and computation methods, banking concepts and terms, and technology processes within a bank. At the banking industry level, these initiatives should be promoted internally to be adopted. There is a business case to benchmark the bank against industry standards such as:

- ISO 20022—business dictionaries and data model
- BIAN artefacts, business object model, and semantic APIs
- Agility, scalability, and resiliency standards provide a cloud service to a bank
- Data privacy and data mutualisation standards prescribed by GDPR and other regulations
- Cybersecurity standards published by multiple regulators in terms of multi-factor authentication, secure applications, digital signatures, and other forms of security such as biometrics
- Best practices standards published by regulators for digital only banks
- Open banking and API standards published by regulators and banking industry bodies globally.

3.5.3 Build Banking AI for the Bank

Building banking AI is a very long journey. The bank needs to consistently invest for many years to build a banking AI corpus and algorithms to deliver the Banking 4.0 vision.

The banking industry has to make industry-level investments to build industry-specific standards and libraries for semantic definitions for products, processes, terms, and computations, etc. The banking industry has consistently lagged in the firm-level adoption of bank-specific knowledge.

This has resulted in limited development and adoption of technology standards and industrialisation. Furthermore, inertia in the development of standards has hindered internal adoption in firms as well as externally by partners and customers. The three most important areas where banking AI makes a big impact are:

- Voice first banking or conversational banking at scale
- Personalisation at scale
- Industrialisation of document management.

The bank may plan investment in banking AI as per the contribution to the Banking 4.0 vision.

3.5.4   Adopt ISO 20022 Standards Internally in the Bank for Every Data and Process

ISO 20022 standards aim to establish software interoperability both within a bank and across banks. It provides a framework to define the metadata repository, messages, computation, banking terms and concepts, and business processes.

To develop banking AI within a bank, the ISO 20022 framework needs to be developed for and adopted by the bank. The semantic capability of ISO 20022, the structured data hierarchies of ISO 20022, should be seen from the perspective of building banking AI into the bank's machines.

3.5.5   Augment IT Governance to Encourage, Enable, and Enforce Paying off Technical Debt

The difference between financial debt and technical debt is that financial debt is raised, serviced, and paid by the same person.

Unfortunately, technical debt is raised by the new application design/architecture team, serviced by the application or process maintenance team (reconciliation and manual efforts and cost), and repaid by future applications and business plans. Therefore, there is a need to augment the IT governance function to encourage, enable, and enforce industrialisation and innovation to pay off technical debt.

ISACA—COBIT has started recognising management of technical debt as a priority to be ensured by the IT governance function. However, unfortunately, ISACA considers the management of technical debt to be an operational issue rather than a strategic one, while for banks, technical debt is a key survival issue that is way beyond a strategic issue.

In many cases, technical debt is never paid off and keeps accumulating. This severely impacts the alignment of industrialisation and innovation engines at banks. IT governance at banks should be augmented to establish process and measurement templates to align all six engines of industrialisation and innovation. IT governance could be augmented with scenario templates to identify engine alignment requirements for each year.

To manage trade-offs between historically accumulated technical debt, and what is being paid as a part of RTB and CTB initiatives and further being added for a future date by architecture, design, technology selection, and prioritisation decisions, IT governance should be augmented.

Augment IT governance to manage the impact of a payoff of technical debt on architecture, design, and innovations. Augment IT governance structure for better collaborations across the value chain, across the products, between RTB and CTB, between owners of the industrialisation and innovation engines, so that different parts of the organisation collaborate to manage technical debt and work together to industrialise and innovate across time and review cycles.

3.5.6 Make Technology All-Pervasive

Technology is all-pervasive at the fourth-generation bank. To create full benefits at no marginal cost, a bank should create a strong culture, organisational structure, and technology for industrialisation and innovation.

The bank needs to upgrade the IT governance, architecture, design, technology process, capital allocation, and budgetary approval process to promote industrialisation, innovation, the platform business, service orientation, collaboration, and custodianship.

The economics of the technology allows full benefits to be reaped at no or low marginal cost. The biggest barrier to entry for the competition is delivering services at no or very low marginal costs. This also works as a barrier to the bank slipping into technical debt.

3.5.7 Continuously Benchmark Innovation

Innovation by the competition and industry is an area over which banks claim that they do not have much control. Leader banks have started gaining significant control over the factors for which banks do not have much control.

To continuously benchmark, learn, and induce innovation in the bank, the leader banks have established innovation centres in collaboration with Fintech, the banking industry, vendors, customers, and cloud providers.

Market leader banks have established innovation and incubation programmes in collaboration and partnership with Fintechs. Leader banks provide innovation as a service to their clients. Banks can engage Fintechs and customers better due to their inherent capability to fund a business.

The technology advancement has completed the full circle from being proprietary (mainframe) to a significant opportunity to participate in the advancement of open-source technology and also interoperability. Banks are promoting, participating, and funding open-source technologies. Fintech firms are at the forefront of advancement in open-source technologies and banks are investing in Fintechs and promoting them to build open-source capabilities ahead of the curve. Cloud providers are further pushing the envelope by providing open-source platforms, making software development much easier while retaining the freedom to innovate for users. Banks are collaborating with cloud providers to align their engines.

3.5.7.1 Benchmarking Case Study—HSBC Partnering with Google Cloud (GCP)

Since 2018, HSBC has partnered with GCP to leverage various GCP products. Many of these initiatives are building banking AI for HSBC on the AI platform provided by GCP.

- Using Google Cloud, HSBC has developed an NLP solution to review Cantonese-English contact centre conversations. HSBC has invested in building machine learning capabilities and industrialised data infrastructure on the GCP data platform.
- HSBC has built an intelligence hub to migrate HSBC data and analytics workflows onto Google Cloud. The bank is designing and building end-to-end data and banking AI solutions.
- HSBC has implemented BigQuery because of its performance over small and large datasets and the availability of an SQL interface and connected sheets to interact with it. BigQuery provides the capability to move data and its schema onto the cloud—without having to manually manage every detail. HSBC had a massive data warehouse which is complex and mission-critical and the existing reference architectures were not able to provide a path of migration. The bank has migrated 30 years of data comprising millions of transactions and 180 TB of data. The DWH ran 6500 extract, transform, load (ETL) jobs and more than 2500 reports, getting data from some 100 sources. BigQuery's capabilities to provide capacity and elasticity helped to solve the problem of capacity constraints.
- HSBC has hosted Corda Enterprise onto Google Cloud to reduce client onboarding times and costs. The bank has built a custody blockchain platform called Digital Vault on R3-Corda. The platform digitises the transaction records of private placement assets from equity to debt, and real estate. Moving the platform to Google Cloud will help HSBC expand its service offerings and enhance customer service.

3.5.7.2   Benchmarking Case Study—Bank Investment in AI Firm H2O.ai

H2O.ai is focused on bringing AI to businesses through software. Its flagship product is H2O, the leading open-source platform that makes it easy for financial services, insurance, and healthcare companies to deploy machine learning and predictive analytics to solve complex problems.

Capital One, Commonwealth Bank of Australia, Wells Fargo, Franklin Templeton, and Goldman Sachs have invested in the firm and are using the platform.

3.5.7.3   Benchmarking Case Study—Mastercard Acquired Brighterion in the Year 2017

To strengthen financial crime management in real-time in the marketplace, Mastercard strengthened its Decision Platform by acquiring Brighterion in 2017.

Brighterion provides real-time artificial intelligence technology to 74 out of 100 of the largest US banks and more than 2000 companies worldwide.

This ability to implement AI internationally on an unprecedented scale was difficult for Mastercard to build internally. Therefore, it decided to acquire the Brighterion platform first to integrate with its platform in 2016 which it ultimately acquired.

Brighterion comes with a distributed architecture and patented, self-learning technology. The platform AI and machine learning secure more than 100 billion transactions annually to help leading organisations manage the credit risk lifecycle and predict delinquency, prevent payments and acquirer fraud, detect healthcare fraud, waste and abuse, and more.

3.5.7.4   Benchmarking Case Study: Citi Has Built a Marketplace of Third-party Fintech Apps

Citi has signed data access agreements of customer-approved accounts with third-party Fintech apps and data aggregators in the marketplace. Citi customers will be provided with a way to permit and share their account information with financial apps and services through the use of API token-based technology.

Through the use of APIs, these agreements will help provide a seamless and secure data sharing experience for Citi customers who choose to share their financial data with third-party apps and services.

3.6 Conclusion—Continuously Rediscover, Benchmark, and Align

Daily new and emerging technologies and business models are eroding barriers to entry into the banking business. The bank needs to proactively map the future and innovate in the BAU mode to keep building the barriers.

To meet the challenge, in order to develop and deliver technologies and business models, the bank has to rediscover, benchmark, align, and implement industrialisation and innovation engines on a continuous and daily basis. Technical debt starts accumulating if there is slippage on rediscovering, benchmarking, or alignment and it is extremely difficult to redeem a bank from a technical debt trap.

Chapter 4
Industrialising Data

4.1 Introduction—Changed Data Requirements at Banks

Fourth-generation banking data infrastructure is undergoing a major shift as financial services firms are facing challenges to deliver digital experience in real time by processing very high data volumes.

Banks are managing real-time voice and text conversations, real-time financial transactions, servicing millions of customers connecting through personal smart devices, connecting to hundreds of marketplaces, complying with privacy and customer protection laws, and delivering the promised real-time digital experience. Self-service customers further accentuate the challenge as customer behaviour varies widely.

To address the challenge, banks are enhancing and making data infrastructure scalable, agile, resilient, and intelligent.

4.1.1 Deliver Digital Experience in Real Time

Fourth-generation banking empowers customers through real-time banking services, personalised service delivery, seamless connectivity to smart devices and marketplaces, and secured voice, video, and text communication.

Banks are leveraging the Internet of Things (IoT) in ATMs, mobile and internet banking logs, weblogs, GPS logs, spatial and cyber logs, etc. to deliver a digital experience and real-time personalised service. To achieve this, banks must collect

© Springer Nature Singapore Pte Ltd. 2022
M. Bhatia, *Banking 4.0*,
https://doi.org/10.1007/978-981-16-6069-6_4

and process exponentially large volumes of log data. Data collection and processing delivery gulp a very large volume of data in real-time.

4.1.1.1   Hyper-Personalised Experience in Real Time

Hyper-personalised self-service needs a very large volume of data to deliver a personalised customer experience. The large volume of data is derived from:

- Connecting with public datasets
- Funnelling social network datasets
- Learning from internal customer datasets

    – transactions with the bank
    – documents and datasets submitted to the bank
    – authentication and authorisation data of customers
    – historical data of services consumed by customers
    – customer Digital ID.

A very large data volume is handled and processed in real time to deliver hyper-personalised service as compared to data volume handled by a third-generation bank.

4.1.2   Process High Volumes of Data

4.1.2.1   Deliver Digital Experience Through Speech, Video, and Text Communications

Delivering customer experience means processing a very large volume of unstructured data in real time. For the past five years or so, year-on-year unstructured data growth has been in the range of 50%.

To deliver customer experience through Speech, Video, and Text communication, the entire data infrastructure—the data pipes, storage and processing, analytics, data visualisation, and machine learning algorithms, etc. need to be upgraded to process high volume of data growing at 50% annually.

4.1.2.2   Deliver Machine Learning Models to Manage and Monitor Complex Financial Transactions in Real Time

To manage the complexity of real-time transactions which are integrated with the marketplace to service thousands of smart devices and applications, banks are developing data analysis and machine learning algorithms.

4.1.2.3 Deliver Granular Data to Regulators

Regulators have changed engagement models with regulated firms. Regulators are demanding data at an extremely granular level (not reports!!) and traceability.

To deliver on the regulatory demand, banks have built microservice-based applications, APIs as an integration tool; bank-wide data search and data catalogues to manage metadata and data governance.

4.1.2.4 Faster Finance, Regulatory, and Compliance Reporting

To comply with IFRS 9 and IFRS 17 finance reporting requirements, BCBS 239 standards for risk reporting are followed, including high-frequency algorithmic trading, surveillance of trader's phone and textual communication, and real-time cyber monitoring, and banks are upgrading technology for a faster near real-time data movement from front to mid and back office.

4.1.2.5 Data and Analytics Volumes at Banks

The banking industry is very different from any other industry. Why? The most relevant differentiator is the volumes of financial transactions handled by the banks every day. No other industry handles the following range of transactions and analytics volumes.

Data and analytics volumes at banks	Volume
Assets size	$50 Bn–1500 Bn
Financial and non-financial transactions every day	2–50 million
Customers serviced	3–200 million
Concurrent users for analytics	1000–3000 users
Analytics jobs executed daily	20,000–40,000 jobs
Analytical system uptime requirement	>99.5% uptime
Transactional system uptime requirement	99.999–99.9999%
Unstructured data—speech, video, document, text, unstructured as a % of total data	>90%
Structured data	<10%

Real-time electronic payments have tripled in most countries in the past five years. Daily real-time payment transaction volume is conjectured to grow by more than five times (2–50 M × 5) in the next five years or so.

At present, real-time transactions are in the range of 50–90% of the total daily transactions (2–50 M) at most banks and the real-time daily transaction ratio is likely to grow to >90% (2–50 M) in the next five years.

Since 2013, regulators have mandated the banking industry to implement data lineage, governance, custodianship, and accuracy, as well as complete financial statements, and risk and regulatory reporting.

The BCBS 239 framework mandates the modernisation of data infrastructure to deliver low latency, high volume processing, accuracy, and completeness of data aggregation and reporting.

The regulatory requirement for data has grown by 10× in the past five years and is estimated to grow by another 10× in the next five years. To improve the sharpness of monetary policy and the effectiveness of central banking decisions, regulators need additional data to manage stress in the economy.

To sharpen their capabilities in managing systemic risks, regulators have implemented legal entity indicators (LEI) for customers at banks globally. Regulators aim to augment their understanding of bank customers by collecting transactions and asset data for each of the bank's customers.

To manage data volume that will be submitted as a result, regulators are establishing data lakes and science labs internally. Regulators are working on plans to implement machine-readable regulatory regimes. Thus, banks need to upgrade their technology infrastructure to cope with the regulatory demand.

4.1.2.6 Industrialisation Has Enabled STP for 90% Transactions

90% of transactions are in straight-through processing	Expected response time
Algorithmic trading	Micro to nano seconds
Trade surveillance	Less than a second
Authentication—including biometric	Seconds
Trading on a platform	Seconds
Payments and financial transactions	1–2 s
Cyber risk and fraud detection	Seconds to minutes
Payment screening	Seconds to minutes

4.1.2.7 Journey Time for STP Transactions Has Dropped by 99%

Banks are implementing IoT in ATM, mobile banking, weblogs, GPS, and spatial and cyber logs. Implementation of IoT involves the collection and analysis of an extremely large volume of logs on multiple tracks for business decisions.

With real-time payments, mobile banking, conversational UI, self-service, algorithmic trading, real-time liquidity, and market risk management, real-time fraud, and cyber risk management, the journey time for data from the front to the back office has decreased by more than 99% in many cases.

4.1.2.8 Automation Has Reduced the Cycle Time of Manual Processes by 50%

Statistical, data mining, NLP, and machine learning-enabled data discovery tools and capabilities help to build intelligence into data quality, custodial, and governance functions by identifying and rectifying errors, applying semantic data definitions, automating reconciliation, adjustment and error rectification, providing identity resolution, and identity matching. Tools also provide data lineage capabilities. Unlike many other industries, the banking industry has many special requirements for data quality and governance, accuracy, and lineage under BCBS 239 standards.

10% of transactions of banks are delivered through human intervened decision-making	Existing decision cycle time
Customer onboarding and credit approval	Minutes to days
Intraday liquidity and trading desk monitoring	Minutes to hours
Financial/GL/sub-ledger closures	Hours to days
Fraud/AML investigation	Hours to days
Clearing and settlement	Minutes to hours to days
Internal and external reporting	Minutes to hours to days

Inbuilt visualisation capabilities in the data discovery process help to automate data integration and empower business users. Patterns and trends discovery capability, along with the use of third-party libraries greatly enhances automation of the integration process and substantially reduces manual intervention, decreasing latency and enhancing data quality and accuracy. This is the single most important capability to aid the industrialisation of a bank.

Banks are automating their decision-making processes by leveraging machine learning and AI techniques in credit underwriting, conversational UI, management of risk and fraud, cyber risk, real-time analysis, alert generation, self-service, reconciliation, marketing, etc.

4.2 Key Indicators of Data Industrialisation

Industrialised data means a scalable, agile, resilient, real-time, intelligent, and contextualised data platform.

4.2.1 Aligned Industrialisation and Innovation Engines with Data Industrialisation Engines

Data industrialisation is a long and iterative process. It requires continuously aligning engines that deliver and redefine business and technology architecture, people skills, and technology implementation or, in other words, the entire target-operating model of the bank.

The iterative process changes take two to five years to show visible business benefits, thus change managers need to communicate with and win the trust of the board of directors and the bank's investors to secure the requisite budget, support, and guidance.

4.2.2 Deliver Data in a Managed Service Mode

A cloud data platform delivers agility, scalability, and resiliency.

- Agility is delivered through enterprise-wide data governance and metadata and data catalogue.
- Scalability is delivered through scalable computing engines and storage.
- Resiliency is delivered through the backup modules and guaranteed high availability of the cloud.

4.2.3 Better Certainty in Data Service Delivery

Automation and orchestration of data resources with agreed service level objectives and indicators for data quality, coverage, timeliness, completeness, lineage, and availability provide more certainty in data services.

4.2.4 Deliver Greater Consistency and Accuracy in Models and Analytics

Cloud-based platforms and analytical notebooks are enabling analytics and models to be embedded on mobile and smart devices. Since the entire business management process is transforming itself to be data-driven, consistency and accuracy are required to build the trust of users.

In the chapter on AI as a service, analytical and modelling patterns were discussed. In the same chapter, we also addressed the industrialisation of machine learning model development, testing, and deployment through modelling pipelines, process orchestration, and APIs; better consistency and accuracy are then built across models and analytics.

4.2.5   Deliver Industrialised Model and Analytics Development, Training and Deployment

Standardisation, consistency, and re-use with a self-service provision.

- Data pipelines and process orchestration to manage data and transformation.
- Machine learning model pipelines to manage their development and deployment.
- Microservices and API to manage application and data integration.

4.2.6   Manage All Data Types

- SQL, NoSQL, file processing
- Wide column, GraphDB, in-memory, and horizontal expansion.

4.2.7   Deliver Conversational Banking at Scale

- Cloud speech to text, cloud text to speech, cloud vision, cloud natural language (both processing and generation), and dialogue management.

4.2.8   Better Data Governance

Data governance aims to reduce duplication and enhance re-usability to reduce data bloat. Data governance enforces consistency in the definition, quality measurement, and quality policy consistency of data. Data governance is enabled by technology tools to provide:

- Data classification, cataloguing, search
- Enterprise data dictionary
- Technical and business metadata management
- Business lineage and business context
- Data quality.

4.2.9   Industrialised Data Privacy Compliance

- Identify PII, enforce privacy requirements, automate linkages with consent and data inventories.
- Identify data residency and enforce privacy laws for cross-border data transfer.
- Encrypt data with the encryption key of requisite strength and key management.

4.2.10   Empowered Business Managers

The industrialisation of data infrastructure changes the data services from a shortage of technical resources to scalable technical resources, from fragmented to agile resources and processes, from managing a supply chain to resiliency to enable business outcomes, from customisation to standardisation, from personal to community resources.

4.3   Industrialise Data Integration

To support the fourth-generation business model, banks are upgrading their data integration capabilities.

With the changing business model and cost structures, integration is required at various points in the process life cycle. For industrialisation, the financial services firm needs seamless integration capabilities for the front, mid, and back office.

Some of the industrialised integration examples are:

- APIs published by the bank for consumption
- APIs consumed by banks
- Integrated data pipelines
- Data integration with data pipelines
- Orchestrated technology process
- Machine learning pipelines
- Integration with public, private, and hybrid clouds
- APIs published by the marketplace leveraging bank's APIs
- Messaging, integration, APIs, and data pipelines with real-time payments
- Integration with regulatory reporting including machine-readable integration.

4.3.1   *Convergence of Data Preparation and Data Integration Tools*

With data preparation and integration now widely spread across the data value chain, tools are converging and becoming more intelligent.

On the technology front, the ingestion, integration, quality, preparation, and transformation of data, feature engineering, data wrangling and cataloguing, among data tools are converging. This is paving the way for a core active metadata informed and ML-enabled data fabric design that transforms data management and integration.

Banks are adopting intelligent data preparation and integration right from data ingestion to data preparation. They are embedding visual exploration to generate exceptions, analytics, and insights on integration, with the end objective to facilitate consistency and accuracy in models and analytics.

The data management function is moving from the technology domain to the business domain. Banks are implementing geospatial visualisation tools for data discovery to empower business users. So, business managers need to be empowered to manage data preparation and integration.

Data preparation and integration tools automate data governance requirements of data quality, metadata management, data custodian functionality, semantic definitions, traceability, and privacy.

4.3.2   *Industrialise Data Preparation*

Data preparation and data transformation consumes 90% of modelling and analytics effort so data preparation is a prime target of industrialisation.

Data preparation for analytics and modelling is an involved exercise. Automation in data preparation and the latter's use in modelling has converged the data preparation methodology and algorithms with modelling methodologies and algorithms. Feature engineering methods to prepare data required for advanced machine learning models can either be considered as a part of machine learning modelling itself or as a part of data preparation.

With the convergence of methods and algorithms and automation in machine learning model development and deployment, we can safely say that more than 90% of the effort in machine learning modelling goes towards data preparation and transformation.

4.3.3   Data Wrangling for Machine Learning Models

Data preparation and data wrangling are processes of data cleansing and data transformation. While the term 'data preparation' is used for transforming raw data, 'data wrangling' means to prepare data for analytical models or machine learning models.

A data wrangling tool has techniques to manage more complex data more quickly, produce more accurate results, and make better decisions. It includes:

- Data cleansing
- Removing extraneous data and outliers
- Filling in missing values
- Conforming data to a standardised pattern
- Masking private or sensitive data entries
- Test for errors.

Data Transformation

- Transforming and enriching data into the desired format
- Enriching means adding or connecting data with other related information to provide deeper insights.

Feature Engineering

- Feature engineering is a process of using banking knowledge to extract features from raw data via data mining techniques.
- These features can be used to improve the performance of machine learning algorithms or analytical patterns. Feature engineering itself is an applied machine learning or analytical pattern.

4.3.4   Case Study: Google Cloud Data Wrangling Tool

Google Cloud Dataprep is a white-labelled, managed version of Trifacta Wrangling. Cloud Dataprep is a managed data service provided by Google for visually exploring, cleaning, and preparing structured and unstructured data for analysis, reporting, and machine learning. It is UI-based so writing code is not required. Cloud Dataprep can be used for interactive data transformation, and is especially useful for working with new datasets.

For large volumes of data or cases in which the set of needed transformations is well defined, Google Cloud Dataflow is a good option for implementing transformations as it supports both batch and stream processing.

Data transformation and wrangling are the processes of mapping data from its raw form into data structures and formats that are required for the consumption of data in the analytical pattern on a machine learning model. Transformations can include the following:

- Replacing missing values with a default value.

- Replacing missing values with an inferred value based on other attributes in a record.
- Replacing missing values with an inferred value based on attributes in other records.
- Changing the format of numeric values, such as truncating or rounding real numbers to integers.
- Removing or correcting attribute values that violate business logic, such as an invalid product identifier.
- Deduplication records.
- Joining records from different datasets.
- Aggregating data, such as summing values of metrics into hour or minute totals.

4.3.5 Industrialised Data Preparation Tools Are Embedded with Statistical and Visualisation Capabilities

Newer data preparation tools are embedded with the following statistical and visualisation techniques to automate the sourcing, integration, transformation, and discovery of data, and feature engineering.

- Forecasting
- Trending
- Exceptions
- Outliers and anomalies detection
- Clustering
- Correlation
- Link analysis.

4.3.6 Case Study: Google Cloud Datalab Tool to Explore, Analyse, Transform, and Visualise Data for Building Machine Learning Models

- Cloud Datalab provides techniques to explore, visualise, analyse, and transform data.
- Cloud Datalab has embedded Python and SQL libraries and works interactively.
- Cloud Datalab has pre-installed Jupyter notebooks to access, analyse, monitor, and visualise data.
- The Jupyter Notebook can also be used with Python, TensorFlow machine learning, Google Analytics, Google BigQuery, and Google Charts APIs.

4.3.7 Case Study: BigQuery Geospatial Visualisation Techniques

For geospatial visualisation, SQL query can be run, and results are displayed on an interactive map. Flexible styling features allow for the analysis and exploration of data.

4.3.8 Embedding Geospatial Visualisation into Applications Empowers Business Managers

Leveraging geospatial visualisation capabilities data preparation and integration for:

- Managing privacy
- Data residency
- Cyber risk analytics
- Fraud detection
- Sanction screening
- Country and political risk
- Legal entity
- KYC
- Currency risk
- Target marketing
- Conduct risk.

4.3.9 Case Study: Data Stream Processing Tools on Google Cloud

Cloud Data Fusion is a cloud-native data integration service. It provides self-service for ETL and ELT process pipelines as well as a re-usable, standardised, validated library of 150 pre-built connectors and transformations. It comes with built-in features like end-to-end data lineage, integration metadata, and cloud-native security and data protection services. Cloud Data Fusion services can be further augmented by a library of custom-made connections and transformations.

Google Cloud Dataflow is a stream and batch processing service to ingest, process, and analyse fluctuating volumes of real-time data.

Cloud Composer is a fully managed data workflow orchestration service to the author and schedule, and monitors software development pipelines across clouds and on-premise data centres. It is used for building directed acyclic graphs (DAGs) in Python.

4.3.10 Embed Data Integration into Applications

Traditionally, only the ETL process was used for integrating raw data from source systems.

With the adoption of more than 15 types analytical models and patterns for technical processes (like machine learning models for data quality, reconciliation, metadata, lineage, data extraction) and business processes (data scrapping, connecting to public datasets, filling of templates, robotic automation); data integration and transformation is required at every step when data is consumed by an analytical or machine learning model.

These analytical models and technical processes are now being embedded in applications and smart devices as APIs. Therefore, data integration and transformation methods are embedded into machine learning pipelines and orchestrated and managed as APIs.

4.3.11 Case Study: Building a Data Pipeline to Migrate Data to BigQuery

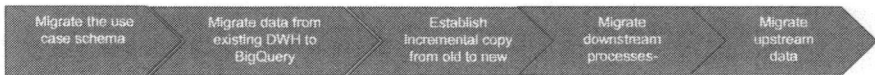

Migrate the use case schema	Migrate data from existing DWH to BigQuery	Establish incremental copy from old to new	Migrate downstream processes-	Migrate upstream data

- Processing data through a sequence of connected processing steps.
- Data transfer from the source system with ETL, data enrichment, and real-time data analysis.
- It can be applied both as a batch processing and a streaming process.
- Orchestration of the data pipeline between source and transactional systems to a data sink or warehouse or other applications.

4.4 Cloud Data Platform as the Data Industrialisation and Innovation Engine

A cloud data platform has a profound impact on data, technology, and business management at banks and is the data industrialisation and innovation engine for banks.

A cloud data platform largely eliminates the trouble with managing the underlying hardware, operating system, and database server infrastructure. Cloud enables data performance, flexibility, agility, scalability, and resiliency for a data platform.

A cloud data platform on cloud is a solution for transactional data and data warehousing, data lakes, data engineering, data science, machine learning, visualisation, building semantics, managing unstructured data, development, training, and deployment of models, and securely sharing and consuming data.

In this chapter, we have discussed data platforms on public clouds Google, AWS, and Azure products. However, our arguments are likely to hold good for other cloud providers such as IBM and Oracle.

A cloud data platform has completely different data management economics. Year on year banks have a very different Banking 4.0 vision. Based on the rates negotiated with the cloud provider and assumptions with regard to Banking 4.0, the business case may differ across the bank.

4.4.1   Cloud Data Platform Optimises Data Integration

Cloud provides fully managed data integration services. It provides building and managing data pipelines through a graphical interface. It provides orchestration services to integrate data integration and transformation. It provides fully managed services to transform and enrich data both in real time and batch mode.

Data storage is migrated to the cloud along with the migration of the data platform. The integration or staging area, result areas, and integration layer are all migrated to the cloud. This creates an opportunity to optimise data integration and remove the circuitous routes by adopting the directed acyclical graph methodology provided by cloud pipelines.

Data pipelines are tied in with a large variety of connectors to connect with different databases using ODBC and JDBC connectivity. When the data pipeline is deployed, DAG is transformed into a series of parallel computations which are executed as separate jobs.

- Approaches to optimise data pipelines

    - Orchestration of data transformation and processing to build data pipelines.
    - Orchestration of multiple data pipelines.
    - Parallelise data pipelines to provide an opportunity to reduce complexity and optimise dependencies.
    - Orchestration is to be reorganised by extracting common tasks into their own DAGs.

4.4.2   Cloud Data Platform Augments Data Storage

Banks are supplementing or replacing their existing data marts and data storage for the following capabilities provided by data lakes. Data lakes technology helps to embed intelligence into data preparation and integration and replace or augment ETL.

- Data integration mode

  - Batch
  - Incremental
  - Log data
  - Near real-time streaming data
  - Flat file
  - DB links
  - Messaging queues or APIs
  - JDBC/ ODBC
  - Flexible

- Data source coverage

  - Product processors
  - Cloud repositories
  - Enterprise data warehouse
  - Unstructured data
  - Streaming
  - Social data and logs

- Data type coverage

  - Structured data
  - Unstructured data
  - Distributed data
  - No-SQL data
  - Graph data.

4.5 Case Study—Cloud Data Platform

4.5.1 Case Study: Google Cloud Data Platform High-Level Architecture

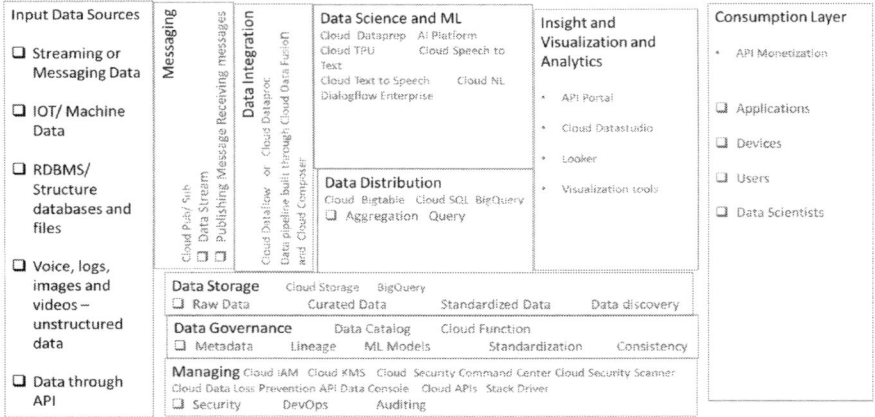

4.5.2 Data Ingestion and Integration Tools from GCP, AWS, and Azure

There are two approaches: One is to process data ingestion in batch mode and the other is to process it in event streaming. All three public clouds provide both approaches.

Data	Coverage	GCP product	AWS	Azure
Event ingestion	Scalable based on message queues	Cloud Pub/Sub	Amazon Simple Notification Service, Amazon Simple Queueing Service	Azure Service Bus Event Hub
ETL tool for both stream and batch processing	Managed service based on Apache Beam for stream and batch data processing	Cloud Dataflow	AWS Glue	Azure Databricks, Stream Analytics

(continued)

(continued)

Data	Coverage	GCP product	AWS	Azure
ETL tool for batch processing with ML capabilities. Cloud Fusion leverages this tool to deliver pipelines	Big data platform for running Apache Hadoop and Apache Spark jobs	Cloud Dataproc	AWS Glue	HDInsight, Batch

4.5.3 Building and Orchestrating Data Pipelines on GCP, AWS, and Azure

Building data pipelines	Code-free, visual data pipeline creation tool with 150 pre-loaded designs for data pipelines	Cloud Data Fusion	AWS Glue	Azure Data Factory
Orchestrating data pipelines	Orchestrating data pipelines	Cloud Composer	Amazon Data Pipeline, AWS Glue	Azure Logic Apps

4.5.4 Data Search on Data Catalog Capabilities on GCP, AWS, and Azure

Data search	Fully managed, scalable metadata management service	Data Catalog	AWS Glue Data Catalog Third-party tool Collibra and Alation	Azure Data Catalog

4.5.5   *SQL Data Modules on GCP, AWS, and Azure*

Data	Coverage	GCP product	AWS	Azure
SQL	Third-party RDBMS on VM	RDBMS on Compute Engine	Amazon Elastic Compute Cloud	Amazon Elastic Compute Cloud
SQL	Regional or BU Level	CloudSQL—MySQL and PostgreSQL	Amazon relational database service	SQL DB
SQL	Horizontally scalable, strongly consistent, relational database service	Cloud Spanner	Amazon Aurora	Azure Cosmos DB

4.5.6   *NoSQL Data Capabilities in GCP, AWS, Azure*

NoSQL	NoSQL database for web and mobile applications. ACID transaction	Cloud datastore	Amazon DynamoDB	Cosmos DB
NoSQL	Third-party NoSQL on VM	Cassandra on a Compute Engine cluster	Amazon Elastic Compute Cloud	Azure Compute
NoSQL	Low latency operational workload —good for hyper-personalisation	Bigtable—wide column	Apache Casandra	Table Storage
NoSQL	Scalable, managed enterprise data warehouse for analytics	BigQuery—DWH and analytics	Amazon Athena	Synapse Analytics, data lake store

4.5.7 Case Study: BigQuery—Industrialised Big Data on Cloud

BigQuery is a serverless, cost effective, multi-cloud data warehouse designed to help turn big data into valuable business insights.

Without industrialised capabilities, 50–75% effort is spent on data management, integration, and developing, training, and deploying models and analytical reports. BigQuery has industrialised data management and integration, as well as management of models and reports.

BigQuery provides APIs and connectors to use BigQuery functionalities; it uses SQL-based ML Query to build and use ML capabilities using SQL. It provides a large array of integration and API libraries and connectors.

A Wide Array of Connectors and APIs

- C#, Go, Java, Node.js, PHP, Python, and Ruby to access BigQuery data
- BigQuery APIs for established third-party BI and data analytics solutions
- BigQuery integration connectors for AI Notebooks, Dataproc, Data Studio, and Looker
- Low cost storage to store the queries results in tables and access the results for tools not provided with APIs and connectors.

Managing BigQuery through a GUI console

- Create and manage BigQuery resources and run SQL queries.
- In UI save jobs and queries.
- UI provides search capabilities based on metadata. Queries are re-usable. Views can be shared for collaboration.

Geospatial capabilities

- BigQuery Geographic Information Systems (GIS) supports geospatial data types and functions that help analyse and operate on any data with spatial attributes.

Multiple ways to develop, train, and deploy ML models, visualisation, and analytics

- Use BigQuery ML to develop, train, and deploy ML models.
- Develop, train, and deploy ML models using SQL tools and skills.
- BigQuery offers connectors to use BigQuery capabilities from within Excel. The BigQuery connector works by connecting to BigQuery, making a specified query, and downloading and propagating that data to Excel.
- APIs and connectors to connect the data science and visualisation tool Looker to BigQuery.
- BigQuery functions can be called from within Looker.
- BigQuery package for R Package can call BigQuery functions.
- BigQuery connector for Apache Beam to transform and enrich both in-stream and in-batch mode data.
- AI Platform Notebook is integrated with BigQuery to run the JupyterLab environment to build ML and data science models.

4.5.8 Data Storage on GCP, AWS, and Azure

Cloud provides data storage as a service. There are three types of data storage services: persistent disks for block storage, filestore for network file storage, and cloud storage for object storage. Each differs by the way storage is accessed.

Data	Coverage	GCP product	AWS	Azure
Block storage—persistent disks as good as a USB drive	Frequent data access is used by all virtual machines	Cloud storage	Amazon Simple Storage Service	Azure Blob
File storage service like network-attached storage	Low latency file operations—fully managed	Cloud Filestore	File Storage	Azure Files
Object Storage service with fine-grained permissions	Infrequent access (once a month or year). Data is accessed through REST API	Nearline or Coldline	Amazon S3	Azure Archive

4.5.9 Analytics and Visualisation on GCP, AWS, and Azure Platform

The analytics and visualisation platform is expected to integrate seamlessly into business workflows, embed into third-party systems, and enable banks to build their own data applications. The visualisation tool is expected to unlock the full value of data capabilities. It should be able to align closely with the business measures.

The best capability of a visualisation tool is its ability to fully leverage the power of a data warehouse in terms of scale and data types. It should be able to integrate, connect, analyse, and visualise data across multi-clouds, connect with underlying data in real time, create a common data model, provide centralised business rules and access via APIs, and embed analytics into workflow and custom applications.

Business intelligence tool to visualise data through dashboards and reports	Connectors with public datasets	Cloud Data Studio	Neptune Workbench	BI Engine
UI and API based	Standardised semantic layer	Looker	Neptune Workbench	Power BI

4.5.10   AI Machine Learning and AI as a Service Platform on GCP, AWS, and Azure

Cloud provides a fully managed end-to-end platform for data science and machine learning. It provides an end-to-end machine learning life cycle. It helps in preparing and building datasets, and building best-in-class machine learning models with or without writing code using open-source deep learning frameworks. It validates models with AI explanation and what-if analysis and deploys models at a scale in the cloud. It manages models, experiments, end-to-end workflows, and pipelines by using MLOps best practices.

Data	Coverage	GCP product	AWS	Azure
Data preparation for machine learning	Data service based on Trifacta to visually explore, clean, and prepare data for analysis	Trifacta	Trifacta	Trifacta
Interactive data visualisation and ML	Tool for data exploration, analysis, visualisation, and machine learning. This is fully managed through the Jupyter Notebook service	Datalab	AWS Data Lab	Azure ML
Service to train and deploy custom machine, learning models	Train, predict, and deploy	AI Platform	Amazon SageMaker	Azure ML
Natural language process	Sentiment analysis, entity analysis, entity sentiment analysis, content classification, and syntax analysis	Cloud NL API	Amazon Comprehend	Azure Cognitive Service
Building conversational interfaces	Can use own libraries	Dialogflow Enterprise	Amazon Lex	

4.6 Industrialise Data Catalog to Deliver Data Governance

4.6.1 Case Study: Data Catalog to Implement Enterprise Data Governance Policy

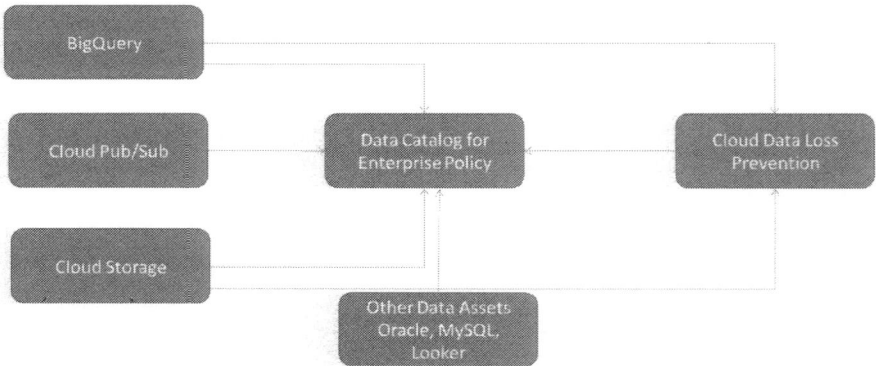

Data Catalog is a fully managed, scalable, metadata management service for implementing technical and business consistency across the data assets. It makes data assets discoverable in business and technical contexts. This helps in drastically reducing data bloating.

Data Catalog tools for delivering enterprise data governance policy:

- Organise technical and business metadata
- Central catalogue: unique IDs up to field level
- Manage sensitive data
- Search and discovery
- Metadata as a service using API
- Ingest metadata from on-premises RDBMS assets
- Integrate metadata from Looker and Tableau
- Integrate cloud storage, Big Query, Pub/Sub, and cloud data loss prevention.

4.6.2 Data Catalog as a Tool for Data Governance

Data Catalog enables and automates building consistency in data management across systems, datasets, classes, and fields within and outside Google Cloud. It helps in enforcing consistent policies, procedures, responsibilities, and controls surrounding data activities.

- Data governance applies consistent principles to manage data during its lifecycle, from acquisition to use to disposal. Data Catalog is a tool that is built and manages enterprise-wide data governance for very large banks.
- Data Catalog metadata building capabilities:

  - Data Catalog is built on Cloud Spanner so it can handle enterprise-level data governance for very large banks.
  - Data Catalog creates and manages both technical and business metadata:

    Technical metadata tags the lifecycle stage of the data
    Business metadata tags the business context

  - The catalogue provides a Unique identifier to data assets and tags source data, external data, datasets, classes, tables, and fields. Data Catalog can extract this information automatically.
  - Data Catalog indexes all the metadata and makes it available through both a user-friendly UI and an API for programmatic integration.
  - API scales the metadata tasks and programmatically integrates with Data Catalog. Technical users can annotate or retrieve metadata in bulk.

- Data Catalog search capabilities:

  - Search capabilities very similar to Google Search capabilities but with filters and predicates for metadata search and contextual search
  - Search metadata access control and data access control work together

- It manages very large data volumes:

  - The expiry date for the fields and classes
  - Metadata tags for a system, datasets, classes, and fields
  - The trust scores for fields and classes

- It manages lineage:

  - Metadata for lineage: the data owners, data source, the business process where the data asset is transformed, or the applications and services involved during the transformations
  - The lineage continues from source data to messaging to integration to storage to access control to ML models to distribution to insights to consumption layers.

4.6.3 Deliver Re-Usable Tag Templates to Build Consistency in Technical and Business Contexts

Tag templates are re-usable structures that can be used to rapidly create new tags. A template is a group of metadata key-value pairs. A consistent technical and business definition-driven tag template enforces consistency and re-usability across data assets.

A technical tag template provides the metadata of the lifecycle stage of the data, applied to both tables and columns.

- ETL template: an ETL job runs successfully. What was the number of rows processed? Did it have any errors or warnings? And so on.
- Data owner: data classification is either public or private; wherein the lifecycle of the data is: production, test, QA, data completeness and quality, and so on.

  - **A data governance tag** with fields for data governor, retention date, deletion date, PII (yes or no), data classification (public, confidential, sensitive, regulatory)
  - **A data quality tag** with fields for quality issues, update frequency, SLO information
  - **A data usage tag** with fields for top users, top queries, average daily users.

The business tag template provides business context metadata

For example, for an individual customer information dataset:

- KYC template: operations manager is interested in the expiry date of the record so that he or she can trigger the KYC review process
- Conduct risk template: the conduct risk manager is interested in data lineage to ensure that age and gender are not used in credit scoring
- PII template: the data privacy manager is interested in complying with access control, encryption, residency, consent, and with privacy laws.

Roll Out Bank-wide Data Governance Policies

- A sample of enterprise data governance policy:

  - Data classification and hierarchies
  - Standardise and re-use business metadata at an enterprise level
  - Data quality
  - Manage sensitive data
  - Data lineage
  - Data assessment and profiling
  - Privacy and other compliance
  - Automate data workflow and model workflow

- Use case policies:

  - Access control
  - Privacy
  - Lineage
  - Re-use
  - Lineage tracking
  - Data quality

- Key management and encryption.

4.6.4 Implement Enterprise-Wide Data Governance on Data Catalog

Tag technical and business metadata:

Tag Technical Metadata for data assets each with unique ids	Tag Business Metadata	Metadata as a service through APIs	Search and discovery	Manage sensitive data

- A flexible and powerful cataloguing system for capturing both technical metadata (automatically) as well as business metadata (tags) in a structured format.
- Provides a unified view and tagging across all assets.
- Synchronises technical metadata automatically and creates schematised tags for business metadata.

Search and discovery:

- A fully managed and highly scalable data discovery and metadata management service.
- Pinpoint data with a simple but powerful faceted-search interface.

Metadata as a service:

- Metadata management service for cataloguing data assets via custom APIs and the UI, thereby providing a unified view of data wherever it is.
- Get access immediately, then scale without the infrastructure to set up or manage sensitive data.
- Tag sensitive data automatically through cloud data loss prevention (DLP) integration.
- Enforce data security policies and maintain compliance through cloud IAM and cloud DLP integrations that help to manage access rights to the sensitive data.

4.6.5 Tag Metadata at Data Asset Hierarchies

Repository of Info Type	Classes are the hierarchy	The policy is defined for info type	Individual fields will be tagged with info type	Additional operations	Insights and Reporting

- Tag consistent business metadata templates at info types, classes, and hierarchies to ensure business consistency
- Re-usable tag templates help to:
  - Create consistent business and regulatory policies

- Implement ML and semantics in data quality, data transformation, aggregation, and insights
- Tagging templates at the info type helps in enforcing:
  - Data retention policy
  - Access control: no access, partial access, and full access
  - Data residency
- Tags at the class level help in enforcing:
  - Consistently managing sensitive data like:

    PII
    Financial data
    Intellectual property
- Using case-level data policy:
  - Conducting risk requirements in ML models, for example, age and gender cannot be used in ML mode for loan approval.

4.6.6 Establishing Business Lineage to Empower Business Managers

1. To establish business lineage in a data catalogue by tagging metadata with a data source, transformation, aggregation, operations, models, and reports.
2. Establishing lineage for info type and info class across data sources starting from data source to transformation to aggregation to additional operations to insights and reporting

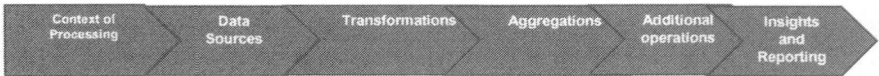

3. Business lineage is very specific to the context of processing. It is established for every model and report. Lineage and tagging rules need to be consistently applied.
4. Business lineage aims to enforce:
   - The data quality assurance that is required in the business context
   - Data class policies for sensitive data, ensuring that data from sensitive classes is not exposed to unauthorised containers
   - A graph of data traversal: in the banking context this is useful to engage a regulator on AML transaction processing, fraud detection, system availability, and regulatory reporting

- Creating explainable ML and AI decisions.

4.6.7 Industrialise the Data Quality Process

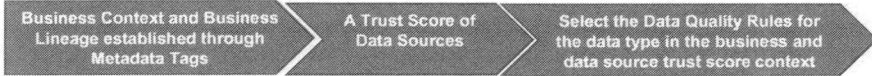

Business Context and Business Lineage established through Metadata Tags	A Trust Score of Data Sources	Select the Data Quality Rules for the data type in the business and data source trust score context

Data quality industrialisation leverages the data integration, preparation, and wrangling modules.

The industrialisation of data integration and data capture, and the embedded statistical and visualisation techniques within the data integration, have made it possible to industrialise the entire data quality process.

The business context of the use case, data sources used in the measurement, and data types are the three pillars of the industrialisation of the data quality process. Without business context and lineage, data quality rules are based only on the data source and data type. The automation of the data quality process results in a large number of false -positives and true negatives, thus impact the delivering of business outcomes.

Business context and lineage helps to deliver data quality business outcomes through the industrialisation of validation and curation process.

Unless the bank has implemented metadata tagging to ensure bank-wide business context and lineage policies, it is very difficult to industrialise data quality validation and the curation process to deliver business outcomes.

The industrialisation of the data quality process is a part of the industrialised data platform.

4.7 The Future of Data Services

The following three case studies provide a glimpse of path-breaking value creation through data as a service by a fourth-generation banking business model.

4.7.1 Case Study: Monitor Customer Behaviour in Real Time

The Tableau Centre of Excellence at HDFC Bank is owned by a central business intelligence unit which is the owner custodian of all performance management data and a single source of truth. HDFC Bank has more than 30,000 Tableau users in the finance, performance, risk, and compliance areas.

The Centre of Excellence was established in 2017 with the primary aim of replacing the MS Excel worksheets of risk, finance, performance and compliance departments and to deliver a visualisation reporting tool to drastically reduce the turnaround time for the availability of reports and also for moving into production of the new reports.

The bank started with a desktop licence of Tableau. As report formats and use cases were established, the bank upgraded its licence from desktop to server.

The CoE supports all the three business lines—wholesale banking, retail banking, wealth management—and covers branch banking and CASA Analytics.

Performance is measured in terms of product, geographical structure, and the relationship manager for customer-wise and branch-wise metrics, aggregated on an organisational structure for a different period including what has changed. Visualised metrics can be accessed on the system or through emails.

The bank has pre-built 1600 views from 28 sources of data covering 50 million customers from five core banking processors. It also includes external datasets and computed fields. Tableau provides real-time drill-down and visualisation, and it enforces governance and responsibility within the bank's data-based decisions.

CoE has separate teams for performance measurement, risk, and compliance.

The bank has built a future roadmap in terms of migration to big data and visualisation to ultimately replace all PPTs. The bank also has NLPC and NLG on its roadmap.

4.7.2   Case Study: An Investment Bank Creating and Selling Thousands of Insightful Datasets Every Year

The Data Science Division of UBS Investment Banking BU has created a separate research laboratory to build datasets for assisting investment banking division analysts and customers of the bank in their business decisions and strategy.

The Data Science Division works as a separate profit centre. The tag line of the division is "converting data into evidence".

The Data Science Lab is available to the IB analysts of UBS and also to clients of UBS and subscribers to Data Science Lab Services.

The lab has 55+ products covering 1000 s of companies globally. The product categories include geospatial, social media, earning analysis through NLP, quantitative modelling, pricing and transactions, digital intelligence, market research, and supply chains.

To make the entire offering focused on business outcomes, the research scope is decided by analysts asking investment and business-related questions, questions that will help the bank's clients in business and strategic decisions. Data scientists and subject-matter experts provide help to uncover new evidence on key issues that inform clients on investment decisions, facilitated by its innovative toolkit of techniques. The report presents the collected evidence. The division produced 3000 such reports last year.

The lab has industrialised big data, AI/ML, and visualisation technologies.

4.7.3   Case Study: The BBVA Bank Data Lab

BBVA bank has established a centre of excellence in financial data analysis. The bank builds datasets and insights by leveraging anonymised internal datasets along with external datasets. The produced datasets help the bank's customers in the identification of fraud, identify marketing target areas, and help in business decisions. The published datasets include:

- Credit card spend in cities
- Footprints of tourists
- Spending money during festivals
- Predicting economic activities and growth

4.8   Conclusion: Industrialised Data Enable Better Alignment of Industrialisation Engines

The purpose of industrialising data is to decouple operational challenges in data technology and build data as a service for consumption in a managed service model. An industrialised data platform helps in delivering scalability, resiliency, and agility for Banking 4.0 services.

A cloud data platform also provides AI platforms. This helps in building banking AI and embedding intelligence into the banking process and technology. An industrialised data platform along with AI platforms help in managing complexities of development, training, and deployment of machine learning and AI models.

Cloud data platform capabilities, benchmarks, and roadmaps are available from the cloud provider and the public domain. This all can help in creating a better vision of Banking 4.0 year on year and in the better planning of the alignment of industrialisation and innovation engines. With cloud data platform capabilities, the industrialised banks will be able to deliver digital experience better by leveraging banking AI built on AI platforms.

Chapter 5
Deliver Digital Experience

5.1 Introduction: Digital Banking

Digital banking aims to deliver a digital experience through modernised and industrialised applications and hyper-personalisation engines. Digital banking is the digital delivery of customer experience, partner experience, and employee experience.

The purpose of application modernisation and industrialisation is to do away with technology complexity to deliver real-time banking services through self-service and personalised digital experience.

Application modernisation means implementing microservices and API-based application design to deliver agility, scalability, and resiliency of business model.

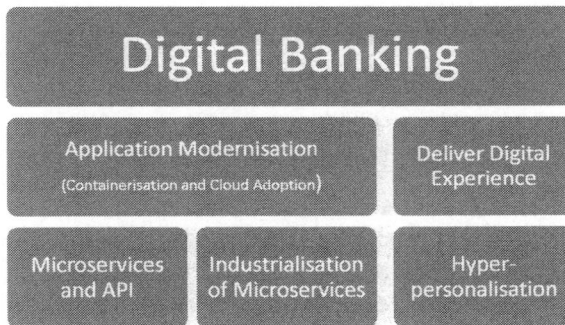

© Springer Nature Singapore Pte Ltd. 2022
M. Bhatia, *Banking 4.0*,
https://doi.org/10.1007/978-981-16-6069-6_5

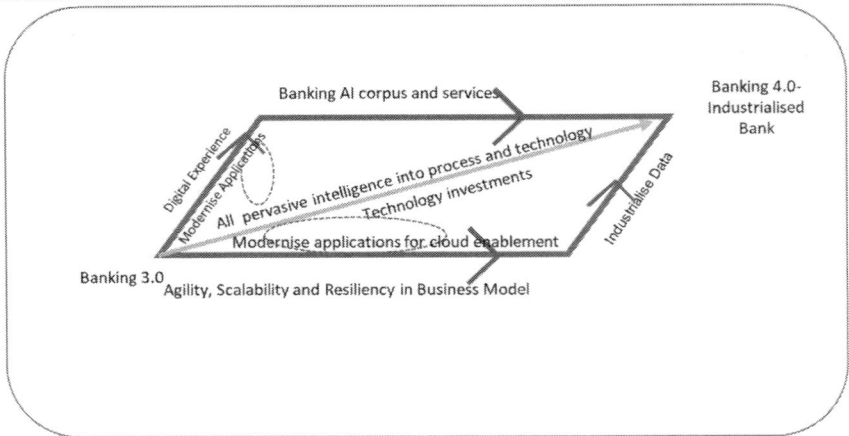

Banking AI corpus and services

Banking 4.0-
Industrialised
Bank

Digital Experience

Modernise Applications

All pervasive intelligence into process and technology

Technology investments

Modernise applications for cloud enablement

Industrialise Data

Banking 3.0

Agility, Scalability and Resiliency in Business Model

Applications Modernisation deliver twin objectives of Industrialised Banking

Every existing bank has hundreds of legacy applications. To deliver digital experience and an agile, scalable, and resilient business model, legacy applications are either modernised or replaced.

Application modernisation and cloud enablement is an iterative process. Banks modernise and cloud-enable legacy applications and monolithic applications by wrapping them in a container supplemented by microservices and API-based modern and cloud-native applications. Legacy applications are cloud-enabled and modern applications are cloud-native.

Application containerisation technology helps in iteratively modernising and cloud-enabling legacy applications. Containers are the lightweight software components that bundle the application, its dependencies, and its configuration on a traditional operating system on a traditional server or in a virtualised environment.

Application containerisation helps in improving application life-cycle management through capabilities such as continuous integration and continuous delivery. Containers are the foundation for cloud enablement. They help in the co-existence of legacy applications with a modern application in the cloud.

To modernise, both Front Office and Back Office legacy applications are containerised and hosted on the cloud. However, Front Office legacy applications are replaced with modernised microservices-based cloud-native applications in a larger proportion and at a faster pace.

The aim of the twin transformation initiative of delivering digital experience and building agility, scalability, and resiliency in the business model of the bank is to industrialise it. Application modernisation is a basic building block in the industrialisation of the bank. Application modernisation is the foundation for delivering digital experience.

5.2 Deliver Digital Experience of Banking 4.0 Services

Customers and partners engage the bank through the Front Office, employees largely work in the Back Office. Fourth-generation banks build digital experience for customers and partners in the Front Office and digital experience for employees in the Back Office. To deliver Banking 4.0 services, the Industrialised Front Office and the Industrialised Back Office is integrated through technology, design, process, and controls for data quality, coverage, timeliness, completeness, lineage, availability, agility, scalability, and resiliency.

Front Office and Back Office technology complement each other to deliver the digital experience to customers, partners, and employees.

Delivering Banking 4.0				
Deliver Digital Experience in Back Office	Industrialised Back Office	Banking 4.0	Industrialised Front Office	Deliver Digital Experience in Front Office
Cognitive reading of documents and data sources Machine Learning and Enterprise Decision Engines	Intelligent Finance 3.0 Intelligent Regulatory Reporting 3.0	Provider, Distributor and of Financial and Non- Financial Services- API Banking and Marketplace Banking	Marketplace and Industry Platforms Digital IDs	Hyper-personalisation Digital Customer Onboarding Conversational Banking API banking Stronger and Contactless Authentication
Integrated risk, compliance and finance- Model development, training and deployment	Risk Measurement APIs	Industrialised Risk Management — Risk 3.0	Integrated Fraud Detection. Engaging customers in collection and complaints and fraud investigation. Risk Measurement Embedded in Front Office	Risk as a Service integrated with Front Office
Financial crime risk model development, training and deployment Low-latency Compliance Data Infrastructure	Risk Based Financial Crime Model Building Public and Shared Data for Cyber, AML and Fraud	Industrialised Financial Crimes Management (FCM 3.0)	Omnichannel cyber resilience	Omnichannel Financial Crime Intelligence
Integrated model development, training and deployment	Industrialised Data Platform AI as a Service	Industrialised Data	Integration with industry utilities, subscribed and public data	Loosely coupled intelligent integration with internal data sources

Deliver Banking 4.0 by integrating industrialised Front Office with industrialised Back Office

5.2.1 Digital Customer Experience

Industrialised banks are building four distinguishable digital customer experiences.

1. Customer self-service for services in addition to payments and transactions. Banks are building a very similar experience whether the customer brings in paper documents or electronic data via:

- Digital onboarding of the customer by the bank and partners. An example is video KYC through the bank's applications.
- API banking and open banking, onboarding is delegated to partners and marketplaces.
- Digital non-financial transactions for SME, commercial, and corporate customers.
- Non-financial service APIs published for integration by customers and partners.

The number of APIs and API maturity is a good indicator of digital customer experience.

2. Digital conversations delivered by banking AI. In Chap. 11 on conversational banking, we discuss in detail the delivery of a digital experience by individually contextualised communication delivered through:

- Question and answer BOTs;
- Textual chat;
- Voice chat;
- Customer initiated communications for payments, transactions, and services;
- The industrialised bank initiated digital conversation with the customers, including conversations for collection, fraud investigation, AML investigation, and related credit administration;
- Real-time digital engagement through text, voice, and video conversation for

  - Real-time financial transactions;
  - Real-time non-financial transactions.

5.2.1.1 Case Study: Implementation of Conversational Banking

Conversational banking planning starts with identifying the business outcomes and measurements. The next step is to identify data sources for customers and products; the solution will serve and identify all channels through which conversational banking will be serviced. Some examples are Alexa, WhatsApp messenger, or a bank that may choose to create its own mobile application. One important challenge in conversational banking is to build real-time data for personalised and contextual conversation. To build conversational AI models, historical transactional and reference data needs to be cleansed and enriched. A conversational solution is integrated with core banking solutions, CRM marketing, analytical solutions, and with live chat for a smooth handover. The next important challenge is to either build or buy a library of banking concepts and computations. Every bank is different in the application of a banking concept to its products and processes. Every jurisdiction may have different rules for each concept. Therefore concepts need to be adopted and continuously trained. Concepts used in the system may also be converted to FAQs for agents and communication.

Conversational banking is deployed on clouds, hybrid clouds, or premises. The most important are:

- Digitisation of banking concepts and computation;
- Drastically reducing latency in the entire data either by feeding in or receiving a feed from conversational banking and making it real time.

3.   Provision of the bank's services through API.

API services are discussed in detail in Chap. 8 on platform banking and API as an integration tool.

And this covers additional services provided to the customers by consuming and integrating third-party APIs with the bank's services and APIs.

4.   Digitised financial transactions include contactless payments, P2P payments, and faster payments.

5.2.1.2   Case Study: HDFC Bank in India Achieved 95% of Customer-Initiated Transactions Coming Through the Internet and Mobile Technology

Customers of the HDFC Bank in India, for the year ending 31 March 2020, initiated 95% of their transactions through the Internet and mobile banking. Customers transacted only 2% through ATMs and 3% at branches. This was possible because the bank had leveraged innovative technology applications, electronic straight-through processing, central processing units, and CRM and analytics to service customers.

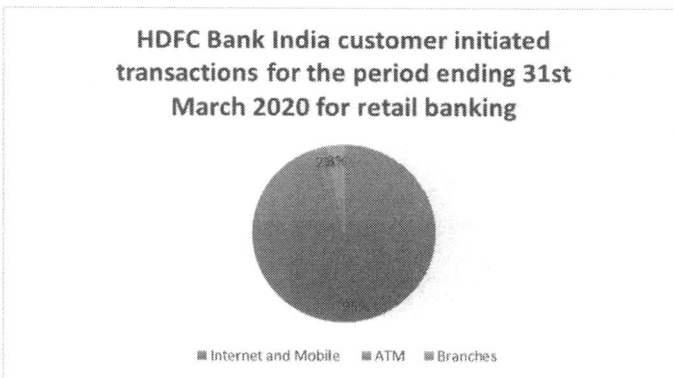

HDFC Bank India customer initiated transactions for the period ending 31st March 2020 for retail banking

■ Internet and Mobile   ■ ATM   ■ Branches

Source HDFC Bank: Annual Report of the Bank 2020

5.2.2   Deliver Digital Experience in the Front Office

1. Delivery of digital experience by industrialised banks necessarily means machines from the bank side engaging with the machines, applications, and devices of the customer.
2. Provision of very similar service levels, experience, and business outcomes when a customer accesses the bank through physical channels, or with the paper document, or uses electronic data, or with human communication, or through electronic channels.

5.2.2.1   Case Study: Back of the Envelope Benchmarks for Digital Customer Experience

The following are the indicative benchmarks for digital experience availed by the percentage of customers at the existing level of industrialisation with banks and customers. Colour-coded cells indicate digital transactions were assisted by human agents.

Assisted by a human agent means: data from documents is partially captured manually, or documents are partially verified manually. It also means some paper documents are also collected and the customer was authenticated against the photo in the identify document on paper.

Product	Digital Customer Onboarding (%)	Digital Customer Enquiries (%)	Digital Financial Transaction (%)	Digital Non-Financial Transaction (%)	Bank initiated communication (%)
Retail — SB - No frill digital native account	90	70	97	70	97
Retail SB for others	70	50	75	50	70
Retail FD	75	50	90	25	30
Retail Credit Card	95	50	97	25	25
Retail Mortgage	70	30	97	30	30
Retail Car	95	30	97	30	30
Retail Wealth	70	30	75	30	30
SME Current Account	50	30	75	30	30
SME Loan	40	30	75	30	30
Commercial Current Account	50	30	75	30	30
Corporate Current Account	55	30	75	30	30

3. Empowering customers by doing away with technology complexity to deliver business outcomes for the customer.

5.2.2.2   Case Study: Digital Experience Makes the Bank Relevant for Every Customer Journey

Digital customer experience is a mindset. Embracing digitisation to transform the bank, from front to back, is to enable it to be nimble and agile, to be faster and scalable, to operate in real time with reduced latency in the data flow across the bank and to be faster in time to market.

Assuming that paper documents are not going to disappear any time soon, the basic driver of digital experience is to provide the customer with a very similar experience whether the customer is using a paper document or electronic data.

The business outcomes expected of digital experience architecture, technology, and design are to embed the bank in the customer journey through digitised experience to grow the revenue and income of the bank, and to build a new stream of fees and other income from low capital pursuits like platform banking.

Reducing the cost of technology and processing would enable the reduction of the overall cost to income ratio to create and sustain a return on the capital for the investor of the bank and sustain a business case for technology transformation through:

- Hyper-personalisation of customer experience;
- Engaging customers through machines of conversational banking, including WhatsApp banking, textual chat, and voice chat.
- Industrialising Back Office processes.

4.   Provision of a very similar service level and business outcome for a customer connecting through a personal device or the bank's application or third-party marketplace application.
5.   Provision of a very similar level of service, experience, and business outcome to all:

- Customer types: corporates, financial institutions, commercials, SMEs, and individuals;
- Channels and products;
- Payments and services.

5.2.3   Industrialised Front Office

Broadly customers and partners engage the bank in the following five areas:

- Customer and partner onboarding;
- Customer and partner initiated communication;
- Financial transactions;
- Non-financial transactions;
- Bank initiated communications.

Except for financial transactions, where the entire process is standardised, roles and responsibilities are standardised, and data interchange is templatised and standardised. The other processes are non-standardised and based on paper documents. Since many processes are on non-standardised documents, banks have built an army of service agents to assist customers in converting paper documents into digital processes.

The industrialisation of the Front Office means the standardisation of roles and responsibilities of parties involved in the transactions, standardisation of data interchange templates, and standardisation of processes and services.

Banking codes and standards in the jurisdiction, handbooks published by regulators, a partnership agreement with third parties, and standards on security and marketplace practices are used by banks to standardise processes and templates for the industrialisation of the Front Office at banks.

The following is an illustrative list of initiatives to industrialise the Front Office:

- Building trust and stronger authentication using biometric techniques, encryption, digital certification, and PKIs.
- To authenticate electronically, integrating with the public database, utilities, and digital ids.
- Building immutability in transactions and contracts by leveraging blockchain technology, encryption, and PKI.
- Publishing APIs for integrating with financial infrastructure, marketplaces, blockchain platforms, digital IDs, payment infrastructures, banking utilities, credit scoring mechanisms, lost data, and scenario sharing mechanisms.
- Delivering a hyper-personalised customer experience, enhanced by digital IDs.
- Embedding in the Front Office an early warning system for credit risk, fraud risk, cyber risk, and resilience.
- Implementing conversational banking for bank initiated conversations regarding fraud investigation, complaint response, and collection.
- Integrating non-banking value-added service with banking services.

5.2.4 Deliver Digital Experience in the Back Office

We have covered the Back Office in detail in other chapters.

Industrialised banks are building three distinguishable digital Back Office experiences:

1. Managing paper documents:

   - RPA and BOTs to manage manual tasks;
   - Cognitive reading of documents and data sources.

2. Automated decision making:

   - Low latency compliance data infrastructure;
   - Data science, machine learning, and enterprise decision engines;
   - Integrated model development, training, and deployment;
   - Data visualisation.

3. Intelligent risk, finance, and compliance management:

   - Integrated risk, compliance and financial model development, training, and deployment;
   - Financial crime risk model development, training, and deployment.

5.2.5 Industrialised Back Office

In other chapters while discussing innovation in a BAU mode we covered in detail the industrialisation of risk, finance, compliance, regulatory reporting, and financial crimes management:

- Industrialised data platforms;
- AI as a service;
- Integrated risk, compliance and financial model development, training and deployment;
- Industrialised Finance 3.0;
- Industrialised Regulatory Reporting 3.0;
- Industrialised Risk Management 4.0:

  - Risk measurement APIs;

- Industrialisation of Financial Crimes Management (FCM 3.0):

  - Risk-based financial crime model leveraging public and shared data for cyber, AML, and fraud.

5.2.6 Deliver Banking 4.0 Services by Integrating the Industrialised Back Office with the Industrialised Front Office

- Provider, distributor, and enabler of financial and non-financial services and API banking:

- API and microservices-based integration;
- Integration with public datasets provided by the government and commercial data providers;
- Integration with social network filters;
- Cognitive reading of documents and data sources;
- Machine learning and enterprise decision engines;
- Digital customer onboarding;
- Conversational banking;
- API banking;
- Stronger and contactless authentication;
- Marketplace and industry platforms;
- Intelligent Finance 3.0;
- Intelligent Regulatory Reporting 3.0;
- RPA and BOTS to automate human tasks;
- Cognitive BOTs, case management tools, and APIs to automate workflow and decision-making process;
- Hyper-personalisation-based predictive model for automated decision making.

- Industrialised risk management: Risk 3.0:

  - Integrated risk, compliance and financial model development, training, and deployment;
  - Risk measurement as APIs;
  - Integrated fraud detection: engaging customers in collection and complaints and fraud investigation;
  - Risk measurement embedded in the Front Office;
  - Risk as a service integrated with the Front Office;
  - Credit risk, collection risk, and early warning alert system embedded in all credit processes;
  - Operational risk and control indicator monitoring and assessment embedded in every process;
  - Visualisation and dashboards for alert disposal and decision making.

- Industrialisation of Financial Crimes Management (FCM 3.0):

  - Financial crime risk model deployment;
  - Low latency compliance data infrastructure;
  - Risk-based financial crime models;
  - Public and shared data for cyber, AML, and fraud;
  - Omnichannel cyber resilience;
  - Omnichannel financial crime intelligence;
  - Fraud risk, financial crimes risk, cyber risk early warning, and alert system embedded in every process;

- Integration with public datasets provided by the government and commercial data providers;
- Integration with social network filters;
- Visualisation and dashboards for alert disposal and decision making.

- Intelligent real-time data platform:

  - Industrialised data platform;
  - AI as a service;
  - Integration with industry utilities, and subscribed and public data;
  - Loosely coupled intelligent integration with internal data sources;
  - Integrated model development, training, and deployment.

5.2.6.1 Case Study: Experience in Digital Innovation as a Single Most Important Reason for an Appointment as a CEO of a Trillion Dollar Asset Bank

UBS appointed Ralph Hamers as Group Chief Executive Officer from 1 November 2020. As per the Annual Report of the bank, the most important consideration in addition to strong corporate governance, proven and charismatic leadership, personality, experience, and strong culture was his knowledge of implementing at ING Group, a fundamental shift in its operating model which is considered one of the best examples of digital innovation in the banking sector.

5.3 Hyper-Personalisation is the Foundation for Deliver the Digital Customer Experience

Banks and FS firms have been servicing their customers through technology channels for the past two decades or so. Providing a personalised customer experience is not a new venture for banks. With the prevalence of smart devices in the hands of customers, the emergence of the digital native generation, and developments in technology, the demand for hyper-personalised customer experience has increased multi-fold. The personalised service expectation is further fuelled by the hyper-personalised experience provided by hospitality, travel, and entertainment industry firms to their customers.

FS firms were the first to offer personalised marketing and sales services. They started their personalisation journey two decades ago. However, like most other firms, personalisation did not progress much beyond marketing and sales. Meanwhile, customers have tested personalised service delivery from other industries. Smart devices in their hands have empowered customers to demand personalised services.

5.3.1 Personalisation of the Digital Customer Experience Has Matured at Banks

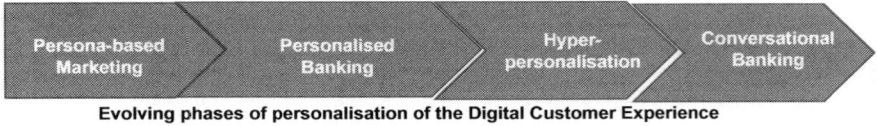

Evolving phases of personalisation of the Digital Customer Experience

5.3.1.1 Digital Experience Enhancement Tool: Persona-based Marketing

Persona-based marketing aims to make tailored offers as per customer needs. Offering financial products to satisfy customer needs improves the marketing conversion rate at banks and is a win–win for both customers and banks.

Persona-based marketing starts by building customer profiles from static attributes like age, gender, education, salary or income level, and address. Banks have gradually extended persona-based product marketing through all electronic channels like call centres, internet banking, branches, ATMs, and mobile banking. Persona-based marketing generally covers retail products like credit cards, personal loans, and wealth management products.

Persona is fitting a customer into a pre-decided segment. Offers are made based on the persona allocated to the customer. The slow-moving personal attributes are used in building personas. Banks using persona-based marketing to deliver customer experience are the banks that have not built customer datasets. This results in very limited input data and a loopback mechanism used for building persona.

A persona-based marketing strategy starts by making purchase recommendations to the customer. A better conversion ratio is an indicator of a better digital customer experience. Unfortunately, at most banks, the conversion ratio is very low. This results in customer fatigue and declining returns. A low conversion ratio is also an indicator that persona marketing is not a tool for delivering customer experience at banks.

5.3.1.2 A Slightly Matured Customer Experience through Personalised Banking

Soon persona-based marketing techniques started providing declining returns because customers were engaged only for marketing and fatigue developed.

In the initial years of computerization, customer data was scarce. The only customer data available was static.

With computerization, banks have started adding transactional, account, credit, and credit history data in electronic form. To enhance the customer experience, banks started adding static services to the individualized or personalised banking services list.

For example, customers can now find out account balances, credit outstanding, SMS banking regarding transactions and balances, account statements, cards lost, nominations, and so on. Information about banks' credit and wealth management products are also included. In some cases, Robo advice is considered a part of personalised banking.

In a nutshell, many of the rule-based push services were introduced.

The division between persona-based marketing and personal banking is blurred at most banks. Banks provide personalised services in addition to marketing based on the persona. Marketing is further expanded to include a relationship manager for a better customer experience of the bank's partner products and basic banking services and greetings.

Customers are also empowered to opt in and opt out.

5.3.1.3 Matured Digital Experience through Hyper-personalisation of Services

Hyper-personalisation aims to enhance customer experience on services and products beyond the realm of marketing and sales. Experience cannot be provided unless customer needs are identified accurately. Based on the targeted customer needs, the bank expands and enables the customer experience.

Every bank has a different business strategy, targeted market, customers, products, and differentiators. Therefore, every bank has a unique way of delivering an individualised customer experience.

Hyper-personalisation is delivered through machines to cover a large number of customer needs, a larger number of customers, and larger customer experience scenarios.

5.3.1.4 The Highly Matured Digital Experience Is Delivering 'Human-like' Conversational Banking

Real 'human' conversational banking aims to provide a human-like exclusive customer experience using machines.

Maturity in conversational banking technology		
Conversational technology	Input data	Digital experience
Personal banking	Customer profile	Multi-channel product promotion

(continued)

(continued)

Maturity in conversational banking technology

Conversational technology	Input data	Digital experience
Personalised banking	Historical transactional account balances, credit and credit history, privacy requirements	Static information about the customer

Hyper-personalised	Historic behaviour and servicing data:
	• Real-time:
	  – Customer behaviour
	  – Location
	• Public data
	• GDPR privacy requirements
	• Social data
		Real-time engines with a feedback loop to learn and improve identification of customer needs and experience
		Augmented data to be used for customer experience communication/conversational engine (chat/call center/messages/human agents)
		Accumulated learning about the customer-driving bank's machine and human behaviour in line with targeted customer experience

Conversational banking	Historical conversation	All of the above

5.3.2 Hyper-personalisation to Deliver Digital Experience

Hyper-personalisation is contextualizing customer experience in real time. Social platforms, the consumer product industry and the entertainment and hospitality industry have been delivering contextualised digital experience in real time to their customers.

With the competition in banking and payment products from social platforms like Google, WhatsApp, and Facebook, unless banks provide contextualised customer experience, they are at risk of losing significance for digital natives.

To remain relevant especially for digitally native customers who spend a significant amount of time on smart devices and social platforms, the banks need to contextualize and enhance customer experience. Banking customers expect a similar experience that the marketplace and social platforms provide.

5.3.2.1 Hyper-personalisation to Identify Customer Needs

The litmus test of personalisation is identifying customer needs accurately in real time and accordingly deliver customer experience. Personalisation aims to identify

the customer needs and accordingly orchestrate and tailor-make the customer engagement across digital and human channels. The purpose of personalisation is to deliver
a win–win for customers and the bank.

Identification of customer needs is not easy. Generally, it starts with segmenting
customers according to the customer's static data and assuming or calibrating certain
'buying' behaviours. So firms focus on buying, as a customer need, and to create
win–win situations by making recommendations.

In hyper-personalisation, the bank goes beyond just the 'buying' needs of the
customer to other services. Accuracy and services need contextual insights about
customers and customer behaviour and enable and execute the customer experience
contextually.

5.3.2.2 Hyper-personalisation to Deliver Individualised Digital Experience

To deliver a highly individualised customer experience, banks build customer context
into hyper-personalisation engines by leveraging customers' financial, non-financial,
and other transactional historical data, and product master and reference data.

Hyper-personalisation engines are contextualised for location and time by leveraging location data, machine and device data, and public datasets. Social influence
on the customer is incorporated by leveraging service context, social networks, and
public datasets.

Digital IDs store financial and non-financial transaction history and other datasets
of the customer. A consent to use and leverage digital ID data can help in delivering
a highly individualised experience.

Some examples of hyper-personalised digital experience are presenting pre-fill
forms by leveraging internal and external data sets, contextualizing conversational
banking for the customer, building a 360-degree view of the customer, and reducing
the number of steps for the customer.

The banks are the most trusted among all players in the marketplace. The strongest
value proposition from banks is the trust it enjoys.

To generate historical data for hyper-personalised services, banks offer digital ID
and authentication services to customers and partners in the marketplace.

This competitive advantage provides banks with access to personal and
behavioural data, and customer needs. All this can be leveraged to design and deliver
a highly individualized customer experience.

5.3.2.3 To Deliver a Better Digital Experience Banks Are Servicing Need-Specific Marketplaces

Banks aim to build a better-contextualised customer experience for previously
identified customer needs and experience.

One of the ways to better identify customer needs is to promote and participate in a need-specific marketplace and subscription economy. This helps in serving the marketplace and covers all customer needs and provides both marketing and customer services. This can help to provide an individualistic and better customer experience.

5.3.2.4 Focus Only on the Customer Needs the Bank Intends to Address

The bank should carefully select the needs it wants to target for the enhancement of customer experience with a hyper-personalisation initiative. The level of impact and the time required to build the expected outcomes will vary according to the level of focus by the bank.

The most important question banks should address is at what level of accuracy and for what needs does it want to build personalisation vectors:

1. Automated recommendations;
2. Behavioural banking;
3. Customer journey map.

As identified needs get elevated from the 'automated recommendation' to the delivery of customer experience, the hyper-personalisation system becomes more complex. Finding a business case in the short run also becomes more difficult.

If the bank is measuring the impact of hyper-personalisation in the short term, it should invest in building a hyper-personalisation system only for additional purchase recommendations. Execution of hyper-personalised customer digital experiences can provide returns to the bank only in the long term. And that also only after cost and revenue structures are changed. Unless structures are changed, it may not provide a direct measurable benefit.

5.3.2.5 To Maintain Competitive Differentiators, Banks Enhance the Digital Experience of Services

Services requiring hyper-personalisation:

1. Communication and engaging customers for the avoidance of penalties and fees;
2. Engaging customers to help or prompt them to improve their finances;
3. Suggesting changes in spending patterns;
4. Suggest benefits in real time;
5. Alert them about transactions, frauds, and collections.

5.3.2.6 Hyper-personalisation Caters to Both Machines and Human Agents

The primary purpose of industrialisation is to build banking AI capabilities in machines to deliver contextualised individual experience.

At the existing level of development and capabilities in banking AI, machines alone at present and in the foreseeable future, may not be able to deliver the entire cycle of the customer experience. Existing banking AI capabilities may not be able to handle complex processes and services. A solution for a smooth handover between machines and human agents is required to build a culture of caring for customer experience.

5.3.2.7   Hyper-personalisation Engines Remember Customer Choice and Communication History

Hyper-personalised data is what chatbot needs to always remember of the customer and this also includes conclusions from historical data. For example, if the customer is not interested in upgrading their credit card, this should enter the memory instead of asking the customer for a credit card upgrade again and again.

5.3.2.8   Privacy Regulation Restricts the Use of Personal Information

On the regulatory front, unrestricted sharing of personal information has been reined in by privacy laws like the GDPR.

5.3.2.9   Banks Are Trusted Institutions and Must Maintain Their Trusted Persona

The most important differentiating value proposition the banking industry brings to the table is that they are more trusted by customers. Banks must maintain their trustworthy persona regarding privacy assurance while providing hyper-personalised services.

5.4   BIAN Framework to Design Application Modernisation

The Banking Industry Architecture Network (BIAN) is a collaborative not-for-profit organisation formed by leading banks, technology providers, consultants, and academics from all over the globe.

BIAN aims to lower the cost of banking by boosting the speed of innovation and automation in the banking industry.

BIAN is a banking enterprise architecture framework that provides standards, benchmarks, and templates for architecture, design, banking processes, services, data, and semantic APIs. BIAN leverages SOA principles to future-proof technology at banks. It is a framework that allows banks to gradually carve out technical debt hidden in legacy systems.

This section discusses the application of BIAN to modernize applications. BIAN Service Landscape 9.1 is the latest version available at:

https://bian.org/deliverables/bian-standards/bian-service-landscape-9-1/.

Readers not familiar with the BIAN framework are advised to read this document.

The application of BIAN Artefacts as the standards for building banking AI is discussed in detail in Chap. 10 on the BIAN Framework to Build Banking AI and Semantic APIs.

The BIAN Framework Defines Service-Oriented Architecture (SOA).

1. BIAN helps to realize the promise of SOA for banks and simplify the integration effort of major projects.
2. BIAN service domains help in identifying data exchanged with other services. This makes BIAN the best practice framework to build internal and external integration.
3. BIAN business object model adoption helps in defining banking concepts, terms, and calculations. This helps in building a semantic layer and build cognitive computing capabilities into an application and makes it intelligent.
4. BIAN adapts open standards to create interoperability.

5.4.1 Case Study: The BIAN Framework

BIAN released version 9.1 in March 2021. This version can be accessed at.
https://bian.org/deliverables/bian-standards/bian-service-landscape-9-1/.
According to BIAN, a bank is an aggregation of 568 business capabilities:

- 5 at the High Level;
- 40 at Level 1;
- 183 at Level 2;
- 345 at Level 3;
- With 186 semantic APIs.

The service domains are at the heart of BIAN design. Each domain is the functional capacity of the bank and represents:

- The elemental building block of a bank.
- An elemental, discrete, unique, and non-overlapping service provided by a bank.
- Service which is consistent in definition across service domains.
- A flexible service that can be provided internally by the bank or by a partner of the bank externally.
- Each service domain provides the right level of generalization and granularity to build a microservice for:

  - Legacy systems
  - Local requirements: privacy, documentation, data residency, etc.
  - Value propositions and differentiators of the bank
  - Customer engagement

- Customer type
- Product type
- Risk and compliance requirements.

BIAN has published the BIAN framework book. The 2019 edition of the book can be accessed at:

https://bian-services.com/books/?v=3a52f3c22ed6.

The book covers all aspects of architecture for the financial services industry. It should support all those involved in helping their bank evolve to be the industrialised bank of tomorrow. The book covers the service-oriented view of enterprise architecture and guides in the fast-evolving API arena.

BIAN has published a value chain view of a bank. It is an organisational view of a bank. This view helps in the easier identification of the control record owner.

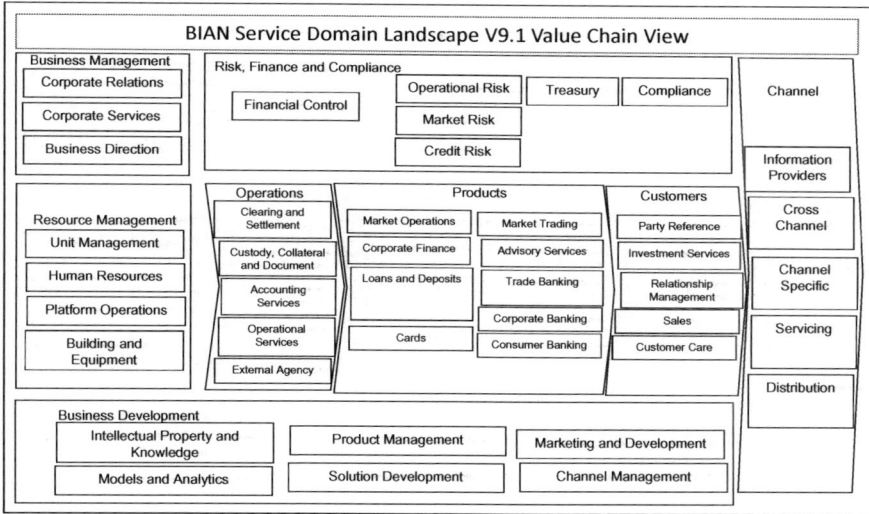

5.4.2   BIAN Framework Helps to Build Consistency and Reusability into Microservices

BIAN has a partitioned business capability that is defined in terms of its business function and the service operations it offers and consumes. Service means: encapsulation of 'data' and 'function'.

To create microservices that are consistent and highly reusable across domains, the service domain is the owner of the control record data.

To provide a framework to design a vendor-agnostic application and information architecture, the bank's technology landscape is mapped in a structured way to the business level BIAN service domains for:

- Partitioning the services and defining elemental level services with a single business purpose. Service partitions are collectively comprehensive, discrete, unique, and non-overlapping and have to perform a single discrete function. Service should support traceability between physical solutions and must-have business purposes and control records. Delegated services should be with other service domains.
- A similar service for a different product or business unit is called 'peer service'. Peer services need to be consistent across products.

5.4.3 BIAN Framework Helps in Identifying Wrappers to Modernize Underlying Applications

Underlying applications mapped to BIAN-defined mutually exclusive business capabilities help in identifying microservices for wrapping.

BIAN has divided banks into mutually exclusive service domains and each service domain further into services. This helps in defining 'what' each service does on a mutually exclusive basis. Since each service and service domain is defined based on 'what' it does, it takes away the source of duplicity due to 'how', 'why', and 'when'. Each of the business capabilities defines the granularity of microservices.

Mapping the underlying technology to business capabilities helps in defining the microservices to be built or exposed:

- Legacy applications: product processors, front-office applications, and back-office applications;
- Channel applications;
- Enterprise service bus;
- Point solutions.

5.4.4 BIAN Framework to Build Microservices

Taking the BIAN framework as a blueprint:

- Partition the business capabilities of an application at an elemental level;
- Identify and define discrete, unique, and non-overlapping service partitions;
- Collectively all services should be a comprehensive set of services;
- Similar services across products are termed 'peer service' sets.

Identify reusable services:

- Identify re-usable services across the service domains and peer sets;
- Provide the same treatment for internal and external services to help in creating flexibility for the business model and reduce fragmentation.

Build flexible and configurable services:

- Flexibility through configuration, better monitoring and intelligence, greater control and security;
- Expose embedded functionality for re-use by building a wrapper;
- Service re-use reduces software development and management costs.

Externalize or delegate service to other domain:

- A service domain delegates service to other service domains through a delegated service call.

For enhancing existing monolithic applications, an incremental approach is required. Transforming all service domains to microservices is an iterative process. Around the monolithic applications, a wrapper needs to be built and continuously upgraded to support the evolving adoption of microservices across service domains.

5.4.5 BIAN as Standard for Designing Microservices

- Standard definitions and approaches;
- Shared business vocabulary;
- Purpose and payload of each service;
- Delay and error management;
- Service operation SLAs;
- Service make-up;
- Operations performance;
- Security requirements.

5.4.6 BIAN Service Domain as a Container

- Aligning application boundaries to BIAN service domains results in an application partitioning that conforms to key microservices principles;
- A service domain can be treated as a container, encapsulating all functions, data, and interactions through asynchronous service exchange;
- A service domain need not be as large as a service domain in BIAN—however, it should be logically split across products and service delegation requirements.

5.4.7   Standardised Integration

- Connecting middleware;
- Routing capabilities for every container;
- To discover and establish all necessary service connections for:
  - Transaction execution;
  - Referential;
  - Command and control;
  - To deliver SLAs as agreed with the provider.

5.4.8   Standardised SLA and Intelligence

- Intelligence to handle:
  - Delays;
  - Errors;
  - Repetitions;
  - Duplicate service calls.

This will help in the externalization of services.

5.4.9   BIAN Delegated Service is a Framework to Build Agility

Externalization or delegation of service or service consumption design principles helps banks to implement information governance. It helps them to define the responsibilities of a service domain (Front Office, product processors, mid-office, Back Office, etc.) in terms of SLAs for service and data quality. Peer-level benchmarks create competition between service production and service consumption.

Analysis for externalization should be done independently of the existing organisational structure of the bank. The present and future business model scenarios should drive the externalization analysis. SLAs, confidence in adhering to SLAs, and SLA contractual terms drive the decision about the externalization of services.

5.4.9.1   Externalization of Service Consumption

- A service domain relies on other service domains for execution through delegated service calls;
- A service domain calling the delegated service becomes a service consumer for the delegated service.

5.4.9.2   The Service Domain Owns and Controls the Record

- Identify discrete functions and assets whose control records are maintained or owned by the service domain;
- A service domain providing a service becomes the owner of the control record;
- The service domain's business purpose and role drive the record ownership;
- Commercial behaviour: the relation of the service with the business model drives the service delegation.

5.4.9.3   Service Production Versus Service Consumption

- Business information governed by the service domain needs to be limited to the logic and information needed to address the life cycle of all instances of its control record directly;
- Benchmark with 'peer services';
- Any service which is to be industrialised should be delegated;
- Identify services for which the service domain is the service provider and what the SLAs are.
- Delegated services governed by SLAs.

5.4.9.4   Delegated Services Are Governed by SLAs

- The service providing the domain should agree that consumption of the service is appropriate;
- The responsibility of the service provider is to deliver the required service within the agreed SLAs;
- Whether to consume a service or not is the prerogative of the service consumer domain.

5.4.9.5   BIAN Framework to Build a 'to Be' State Information Architecture

Application modernization at banks is a continuous journey. Technology debt cannot be paid in a day or a year. For application modernization, the architecture council at the bank has to agree and adopt BIAN design principles with a timeline to remove redundancy and duplicity. All peer services should adopt similar designs and the BIAN business object model which can be translated into banking standards like the ISO 20022 data model. The high-level implementation steps are:

- Provide an inventory of applications and databases and this includes for each application and database:

- – Document business processes within the bank. Map them to BIAN business capabilities.
- – Document:

    Business architecture;
    Application architecture;
    Information architecture.

- – Map application and database to the business process and BIAN capabilities.

- Map a logical group of business process to BIAN services:

    - – Use BIAN functional patterns to create business operations in terms of:

        Management and support capabilities;
        Resource management;
        Activity oversight;
        Resource assignment;
        Production.

    - – Identify gaps in the BIAN framework and document enhancement for the framework used by the bank.
    - – Document a BIAN technology blueprint at a business domain level:

        Identify the BIAN service domain needed;
        Adapt the BIAN design;
        Distribute duplicate business facilities in an organizational 'blueprint'.

    - – Extend the technology blueprint for business and technical changes:

        Targeted point solution:

            Assessing and implementing point solution;
            Product launch;
            Core system repurposing;
            Vendor solution alignment.

        Enterprise analysis:

            Application portfolio rationalization;
            Mergers and acquisition;
            Investment planning;
            Outsourcing and insourcing.

- Identify scenarios for delegated business functions:

    - – Identify scenarios for delegated business functions, internally or externally;
    - – Map identified services to BIAN service domain;
    - – Identify roadmap for delegated services.

- Identify microservices to be built:

  - Map open banking standards for business logic and endpoint data to BIAN microservices;
  - Document business logic for each microservice with an endpoint;
  - Provide an inventory for BIAN microservices.
  - Develop the technical specifications for three scenarios:

    Core/host/legacy;
    ESB enabled;
    Cloud and microservices.

- Document design patterns:

  - Estimate the volume of each service endpoint for:

    Add;
    Update;
    Retrieve;
    Delete;
    Others.

- Map data elements to the ISO 20022 data model.
- Real-time services and batch services.

5.4.9.6   Case Study: BIAN Presented as a Coreless Banking Pilot at SIBOS London in September 2019

BIAN has put banks in the driver's seat, giving them a role in the development of services that are more relevant to the needs of their customers. The main objectives are:

1. Developing a future-proof, regulatory-compliant, and universally compatible banking infrastructure based on BIAN microservices.
2. To promote a more efficient and effective approach to modernising banking software.
3. Solve the perpetual challenges presented by legacy core infrastructure, and allow for faster, more cost-effective development of services that are more relevant for today's digital-first customers.
4. The initial focus of the pilot is to develop API-based microservices covering:

   (1)   Consumer payments;
   (2)   Customer offers;
   (3)   Consumer loans.

5. Complete plug and play functionality, to ensure no impact on user experience.
6. Fully deployable to the cloud, so users can take advantage of modern software development techniques.

7. Bank consumable API interface to orchestrate BIAN APIs (where necessary) and reduce network traffic.
8. Cross-domain orchestration to also reduce network traffic.

5.4.9.7   Banks Should Adopt and Participate to Strengthen the BIAN Framework

The banking industry has not yet established any forum or framework to standardise API technical standards at the industry level. As banks start publishing APIs, unless they build and comply with technical standards for APIs, this may soon become non-manageable.

Banks are sitting on billions of dollars of technical debt. To modernise applications, the banking industry needs a business capabilities framework to benchmark its microservice granularity. Benchmarked granularity can help in standardising APIs in the banking industry.

Therefore, participation in the BIAN framework may ultimately help in establishing API technical standards.

5.5   Modernise Applications to Deliver Digital Experience

5.5.1   Three Approaches to Application Modernisation

1. Retire legacy applications;
2. Extend legacy applications;
3. Develop cloud-native microservice applications.

5.5.1.1   Retire Legacy Applications

For first, second, and third-generation banking applications, the business case for retirement is very strong in terms of high TCO and not being able to support customer experience delivery. The business case for retirement gets stronger with the spread of digitisation within and outside a bank.

All existing technology cannot be immediately replaced with a digital technology or architecture. Neither will there be an immediate business case for the replacement of existing applications with digital native technology.

Legacy application replacement is planned over time, supported by the necessary investment and capital allocation and implementation timelines.

Legacy applications are re-used most of the time.

To enable the delivery of the digital experience, and to enable the digital banking business model, legacy applications are modernised by a building wrapper for functionality and containerized to deliver continuous integration and continuous deployment.

5.5.1.2 Build a Roadmap to Extend and Retire the Legacy Applications through Repackaging, Replatforming, and Refactoring

Banks cloud-enable their applications and infrastructure to deliver a digital experience. Cloud enablement helps in scaling, resiliency, agility, and provision of machine learning platforms.

On-premise legacy applications, in a legacy data centre infrastructure, impact on delivery speed and agility. To address these issues, banks enable legacy applications so that the private cloud can exploit cloud scalability, agility, and resiliency.

Banks adopt a hybrid cloud model–public cloud to deliver the Front Office customer experience and a private cloud to host the Back Office legacy applications and to secure the privacy of customer data.

The primary aim for application modernisation is to build agility into the technology and applications and address the requirement for faster time to delivery and the demand to achieve the business outcomes. This is enabled by the containerisation (Kubernetes, Docker) of applications and microservice architecture. Containerisation does away with the complexity of deployment and brings execution consistency. Microservices ensure ways to deliver scalability and continuous integration and deployment. All this is required to support and deliver business outcomes.

5.5.1.3 Repackaging Applications into Containers

Applications are repackaged into containers to provide a significant cost advantage and technology operation benefits in terms of simplified upgrades, portability, development and deployment, patch management and compliance, traceability and immutable images, and CI/CD integration. Containerisation does not change in the application architecture and this is a simpler and faster way to improve operational efficiency. The next-generation containers with software-defined infrastructure are further improving the time-to-market and security position.

5.5.1.4 Application Replatforming

One approach is to lift and shift the application to containers and deploy them on a modern deployment platform.

An application to be replatformed is containerised. Containerised applications are deployed like cloud-native applications. Replatforming and containerisation help in reducing application duplicity and further enhance security positions.

Lift and shift to containers does not modernize the application. It only provides a time buffer so as to refactor an application.

To modernise a containerised application, the bank augments the application with a new layer to enable the gradual modernisation of the application architecture. An augmented layer helps:

- To deliver the application on mobile and other channels;
- In making existing application functionality accessible to cloud-native applications.

5.5.1.5   Application Refactoring

Application refactoring is the re-architecting of all or parts of monolithic applications using cloud-native principles to produce a distributed microservices-based stateless application. Banks generally refactor monolithic applications over some time. They initially start with providing a wrapper to legacy applications and exposing certain functionalities of the wrapped applications as microservices or APIs.

Banks create a new layer of application software that wraps the existing application functionality and data with an interface that is accessible to new cloud-native applications. Generally, no extra business logic is inserted in the new or augmented layer.

Over a period, the bank starts breaking the monolithic legacy application and keeps building the microservices and APIs. However, it should be noted that the required level of granularity of the wrapped back-office application is quite coarse.

5.5.1.6   Develop a Cloud-Native Microservices-Based Application

These applications are architected and developed on cloud-native technology. They are designed for agility, scalability, and high availability. These applications are built on a distributed microservices-based stateless design. The stateless design makes the application highly orchestratable. The approach is to build a new application on digital technology and make application functionality available through APIs. An adapter microservice is built to call these APIs. Other applications use adapter microservices to call functionality APIs.

5.5.2   Aims of Application Modernisation

5.5.2.1   To Pay Off Technical Debt

Paying off technical debt is financing an application modernisation program with a business case to industrialise the bank.

5.5.2.2   To Reduce Duplicity for a Faster Processing Cycle

Duplicity is created with the false belief that by duplicating application and data, the movement of data across the process and the release of changes to a production environment is fast-tracked. This may be so for a portion of the particular process. But duplicity increases complexity and exponentially slows down the end-to-end process. At an overall level of application and data, duplicity slows down many other processes. Any step to reduce copies of applications and data is a part of the application modernisation effort.

5.5.2.3   Mutualise Data

Data in banks annually are growing at 20%++ on a very large base. This is largely due to duplicate data in the bank. Tens or hundreds of data definitions and much duplicate data exist in every bank. The unintended benefit of the GDPR requirement to maintain up-to-date consent of the subject is forcing banks to mutualise customer data and hence reduce copies of PII data within the bank. The principles of data mutualisation need to be extended beyond PII data.

5.5.2.4   Make External Integration Agile

For legacy and monolithic applications, only internal integration is designed for.

To support the new business model, the bank has to integrate with millions of personal devices, applications, and APIs of the customers and partners so as to deliver:

- Customer digital experience;
- Marketplace;
- Digital banking;
- Customer self-service;
- Integration with Fintech;
- Virtual banks.

Application modernisation and the creation of APIs help in the modernisation and creation of external integration, which is agile, scalable, resilient, and continuously deployed.

5.5.2.5   Deliver New Business Model

Every time a business comes up with a proposal, several components of technology are identified for change. If these changes are accounted for in the project cost, it makes many of the new business projects non-viable. Thus the bank loses business opportunities and over a period this may lead to them losing market position.

Application modernisation should be financed through a separate capital allocation as a business strategy to deliver the new business model.

5.5.3 Scoping an Application Modernisation Program to Deliver an Industrialised Bank

The primary reason for duplicity is monolithic applications. Reducing application size and making it standardised, flexible, and loosely coupled can reduce duplicity to a large extent. Loosely coupled applications interspersed with 'everything as a service' is the basic tenet for delivering an industrialised bank. To do this, application modernisation scope is defined in terms of:

1. Ease of management: digital enablement of application means automate installation, scaling, and management of workloads and services.
2. Portability: application portability means the ability to run uniformly and consistently across any platform or cloud or on a hybrid cloud.
3. Agility: means the use of DevOps tools and enables rapid application development and enhancement.
4. Fault isolation: each application is isolated and operates independently of others. The failure of one application does not affect the continued operation of any other application.
5. Security: since the applications are isolated, this prevents the invasion of malicious code from affecting other containers or the host system.
6. Building scalability into technology is the ability to add computing resources to grow and manage increased demands. Computing resources cover process, network, software, or appliances. Scalability is one of the most important features of cloud computing.
7. Building microservices platforms. We have discussed this in detail in this chapter.
8. Building APIs as an integration fabric to extend the digital core. We have discussed this in detail in Chap. 9: APIs Are the Public Persona of an Industrialised Bank.

5.6 Application Modernisation Through Microservice-Based Architecture

The most important reason for adopting a microservice-based architecture is to overcome the challenges that a monolithic application faces:

- A monolithic application is slow in adapting to business changes due to the large codebase and inherent testing and code promotion formalities.

- From a business perspective, adapting services for new customers and business is a priority.
- Monolithic applications make agile development, deployment, and operations difficult.

A microservice is a small, autonomous service, fulfilling a business/domain task. A microservice is designed to work cohesively towards achieving a business goal. It is an approach that builds systems from small services developed and deployed independently of the other, focused on performing a small task well, each consisting of its processes, communications, and database.

5.6.1 A Microservice Is Small Enough to Enable Agility, It Is Large Enough to Deliver Business functions

'Micro' is a size given in comparison to a monolithic application. Smallness is not an absolute measure. The definition of smallness varies across the applications:

- It should be small enough to enable re-usability;
- It should be large enough to cover the scope and purpose of the business function;
- It should not be so granular that the integrating overheads exceed the benefits.

BIAN artefacts help in deciding the appropriate level of granularity. In this chapter and a separate chapter, we have discussed the adoption of the BIAN framework to modernize applications.

5.6.2 The Microservice Has to Be Agile, Flexible, Resilient, and Quickly Adjustable to Customer and Market Realities

From a development perspective too, a microservice has reduced operational overheads, minimal coordination between teams, and adaptability to automation.

5.6.3 Microservice Design Builds Agility into the Banking Business

The service boundaries in a microservice (MS) should be aligned to the achievement of the business task. The functional mapping helps in reducing duplicity and redundancy in the bank. The MS should be small enough so that is re-usable. At the same time, it should be big enough that there is no other MS executing the same business logic. The same service can deliver different values in a different context. However, the boundary needs to be well defined to contextualise the business logic for the same nomenclature and reference to the same object.

An MS does more than simply break up things into smaller pieces. It has implications for architecture, business and technology processes, business outcomes for the bank, and much more. Microservices enable banks in making better use of cloud-native technology advances and increase their pace of innovation, industrialisation, and new business models.

Smaller MS components can be changed in isolation to create greater agility, can be scaled individually to better use a cloud-native infrastructure, and managed to provide resilience.

MS finer granularity is required for Front Office online applications. Composition/aggregation with other services can form a completely new paradigm.

5.6.4   Core Benefits of Microservice Architecture

1. Greater agility: MS are small enough to change independently and large enough to make an impact on the outcome.
2. Scalability: the required business outcome defines the resource usage. It is scalable so as to work for business outcomes. For example, the business requirement of providing connectivity to x million personal devices will drive resource usage.
3. Discrete resilience, unlike monolithic applications where the entire application has to be resilient, changes to one MS and does not impact on other MS.

5.6.5   Case Study: Microservice Architecture for Regulatory Reporting

According to one estimate, in a regulatory reporting application, 10–20% of overall fields or computation is updated by the regulator annually. Banks are adopting microservices to manage frequently mandated changes.

For this design, microservice architecture with minimal interdependence on other services is used so that the services perform independently. Each microservice is loosely coupled and can be individually replaced with the modified microservice and with the need to make a minimum change in anything else. That is all related properties are placed with a microservice so that one change will enable all changes to be made quickly.

Following are the principles for the regulatory reporting of microservice design and architecture:

- In a regulatory reporting application, the following microservices are the likely candidates for frequent changes:

- Data, programming logic, and calculation engine;
- Computational logic for aggregated reporting, specific canned reports, and user-defined reports.

- It takes minimum effort and time to rebuild, retest, and redeploy a new microservice.
- There are minimum end-point changes so that consumers are not impacted by changes in data, logic, switching, or modifying the system of records which has a minimum downstream impact.
- Microservices are independently deployable, scalable, and distributed.
- To build an API, identify the appropriate level of granularity. Fine granularity increases the service calls. The orchestration of the process and accuracy testing becomes a major challenge for granular level APIs, adding overheads everywhere.

5.6.6 Applications Fit for the Adoption of Microservice Design

All applications which require greater autonomy are fit for the adoption of microservice design. All cloud-native applications are fit for the adoption of microservice design. The following is an illustrative list of applications that are strong candidates for microservice design:

- A high amount of data in memory;
- High usage of CPU operations;
- Inability to scale a portion of the application, hence the entire application needs to be scaled;
- Applications with very high code dependencies and therefore difficult to manage.

5.6.6.1 An Application Integrating with Multiple Technologies Is the Stronger Candidate for the Adoption of Microservice Design

- Coexistence of multiple technologies (system platforms, development languages, communication methods, storage technology).
- Allows the flexibility to select the correct tools for the requirements as it can adopt new technologies or newer versions of the technology stack for development without disruptions.
- Allows different technology elements among services:
  - Customer services;
  - Catalogue services;
  - Recommendation services;
  - Minimal centralised management.

5.6.6.2   Common Basic Services Are a Stronger Candidate for Adoption of Microservice Design

- Authentication, access controls, and account management;
- Common edit checks, reconciliations, and validations;
- Common caching, data lineage, and programming logic;
- Portal uploading services;
- Audit logging.

5.6.6.3   Applications Following a Layered Approach Are Stronger Candidates for Adoption of Microservices

- Client-side screen computations (Java scripts, HTML pages, browser).
- Server-side operations processing (handle HTTP requests, implementing domain logic, handling data distilled from the DB, creating HTML display for client-side browser).
- Databases (data manipulation, management, relational DB, handle individual operation functions).
- All logic handling requests can be dealt with as a single process.
- Applications are divided by each class and function.
- High traffic requirements:

  - Deliberate separation of deployment;
  - CQRS (Command Query Responsibility Segregation): differentiates MS for commands vs queries.

- Implementing changes to such layered architectures without impacting other parts of the system is easy.

5.6.6.4   Managing a Big Ball of Mud Syndrome

Certain applications are not good candidates for MS specifically where:

- Dependencies criss-cross the system;
- Very difficult to establish traceability;
- The system works based on contingent logic.

In such cases, it is advisable to break down the application into its components and use the strangler principle. That is the new system captures and intercepts calls to mature applications in coexistence, routes them to other handlers, and gradually replaces them altogether, as rewriting the entire application for cutover is quite risky.

Wrapping the application and exposing application functionality as API is required to:

- Improve control over the runtime environment and database schema;
- Enhance performance;

- Improve reliability of services;
- Improve overall availability, scalability, and fault tolerance;
- Prevent failure of collaborating services having an SLA impact.

5.7 Industrialisation of Microservices

To industrialise a bank and to modernise applications, the first step is to build a microservices-based cloud-enabled application design. To automate application life cycle management, there is a need to standardise all technology processes relating to the building, release, and deployment of microservices. Standardisation aims to create re-usability and faster deployment. Standardisation means segregating variation and managing it separately.

Standardisation and automation of technology process management aim to deliver the industrialisation of microservices. The following is an illustrative list of the standardisation and automation of technological processes and microservices design.

5.7.1 Manage Version Control of Codebase to Re-use Code Repository

Every application must have one codebase, so there is a need to maintain a code repository. Multiple applications can use the same codebase through libraries. Also, there is a need to maintain a version control of the codebase in the library and across the deployments using version control systems like GitHub's automated library management.

5.7.2 Managing Dependency on Another Library or Package

Manage dependency on another library or package of services by explicitly declaring every dependency. No implicit dependencies on package and libraries can be assumed.

5.7.3 Separation of Configuration from Code

This helps in the reuse of code. Further, configuration is specific to the deployment. Segregation of configuration helps in re-using code and applying the local configuration. Separation helps:

- To make provision of resources for the database and cached memory, making database scalable;
- In segregating the credentialisation to external services such as cloud services for better access rights management;
- Per-deploy values such as the canonical hostname for the deployment.

5.7.4   Backing Services

Every microservices application consumes other services as a part of normal operations. These are called backing services. Each service consumed may vary across the deployment and network. So it needs to be loosely coupled and segregated. Segregation of backing services makes microservices reusable. This also helps in standardising the backing service as a separate service. This makes the management of consumption of internal and third party services very similar. The following are some examples:

- Datastores;
- Messaging;
- SMTP for outbound;
- Caching system.

5.7.5   Managing the Services Version

To manage the services version, the bank should strictly separate the development, staging, and production environment:

- The development stage converts a code repository into an executable bundle known as a build. The build stage fetches dependencies and compiles binaries and assets. The code is version controlled.
- The staging stage applies configuration to the build and is ready for immediate execution in the execution environment.
- At the production stage, the service is run in the execution environment, by launching some set of the applications processes against a selected release.

5.7.6   Segregate Process from the State

The approach is to segregate the process from the state and assume a stateless service. Building a stateless service makes services truly re-usable. The assumption is that the service shares nothing and any state or data that need to be shared or persisted, should be stored in the stateful backing service or database. Stateless service never assumes that caching anything in memory or cache memory will be available for future jobs.

5.7.7 Port Binding

Port Binding Export services via port binding. This helps in making one service a backing service for another, thus standardising the backing service.

5.7.8 Scale-Out

Scale-out is via a process model. It shares nothing, though horizontal partitioning can help in handling diverse workloads.

5.7.9 Disposability

This maximises robustness with a fast startup and graceful shutdown. This facilitates faster scaling and rapid and robust code deployment.

5.7.10 Development Production Parity

Keep the development, staging, and production environment as similar as possible. Reduce the time gap to move code to production; make the developer who wrote the code move it into production and let them watch the behaviour of the code; let both environments have the same tools and versions. This parity is very important for the database, queuing system, and cache.

5.7.11 Treat Logs as Event Streams

Logs are the stream of aggregated, time-ordered events collected from the output streams of all running processes and backing services. Logs or usage analytics is required by both. This helps in:

- Finding a specific event in the past;
- Graphing trends;
- Active alerting according to user heuristics.

5.7.12   Run Admin Tasks as a One-off

Run in an identical environment as the regular long-running processes of the application. They run against a release, using the same code base and configuration as any process running against that release. Administration code must ship with the application code to avoid synchronisation issues.

5.8   Conclusion: Deliver Digital Experience by Modernising Applications

Application modernisation aims to deliver digitisation objectives, to build the foundation for AI as a service, to complement API as an integration tool, to industrialise the bank, to empower managers to pursue and achieve business outcomes, and to do away with the complexity of technology.

Modernisation of applications, hyper-personalisation of customer engagement delivery, and implementation of the BIAN framework are tools to digitise banks:

1. Make provision for similar experience and business outcomes or service levels and whether the customer is engaged through the paper document or electronic data or human communication.
2. Make provision for similar business outcomes or service levels and whether the customer is connecting through personal devices or the bank's applications or third-party marketplaces.
3. Empower customers and partners through self-service to achieve business outcomes and remove the complexity of technology management.
4. Build agility into the business model with a faster time to market.

We also suggest supplementing this chapter by reading Chaps. 9, 11, and 12.

Chapter 6
Cloud Adoption: A Foundational Engine

6.1 Introduction: Cloud adoption—A Foundational Engine

In the past five years or so, cloud computing has become the key enabler for innovation at banks. Cloud is enabling banks to leverage new service models and new technology capabilities, implement microservices, and deliver API to significantly improve digital experience and business outcomes by building agility, scalability, and resiliency into the business model. It is the foundation to industrialise data infrastructure to process a very high volume of data in real-time and deliver banking AI as a service by leveraging AI platforms provided by cloud service providers (CSPs).

Cloud lays a foundation for the industrialisation of the bank and for the transformation of the bank's business model.

© Springer Nature Singapore Pte Ltd. 2022
M. Bhatia, *Banking 4.0*,
https://doi.org/10.1007/978-981-16-6069-6_6

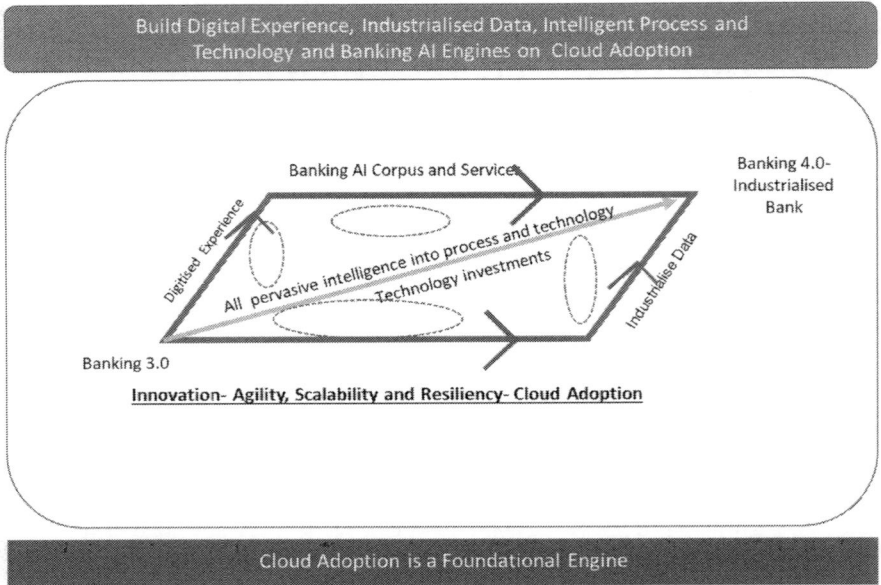

Build Digital Experience, Industrialised Data, Intelligent Process and Technology and Banking AI Engines on Cloud Adoption

Banking AI Corpus and Services

Banking 4.0-
Industrialised
Bank

Digitised Experience

All pervasive intelligence into process and technology

Technology investments

Industrialise Data

Banking 3.0

Innovation- Agility, Scalability and Resiliency- Cloud Adoption

Cloud Adoption is a Foundational Engine

'Cloud' is a broad term, and stakeholders have interpreted it differently. Cloud encompasses a range of IT services provided in various formats over the Internet, including public cloud, virtual private cloud, hybrid cloud arrangements, and the banking community cloud.

Cloud adoption has three levels of maturity. It starts with the adoption of infrastructure as a service (IaaS), and as banks mature in cloud adoption they move to platform as a service (PaaS). Then, as banks become industrialised, they move to software as a service (SaaS).

The most important contribution of cloud adoption is that it empowers banks to compete with Fintechs.

6.1.1 Cloud Adoption Lays Foundation for Industrialisation and Innovation at the Bank

Managing the cost of technology (storage, computing, database, services) resources through cloud adoption is only a small part of the story. Cost may be a good story at the level of IaaS. For a large bank or in the long term, the sustainable story is that cloud enables industrialisation and catalyses innovation.

The real benefits of the cloud come when it is used to build SaaS or BaaS. Cloud capabilities industrialise a bank by abstracting the technology capabilities as business capabilities, doing away with technology complexities, and focusing on business outcomes.

- Cloud provides capabilities to orchestrate a technology process across cloud products in terms of data ingestion, data storage, data distribution, ML models, and insights.

  - This helps to enforce standardised business policies across the technology process chain.
  - It reduces uncertainties in technology services.

- Cloud provides a platform to manage structured, unstructured, and semi-structured data.

  - This helps to manage documents, voice, and textual chats and hence delivery of the digital experience.
  - It helps to digitise the front office of the bank for better customer engagement.
  - It helps in the industrialisation of the front and back office.

- Cloud provides capabilities to manage metadata across cloud products, clouds, and on-premise technology assets.

  - Metadata management at the technical and business level along with data search capabilities helps to reduce the data duplicity and mutualisation of data for better security and privacy management.
  - Automation of metadata management helps to drastically reduce technology resource requirements and the complexity of managing systems, as well as enables straight-through processing, and self-service and reusability of technology assets.

- API/ microservices/ software-based interactions with applications, data, and infrastructure.

  - This helps to create SaaS and empowers business managers, customers, and partners.

- Cloud provides technology to deliver legacy application modernisation.
- It enables and delivers business innovation in a BAU mode.
- It enables continuous delivery of integration and delivery of applications.
- It provides a platform to build microservices and API-based modern applications.

6.1.2 *Iterative Cloud Adoption Process Aligns Other Engines*

The challenge with existing technology is that it has fragmented information architecture built-on legacy applications. Transformation to an industrialised bank is necessarily iterative. Cloud adoption is an iterative process to deliver banking as a service—the industrialised bank of tomorrow.

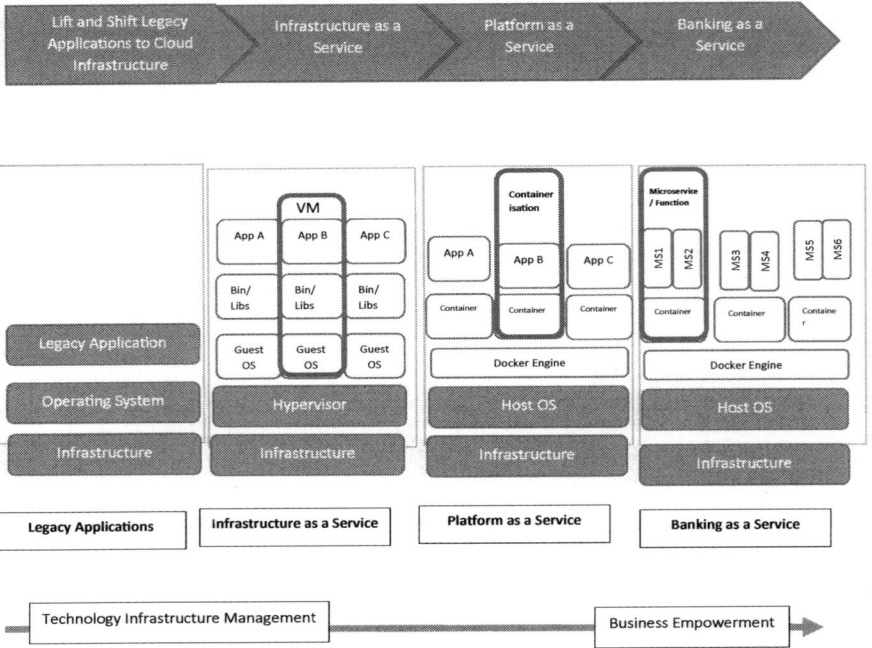

| Lift and Shift Legacy Applications to Cloud Infrastructure | Infrastructure as a Service | Platform as a Service | Banking as a Service |

| Legacy Applications | Infrastructure as a Service | Platform as a Service | Banking as a Service |

Technology Infrastructure Management ────────────────────────────── Business Empowerment ▶

Infrastructure as a SERVICE	Platform as a service	Banking as a service
Resiliency—fault tolerance and resiliency	Loosely coupled microservices, APIs Containerisation to deliver fine-grained resiliency	Design and architecture of technology, business process with inbuilt redundancy, and decentralised organisation to deliver resiliency
Agility—infrastructure in a managed service mode	Integrated cloud platform and service catalogues to automate, develop, and deliver agility	Agile Integration—API-based business-to-business integration
Scalability—horizontal scalability	Container orchestration capabilities to deliver scalability	Fully re-factored applications with inter and intra application APIs
Virtual machines for manage network, storage and processing	Database as a service AI as a service Data movement as a service Security services Development services Event-driven services Message queue services Monitoring services Archival services	APIs for service fulfilment APIs for customer onboarding APIs for loan approval APIs for payment APIs for data

6.2 Cloud-Native Applications (CNAs) Designed to Deliver Business Outcomes

Cloud-native applications are microservices-based applications, run on a containerised and dynamically orchestrated platform. They are built to take advantage of cloud computing capabilities of agility, scalability, and resiliency. Cloud-native is not an attribute of application deployment. It is characteristic of application design, architecture, development, orchestration, deployment, and management.

6.2.1 Cloud-Native Applications Are Modular

Cloud-native applications are built-on modularity principles. Microservice architecture provides the foundation to build modularity, a design level principle, into applications. Modularity is exploited in architecture, development, orchestration, deployment, and management to deliver continuous integration and deployment of applications to build agility into the business model.

6.2.2 Cloud-Native Applications Leverage APIs as an Integration Tool

Cloud-native applications being built with modularity design on microservices are loosely coupled and delivered as APIs. API-based modular design allows communication via service interface calls over the network, avoiding the risks of direct linking, shared memory models, or direct reads of another team's datastore. This design extends the reach of applications and services to different devices and forms.

6.2.3 Containerisation Makes Cloud-Native Applications Horizontally Scalable

Cloud-native applications are built to scale horizontally, on demand, portable, and container-centric. Container technology uses operating system virtualisation capabilities to divide available computer resources among multiple applications while ensuring that they are secure and isolated from each other. Containerisation technology abstracts and simplifies access and management of the underlying infrastructure. It can manage the entire life cycle across on-premise, private clouds, and public clouds. Containerisation offers self-service, automation, and life cycle management capabilities.

6.2.4   Cloud-Native Applications Enable Continuous Deployment

Containerisation helps development, deployment, and operations in self-service and on demand. This helps developers focus on building applications without the obstacles and delays associated with provisioning infrastructure.

6.2.5   Cloud-Native Applications Are Built-On Reusable Components

All re-usable components such as the caching service, rules or workflow engines, integration connectors, mobile and API management capabilities, data virtualisation service, messaging broker, or serverless frameworks are standardised and re-used by integrating with the underlying container-based infrastructure. Continuous integration (CI)/continuous delivery (CD) enables the fast feedback loop and extends the infrastructure automation to an end-to-end automated delivery, automated testing, vulnerability scanning, security compliance, and regulatory checks. The goal of building automated delivery pipelines is to update without affecting operational capacity, reducing delivery risks.

6.2.6   Cloud-Native Applications—Designed to Deliver Business Outcomes

The focus of cloud-native applications is business outcomes and reaching them more quickly. To speed up the process, the bank adopts collaborative, continuous integration, and continuous development teams with short and continuous cycles.

Evolving to the cloud-native application is a journey. In addition to technology and architecture, it needs a technology process and a mindset to benefit from cloud capabilities.

6.2.7   BIAN Is a Design Template Used to Build Cloud-Native Applications

We have discussed in detail in other chapters about leveraging the BIAN framework to identify and build domain-driven microservices and semantic APIs.

6.3   Managing Risks in the Cloud

The adoption of cloud is exposed to risks of information security, contractual terms, reliance on the terms of the cloud provider, appropriate risk assessment, and risk control monitoring. An illustrative and non-exhaustive list of scenarios considered for risk management are as follows:

6.3.1   *Security Design and Architecture at Banks Must Complement the Security and Privacy Posture Provided by CSPs*

- Understanding the network access and inherited security and privacy control posture provided by CSPs and the intermediaries.
- Designing the security and privacy controls to complement the security and privacy control posture provided by the CSPs and intermediaries to comply with the security and privacy requirements of the regulator, and to manage the risk and control scenarios and use cases as per the security, privacy, and control policy of the bank.
- Designing the compensating security and privacy controls as required to manage the risk, control, security, and privacy.

6.3.1.1   Case Study—Security, Design, and Architecture Posture of CSPs Varies with Cloud Services

As the cloud services mature from IaaS to PaaS to SaaS, the security and privacy posture of CSPs and complementary security design and architecture adopted by the banks vary.

Unfortunately, none of the public cloud providers has moved beyond infrastructure as a service. Some of the Fintechs have started providing banking as a platform.

For SaaS-technology infrastructure or virtual machines, since database and application management are all on the cloud, the risks are higher.

Inherent risk is high on the public cloud involving systems of record that maintain information essential to determining obligations to customers and counterparties, such as current balance, benefits, and transaction history.

Areas of responsibility	Type of cloud service		
	Infrastructure as a service	Banking as a platform	Banking as a service (Fintech SaaS platforms)

(continued)

(continued)

Areas of responsibility	Type of cloud service		
	Infrastructure as a service	Banking as a platform	Banking as a service (Fintech SaaS platforms)
Continuous and real-time monitoring of operations and effectiveness of security and privacy controls	Bank	Bank	Bank
Customer side information security	Bank	Bank	Bank
Data quality	Bank	Bank	Bank
Application management	Bank	Bank	CSP
Virtual machines and networks	Bank	CSP	CSP
Cloud infrastructure	CSP	CSP	CSP

6.3.2   Continuous and Real-Time Control and Risk Monitoring by the Bank and CSP

- Design and implement continuous and near real-time control monitoring of operations and effectiveness of the security and privacy controls of the bank.
- Design and implement continuous and near real-time control monitoring of the cloud provider's operations relating to the cloud-based information system of the bank and assess the system's security posture.

6.3.3   Clearly Defining and Action Items and Contractual Terms

- Clearly defining and implementing the roles of CSPs and bank to manage the co-mingling of roles and responsibilities.
- Managing multi-tenancy—under multi-tenancy arrangements, computing resources like storage, processing, memory, network bandwidth, and application are pooled to serve multiple consumers. Resources are managed physically, virtually, and dynamically assigned and reassigned. Dynamic assignment of resources makes the management of the cloud complex. The need to manage data and

system protection in the context of logical and physical boundaries and data flow separation is heightened.

- Multi-tenancy is an orchestration of container deployment. There are conflicting goals in the container deployment orchestration process.

  - One goal is to optimise the use of underlying resources which need less restrictions on container deployment. Security and privacy requirements need more and granular level restriction and complete segregation of deployments.
  - Resources may be available across countries. Data residency requirement is to store and process all data within a country. Residency is managed through *geolocation* methods. Unfortunately, existing geolocation methods are not accurate at most of the CSPs, which require close monitoring and management of operational controls and currently are neither fully automated nor scalable. Therefore, there is a need to establish and continuously monitor data residency. The bank may also build the data residency as a part of configuration management and policy enforcement.

- Managing data residency as per the banking regulatory and privacy requirement. Data residency is a requirement to store or process data in a particular geography or location or jurisdiction. Regulators are driving this requirement world over. For example, payment system providers must store and process all data related to payment systems within India. There are similar requirements in the UAE and many other countries. Financial, personally identifiable, and healthcare data are mostly covered by data residency requirements, which are managed through the creation of a data catalogue and by identifying all data assets in the bank. Data residency requirements for each asset and monitoring data residency are defined through automated controls, CSPs and their contracts, and intermediary declaration and auditing.

6.3.3.1 Scale, Dynamics, and Complexity of Cloud Pricing Models

Understanding the relationships and interdependencies between the different cloud computing deployment models and service models is critical to understanding the security risks involved in cloud computing. The differences in methods and responsibilities for securing different combinations of service and deployment models present a significant challenge for cloud consumers. They need to perform a thorough risk assessment, accurately identify the security and privacy controls necessary to preserve the security level of their environment as part of the risk treatment process and monitor the operations and data after migrating to the cloud in response to their risk control needs.

The primary factors driving the pricing are listed below.

- Type of cloud service delivery model

  - IaaS

Low priority, preemptible
Reserve—no upfront to partial upfront to full commitment or subscription-based
On demand
Bare metal
Host Services

- SaaS or PaaS

    The user commits a minimum subscription and revenue to the cloud provider

- Banking as a service or code on demand

- Value spectrum
- There is some upfront cost and ongoing cost. There are three types of pricing models:

    - Subscriptions for a pre-defined period
    - Pay as you go
    - Combination of subscription and consumption.

6.3.3.2   Case Study: Consumption-Based Pricing Model for Google Cloud Platform

The rate for size machine or server used for time	Storage volume (TM)	Number of operations on storage	Network usages (TB)	BigQuery (TB)	Dataproc/dataflow/cloud composer	Pub/Sub	SQL/spanner
CPUs and RAM	Cloud storage	Class A operations—writing to memory	Ingress—upload (Internet and VM to VM)	Storage	Master node size	Message volume in terms of TB	Nodes
Nodes	Nearline		Egress—download (Internet and VM to VM)	Query in terms of TB	Worker node Size	Published	Storage
GPU	Coldline	Class B operations reading memory	Data retrieval from nearline, coldline and archival	BigQuery ML—creating model, testing model, and serving model (in terms of TB)		Retained	
TPU	Archive					Snapshot	
	File Storage (standard and premium rates)	Standard and premium rates					

Adoption of cloud technology does not, in itself, alter the regulatory obligations of the bank. Regulatory compliance with electronic banking, conduct risk, and payment systems requirements does not change and continues to be the primary regulatory requirements for cloud.

6.3.3.3 Pricing Approaches Adopted by the Cloud Service Provider

Resource-based pricing.

- Discount pricing
    - Early payment
    - Off-season
    - Build purchase
    - Retail discount
    - Cash discount
    - Trade-in allowance

- Promotional pricing
- Freemium pricing
- Volume or material-based pricing
    - Methods to compute volume
    - Defined granularity of the task
    - Bundled tasks volume
    - Slab-based volume
    - Optional features

- Time and material
- Discriminatory pricing
    - Customer segment
    - Customer geography
    - Product-based
    - Dynamic or surge price
    - Loyalty price

- Value-based
    - Bundled features
    - Free upfront and pay later or freemium
    - Pay as you use
    - Pay per task (task as a measurement unit)
    - Pay as you go (time and material)
    - Pay as you like (feature).

Value-based pricing is used for stateless shared software resources.

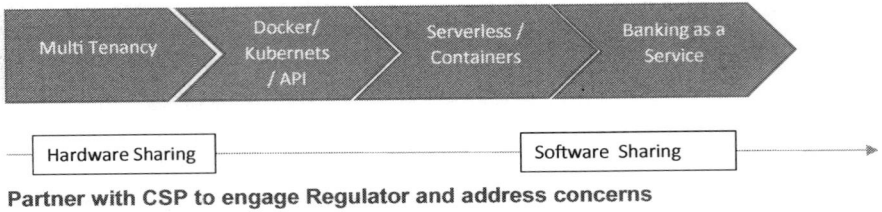

Partner with CSP to engage Regulator and address concerns

6.3.3.4   Partner with CSP to Engage Regulator and Address Concerns

Regulators are concerned about the risks associated with cloud technology. CSPs and Banks are engaging regulators to reconcile regulator's perception about cloud technology risks with their perception and experience. In all jurisdictions, regulators are participating in the dialogue on cloud technology risks.

Banks are managing cloud technology risks by carefully managing consistency, security, and risk while migrating their services to the cloud. They are also revisiting their cloud-specific controls.

6.3.3.5   Case Study—APRA Designated Extremely High Inherent Risks

Infrastructure as a service. This service typically involves the sharing of physical hardware arrangements involving storage, servers, networking, or virtualisation.

Platform as a service. This service typically involves providing operating systems, middleware, database, or runtime services.

Software as a service. This refers to the provision of software for business users. Examples include customer relationship management, enterprise applications (e.g. payroll, human resource management, and general ledger) and productivity applications (e.g. word processing, spreadsheets, email).

As with any outsourcing arrangement, it is prudent for an APRA-regulated entity to only enter into cloud computing arrangements where the risks are adequately understood and managed. This includes the demonstration of the ability to continue operations and meet obligations following a loss of service and a range of other disruption scenarios; preservation of the quality (including security) of both critical and sensitive data; compliance with legislative and prudential requirements; and absence of jurisdictional, contractual or technical considerations which may inhibit APRA's ability to fulfil its duties as the prudential regulator, including impediments to timely access to documentation and data/information.

The nature of the services consumed also presents different risk profiles. Offerings can be broadly classified into IaaS, PaaS and SaaS arrangements. With the consumption of these services, APRA regulated entities are placing reliance on the providers to manage an increasing aspect of the technology stack. Conceptually, this adds greater layers of abstraction and opaqueness, which can inhibit effective risk management.

6.3.3.6   Public Cloud Versus Banking Community Cloud

Public cloud is an environment that is also available to non-financial industry entities. Security requirements, risk profiles, and risk appetites of the other users of the public cloud are substantially different from the bank using the same public cloud.

In a banking community cloud, all users have a similar level of security requirements, risk profiles, and risk appetites. Cloud ServiceProviders (CSPs) the world over are building banking community clouds, which helps to create a base level of security and trust as required by financial services regulators. Banking service cloud providers (BSCPs) pre-configure risk and control postures for adoption by the banks as per the risk profile of a bank. BSCPs provide tools to monitor the control of data with encryption and security standards, to monitor mission-critical systems in real-time, and to monitor the governance and change management process to deliver regulatory compliance.

a.   A banking community cloud provides the design and architecture of applications, security, privacy, and monitoring to deliver the risk profile and risk appetite. It provides automated tools to manage risks and controls for continuous monitoring, visibility, and control.
b.   A banking services cloud provider generally provides the following compliance measures:

   - Continuous validation of the effectiveness of cloud-specific controls as identified by the banking community.
   - Continuous monitoring and sharing of data and results for compliance with policies, processes, and controls.
   - Continuous monitoring of security controls.
   - ISO 27001 and ISO 27002—adoption of security management best practices.
   - ISO 270017—cloud-specific information security controls.
   - ISO 270018—protection of personal data in the cloud.

c.   PCI DSS Level 1—PCI DSS applies to entities that store, process, or transmit cardholder data (CHD) and/or sensitive authentication data (SAD) including merchants, processors, acquirers, issuers, and service providers. Banks are empowered by the cloud service providers to manage security, risk, and controls:

   - Banks decide on what is stored and processed on the cloud.
   - The type of cloud services used by the bank determines the design and architecture of cloud adoption.
   - Geographical boundaries within which to store and process the data.
   - Anonymisation, masking, and encryption of data—the techniques and keys used are determined by the bank.
   - Access control, access rights, grants, management, and revocation.

- Security and trust across environment policies and controls which are required to meet regulatory compliance obligations regarding complete control of data, encryption and security control of intellectual property, and control of mission-critical systems portability and consistency across private and public environments.

6.3.3.7 Cloud Service Providers Have a Major Role in Regulatory Compliance

Technology capabilities, SLAs, and contracts with CSPs need to be architected and drafted to support banking regulatory compliance requirements. Contracts and SLAs must include thorough oversight of the service provider, allocation of responsibility, that staff have sufficient skills and resources to oversee the service provider, and suitable arrangements are in place for dispute resolution.

6.3.3.8 A Key Expectation of a Banking Regulator

The key expectation of a banking regulator from a bank is that the bank understands the Cloud Contractual Terms and Cloud Security and Privacy Posture and the risks and controls to manage cloud risks. The bank can manage these risks on an ongoing basis including risks during the migration.

The bank has sufficiently built flexibility into its design, architecture, and contractual terms and should be able to revert back to on-premise or switch the applications hosted on the cloud to another CSP. Banks are cloud-enabling their existing applications or building a cloud-native application to enable them to control their intellectual property.

- The use of open source technologies, platforms, and container technologies, to promote application portability, enables the bank to move more easily from one cloud provider to another.
- Banks should also establish the right of their regulators to audit the CSP with the same levels of access as banks have through their contracts and SLAs with CSPs.
- When migrating critical business applications to the cloud, banks need to fully understand the ability to access and run those applications that affect the capacity to provide service to their customers.
- SLAs in the contracts with CSPs have to be definitive, to ensure business continuity in case of any issue.
- BCP and residency of all data within the country, so that a bank is compliant with the data residency requirements at all times.

6.3.3.9   Cloud Security Has Matured in the Past Five Years

Cloud security has matured and cloud security risks are comparable to those on premises. Public cloud services are scalable to a significant level. Resilience, scalability, speed, and security are the core building blocks of public cloud offerings. All four are the core business of a public CSP. Public CSPs are making significant investments in providing the strictest and newest security standards to meet the evolving threat vectors and actors.

6.3.3.10   Cloud Risk Management Framework for Banks

The scale of technology risk exposure is higher for the cloud. Broadly following technology risks are cloud risks:

- Protection of personal data including data localisation and prevention of cross border data flow, and retention of a local copy of data.
- Information, data, and cloud security.
- Technology risks including continuity of business.
- Cyber risks and resilience.
- Additional operational risks—inadequate or failed internal processes, people, and systems at CSP—including fourth parties sub-contracted by CSPs.
- The risk to data access by the regulator is part of cloud risk.

Depending on the criticality of the service and the sensitivity of the data involved:

- Banks can choose different levels of encryption
- Manage passwords and encryption keys in various ways
- Leverage 'security as a service offered by the CSPs.

6.3.3.11   Designing Personal Data Protection on Cloud Is a Joint Responsibility Between Bank and Cloud Service Provider

- Design and responsibilities must be reflected in contracts.
- Cloud provider provides the following services for data protection and these services can be adapted and configured based on risk and assessment of technology features provided, and cost of implementation in the light of nature, scope, context, and purposes of system:
  - Data and application inventory management
  - System security and data protection technology capabilities
  - Data deletion
  - Records and logs of processing and changes
  - Notification of data breaches
- Cloud provider implements security programme and continuously monitors security for the entire cloud. Monitoring alerts can be suitably used by the bank.

- Provide data storage and data processing within a certain country.
- Cloud provider must be audited and demonstrate compliance with the data protection standards of a country.
- Notify the bank if and when there are data breaches.

6.3.3.12 Case Study: Data Privacy and Data Protection Services Provided by AWS Public Cloud

Security and Data Protection

- Access control and security over cloud resources:
  - Resizable computing facility (EC2) and block store
  - Storage capacity (S3)
  - Relational database service (RDS)
  - Identity and access management (IAM)
  - Governance, operational audit trail, and audit trail (cloud trail)
- Can integrate with third-party tools for advanced threat analytics, application security, identity and access management, server endpoint protection, network security vulnerability testing.
- Machine learning to detect and encrypt sensitive data.

Encryption Services

- Encryption of storage—server- and client-side
- Data used in computation—to blocks and storage
- Encryption of in-transit data—to storage and computation
- Inbuilt—centralised key management
- Using third-party key management
- Stronger keys—AES256.

Record of Processing and Changes

- Encryption of storage—server- and client-side
- Data used in computation—to blocks and storage
- Encryption of in-transit data—to storage and computation
- Inbuilt—centralised key management
- Using third-party key management
- Stronger keys—AES256.

6.3.3.13 Case Study: FCA Recommendations on Data Security

- Banks to agree a data residency policy with the provider upon commencing a relationship with them, which sets out the jurisdictions in which the firm's data can be stored, processed, and managed.

- Bank to understand the provider's data loss and breach notification processes and ensure that they are aligned with the firm's risk appetite and legal or regulatory obligations.
- Bank to consider how data will be segregated—if using a public cloud.
- Bank to take appropriate steps to mitigate security risks so that the firm's overall security exposure is acceptable.
- Bank to consider data sensitivity and how the data are transmitted, stored, and encrypted, where necessary.
- Regarding data protection, a firm should comply with the GDPR and any associated guidance.
- Firms should require prompt and appropriately detailed notification of any breaches or other relevant events that arise, including the invocation of business recovery arrangements, and ensure the contract(s) provide for the remediation of breaches and other adverse events.

6.3.3.14 Case Study: Hybrid Cloud Is Inbuilt into Regulatory Requirements—FCA Requirements for BCP and Exit Strategies

The bank should:

- Have exit plans and termination arrangements that are understood, documented, and fully tested.
- Know how it would transition to an alternative service provider and maintain business continuity.
- Have a specific obligation placed on the outsourcing provider to cooperate fully with both the firm and any new outsourced provider(s) to ensure a smooth transition.
- Know how it would remove data from the service provider's systems on exit.
- Monitor concentration risk and consider what action it would take if the outsource provider failed.

6.4 Conclusion—Cloud Adoption Enables Alignment of Other Engines

Cloud adoption and cloud enablement are the key enablers for connecting a bank with customers who are already residing in marketplaces and the cloud.

Cloud adoption at banks is an industry-wide trend and banks are doing so to bring scalability and agility into a business model, improve resiliency, and make their business model cost efficient.

Thus, cloud adoption helps banks to seamlessly connect with customers, other banks, and Fintech.

Cloud adoption exposes the bank to additional operational risks. Banks need to manage cloud risks to successfully achieve their business objectives.

Chapter 7
Industrialise to Manage Changes in the External Environment

7.1 Introduction

Every bank has different priorities, the burden of technical debt, competitive advantages, relationships with the customers, and financial metrics. Based on the strengths and strategies, banks draw up their plans for industrialisation.

7.1.1 An Inside-Out View of the Industrialisation of Banks

The industrialisation of the Front Office is discussed in Chaps. 1, , 2, 11, and 12. We have also discussed the industrialisation of the Back Office in Chaps. 4 and 6.

A Front Office and Back Office industrialisation is supported hand in hand with the bank-wide transformation of the bank in terms of implementing APIs as an integration tool, adopting BIAN artefacts as templates, and paying off technical debt.

All these chapters together provide an inside-out view of the industrialisation of a bank, which is more focused on the industrialisation options the bank has though it may not cover industrialisation requirements.

© Springer Nature Singapore Pte Ltd. 2022
M. Bhatia, *Banking 4.0*,
https://doi.org/10.1007/978-981-16-6069-6_7

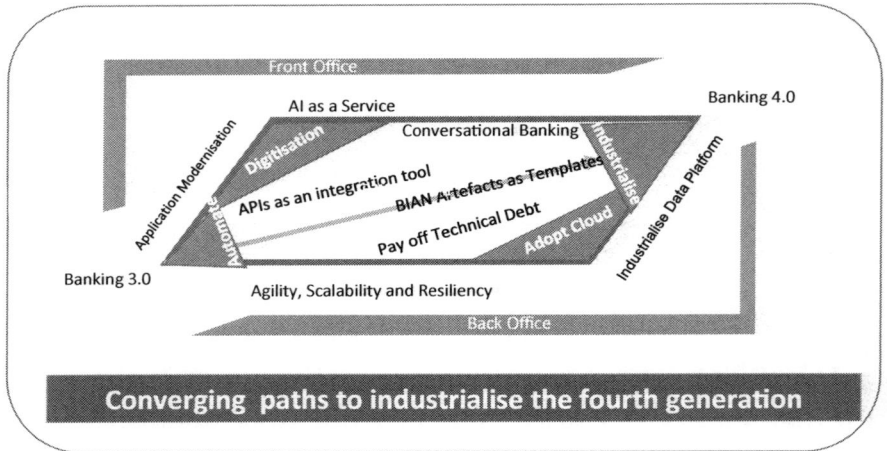

Converging paths to industrialise the fourth generation

7.1.2   Outside-In View of the Industrialisation of Banks

In Chap. 8, we attempt to define how the market place is driving the industrialisation path and its requirements. Platform banking requirements are driven by competition and market opportunities. In Chap. 13, we attempt to identify how fintech is driving the industrialisation strategy of banks. Both are outside-in views. Both chapters define the industrialisation requirements needed or driven by the external environment.

Banking is a highly regulated industry, where, privacy, conduct, data and information sharing, risk management, financial and capital requirements, and regulatory reporting and compliance requirements are driven by regulators.

In this chapter, we will take forward the outside-in view for regulatory and market requirements driving the industrialisation of banks.

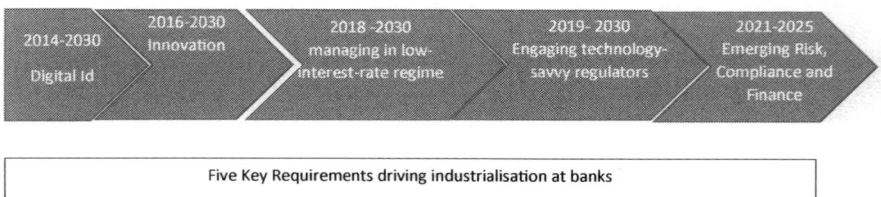

Five Key Requirements driving industrialisation at banks

7.1.3 Banks not Industrialising Are Likely to Lose Market Share

The financial services industry is still highly fragmented. Ongoing margin pressure, a low-interest rate regime, a dearth of capital, the search for cost efficiencies, and the increasing scale advantages resulting from the fixed costs of technology are the key drivers for consolidation in the industry:

- Consolidation is more likely to be seen in Asia and emerging markets as banks from the developed world are searching for exposure and access to regions like Asia and emerging markets with attractive growth profiles.
- Consolidation may happen through acquisitions or partnerships. The partnerships will be of white-label technology of fourth-generation banks to sell the products of third-generation financial institutions.
- Non-core technology assets at a bank are reviewed for their role in the digitisation and industrialisation journey. The assessment template is completely different from the past.
- Partnerships or acquisitions with fintech firms gain an edge over competitors in terms of technology, cost efficiency, and service quality.

7.2 Digital ID Creates Trust in the Marketplace

Digital identity includes identification data, authentication data, and personal, commercial, financial, contractual, and asset data or documents that ID holders would like to share in a controlled manner with other individuals or entities.

To deliver customer experience on channels and the marketplace, the use of digital identities is widespread. In many discussions, 'digital identity' is synonymous with the collection of data generated by the ID holder's online activity.

7.2.1 Data Coverage of Digital ID

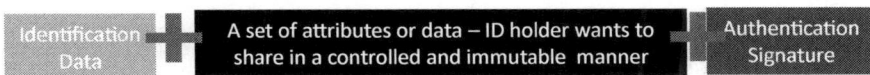

Identification Data	A set of attributes or data – ID holder wants to share in a controlled and immutable manner	Authentication Signature

Digital ID for the individual	Personal data and address
	Personal identification data
	Contact data

(continued)

(continued)

	Government and privately issued ID data
	Biometric data for authentication
	Electronic data for authentication
	Financial IDs
	Financial data and asset data
	Health data
	Historical crimes data
	Historical behaviour data

Digital ID for the entity	Entity data and address, contact details, government and privately issued ID data, electronic data for authentication
	Owners and controllers—digital ID data—personal data, identification, biometric data
	Entity contact data and contract execution data
	Entity financial data
	Entity commercial data

Digital ID for the asset	Asset owners—digital ID of individual owners and controllers—personal data, identification, biometric data
	Asset owners—digital ID of entity owners, entity—data, entity commercial data and entity financial data
	Asset data
	Financial data of asset
	Historical data about asset and ownership

7.2.2 *Digital ID Builds Trusted Marketplaces*

Identity networks build a trusted environment on the Internet to share data in a controlled manner:

- Digital identity is an important tool to build trust and security in the electronic world and is an enabler of data protection and prevention of online fraud.
- Digital identity can guarantee the ambiguous identity of a person and make it possible to get services delivered to whom it should be.
- Digital identity may be useful in the cross-border interoperability of IDs and help in building digital markets.
- Digital identity is an important ingredient for the traceability of transactions, services, and goods.

- Digital identity can help accumulate other attributes of the entity beyond name and government identity.

7.2.3   Digital ID Delivers Industrialisation

Digital identity is the data of an individual or entity representing the ID holder. Digital ID builds and delivers trust in the marketplace and online activities. 'Trust' smooths the online and marketplace business process. Trust creates belief in a straight-through process. Trust creates belief in the machine interface and automation. Both automation and straight-through processing are the deliverables of industrialisation. Hence digital ID creates trust for industrialisation:

- Digital ID provides stronger, contactless authentication for better trust and convenience.
- Digital ID enables stronger authentication to provide trust to straight-through real-time transactions and services.
- Digital ID shares behaviour and other financial data of the ID holder. This provides a 360-degree view of the customer and helps machines to deliver hyper-personalised products and services.
- Behaviour and historical data improve predictive and machine learning models to automate the process, grow revenues, and for better risk management.

7.2.4   Case Study: Aadhar ID Has Industrialised Customer Identification and Authentication

Since its inception, GOI has built the Aadhar platform to provide unique IDs to every Indian resident. With the government mandate, Aadhar now has more than 1.22 billion ID holders.

Telecom operators have linked SIM with Aadhar. Banks have linked customer IDs with Aadhar. Tax authorities have linked tax IDs with Aadhar.

Aadhar is essentially a paperless online anytime-anywhere identity assigned to a resident to cover his or her entire lifetime. The verification of identity is done online with the help of authentication devices which connect to UIDAI's central identity repository which returns only a 'yes' or 'no' response to the basic query: 'Is the person whom he/she claims to be?" based on the data available within UIDAI.

The Aadhar platform identifies and authenticates Indian residents. It provides the following services:

- Virtual IDs and Aadhar IDs: the platform restricts access to Aadhar IDs only to entities that require ID for the discharge of public duties. All other entities are provided with virtual IDs. Here the entity can only store the virtual ID and cannot store or have access to Aadhar IDs. A virtual ID is valid only for the data recipient, only for the specific purpose for which the ID was obtained, and is not valid for further sharing.

- Authentication of ID holder: through a biometric signature; and it provides a token for the verification of demographic details (fields). Some data recipients can store their Aadhar ID and all others can store verification tokens received. No one can store the biometric signature of an ID holder.
- Delivery mode: by Aadhar letter on paper; e-Aadhar, digitally signed; m-Aadhar on mobile; a virtual ID, and Aadhar based authentication.
- Restriction of IDs: no sharing of Aadhar numbers, no storage of Aadhar numbers, only tokens for authentication; a virtual ID as a token for authentication and the locking of biometric authentication.

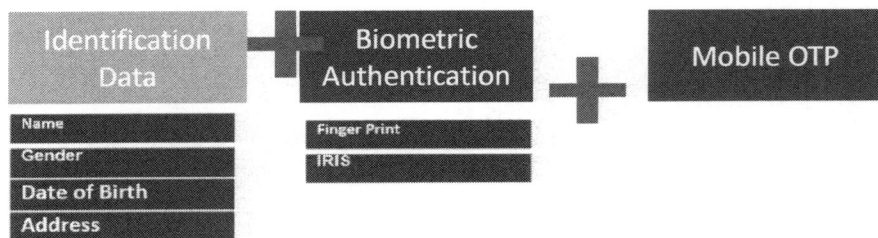

7.3   Industrialise to Deliver Innovation as BAU

The innovation aims to reduce cost, grow additional sources of revenue, and better manage risks. The aims of industrialisation are similar. Industrialisation and innovation add to each other and create a virtuous circle.

Industrialised and configurable technology infrastructure with in-built scalability, agility, and API-based integration capabilities help in delivering and maintaining innovation CoE.

The establishment of well-functioning innovation CoE in an industrialised bank reduces innovation cost drastically and performs innovation as BAU.

Considering the disruptions that fintech, regulators, technology, and consumers create, banks need to build a culture of innovation BAU.

7.3.1   Case Study: PNC Bank, USA Is Industrialising to Embrace Innovation

The bank has adopted BIAN artefacts as templates to industrialise. To adopt BIAN artefacts, PNC Bank inventoried and reviewed every application in the bank and mapped it to BIAN service domains or capabilities in an enterprise architecture management tool. This helped in identifying overlapping capabilities. It also helped in identifying a control record for each service domain.

BIAN is a framework to build a design to componentize the core banking solution and build a logical roadmap to manage and prioritize the transformation to implement business strategy.

Mapping an application portfolio to capabilities helped in setting up a roadmap for the innovation, digitisation, and industrialisation of technology.

PNC Bank is evolving core banking capabilities into a componentized framework so that it embraces the changing business model and customer demands. In this way, the bank is retiring monolithic applications and adopting API-based architecture.

7.3.2   Case Study: To Embrace Innovation UBS Is Replacing 20% of the Application Portfolio

UBS is replacing 20% of its applications and is planning to save 20–30% of the annual IT budget and 20–30% of FTE deployed on the applications. This saving will help it to invest in the industrialisation of the bank.

7.3.3   An Illustrative List of Innovation Vectors on the Industrialisation Foundation

7.3.4   Industrialising the Processing of Petabytes of Data Added Every Year

Banks with an asset size of USD1 trillion every year accumulate additional data of hundreds of petabytes. Industrialisation means scalability in computing power, storage, data pipelines, and applications to process and action this quantum of data.

7.3.5   Blockchain Platform for Cross-Border Commerce, Payment, Banking, Clearing, and Settlement

Blockchain platforms for cross-border commerce, payment, financing, clearing, and settlement are replacing intermediaries in the value chain and are automating the entire process and replacing paper documents and contracts with smart contracts. The platform replaces contract immutability with blockchain technology.

Cross-border blockchain platforms disrupt the business models of correspondent banking, trading, foreign exchange trading and clearing, cash management, trade financing, and custodian services.

Banks need to upgrade and make their target operating model for cross-border banking services agile.

7.3.6 Integrating Alternative Data Sources to Improve the Predictive Power of Models

Banks are using alternative data sources to improve the predictability of credit scores. Alternative data sources include historical transaction data with the same bank and other banks, saving behaviour, and social media behaviour. The aim is to achieve better risk separation.

Historically, these data sources were not available. Some of them have become available due to API banking, others due to big tech social media subscriptions, and others due to the electronification of public records. Similar initiatives are likely to grow. Banks' industrialisation designs must consider sharing data both ways.

Some of the fintech lenders are sharing the data of customers who were declined credit with other players to improve their credit, collection, and fraud modules.

7.3.7 ML Models to Enhance the Discriminatory Power of Credit Risk Models

The most important impact of big data and ML methodologies is on the finer risk measurement and discrimination of borrowers:

- ML methodologies have the potential to dramatically improve the screening of risky borrowers. And this at every risk category level. The primary differentiating and value proposition of fintech firms is ML methodology so as to better measure and price risks.
- ML techniques help in the finer discrimination of borrower risk. It can split borrowers from a risk category into better and worse categories.

The question to be decided is: Does the bank have the requisite technology to support ML models? For this, the entire technology process chain has to be geared up to support the ML methodology:

- Read internal and external data sources, public datasets, documents, and web pages in the volume, at the latency required.
- Faster deployment of models into production, so that default and discriminating experience can be fed into a model daily and models are continuously trained on

discriminating data samples. Faster deployment may be as fast as daily or multiple times in a day.

If a bank does not have strong ML methodologies, better customers will fly to the competition, since they will offer better rates. Banks will always be left with higher risk customers and prospects. In the absence of ML methodologies, the bank will be able to detect higher risk only in hindsight, increasing its risk losses.

If a bank does not upgrade its technology, it will start losing market share and lower risk customers to the competition with fintech impacting on its growth trajectory, revenue, and cost. Soon, it will be a target for consolidation. Otherwise it will have to white label the technology platform of fintech or the competition to service the existing customers. So, there is no option for a bank. Adopt the new technology today, or tomorrow the bank will be acquired or white label the technology of the leaders.

7.3.8 Cloud Technologies Moving to the Mainstream

- Cloud services are increasingly important for innovation. Banking services are increasingly likely to be hosted online on the public cloud.
- Cloud enablement can spur innovation. The cloud provides flexibility, scalability, and agility and reduces entry barriers for fintech and innovation. Combined with digital customer experience capabilities it cuts the cost and time to market drastically.
- McKinsey estimates in the next ten years 40–90% of banks' workloads will be hosted on the cloud or will be using software as a service. The cloud will be increasingly used for the Back Office and risk finance and compliance functions.
- The cloud also provides better cyber resiliency. Cloud providers have better design and investment in security capabilities. The cloud by design has diversified storage and multiple back-ups thus reducing the chances of a complete outage. Cloud providers have also deployed cutting edge tools to protect the network against service attack.

7.3.9 The Level of Disruption and Innovation May Vary Across the Product Portfolio

- The degree of value chain unbundling and market disruption varies across products.
- Fintechs largely focus and exploit payment and SME lending markets which are larger, easy to contest, and easier to enter.
- Custody and settlement markets may be difficult to disrupt because of the long-term relationship of customers with banks.

7.4 Industrialise to Manage Low-Interest Rate Regimes

7.4.1 Create Scale Through Industrialisation to Service the Cost of Capital Under Low-Interest Rate Regimes

- Change the business model to improve efficiency, resiliency, and customer experience.
- According to estimates of the financial stability board, 30–50% of financial intermediation within retail asset classes is now happening within non-banking institutions.
- Scale is more important in the low interest and profitability regime. The scale helps in reducing the cost. Industrialisation creates scale and reduces cost.
- Cost savings created by industrialisation directly add to the capital; savings help in augmenting the CTB budgets.

7.4.2 Low-Interest Rate and Bank Profitability Regimes with High Disruptable Business Segments

- Banks will become more modularized with services primarily provided through a marketplace and outsourced partners.
- There are three options for the banks:
  - Fintechs front-ending the banks for customer acquisition. Banks ending up as a low margin back end utility, lending the regulatory franchisee to fintech.
  - Being non-industrialised, smaller size or with high-cost and therefore getting merged/consolidated, and being acquired to build scale.
  - Industrialised banks who have established industrialisation and innovation in the BAU mode and who are able to manage cost curves, grow revenue curves, and manage the changes demanded by the external environment.

7.4.3 Skill Distribution at Industrialised Banks

Skill requirements at fourth-generation industrialised banks are very different from third-generation banks. In future, there are likely to be only three skill requirements:

- Skills to market and engage partners, marketplaces, customers, and prospects in the digital environment.
- Skills to innovate; manage digital innovation; design, develop, transform, and update technology, channels, tools, and the business model of the bank continuously. Managing digital innovation is likely to be at a premium soon.

- Identify and manage existing and new risks; manage capital, liquidity, and finance; manage compliance, controls, and regulation.

Industrialisation drastically changes the skill mix of people at banks. One of the scenarios of the skill distribution for risk, finance, and compliance control function is:

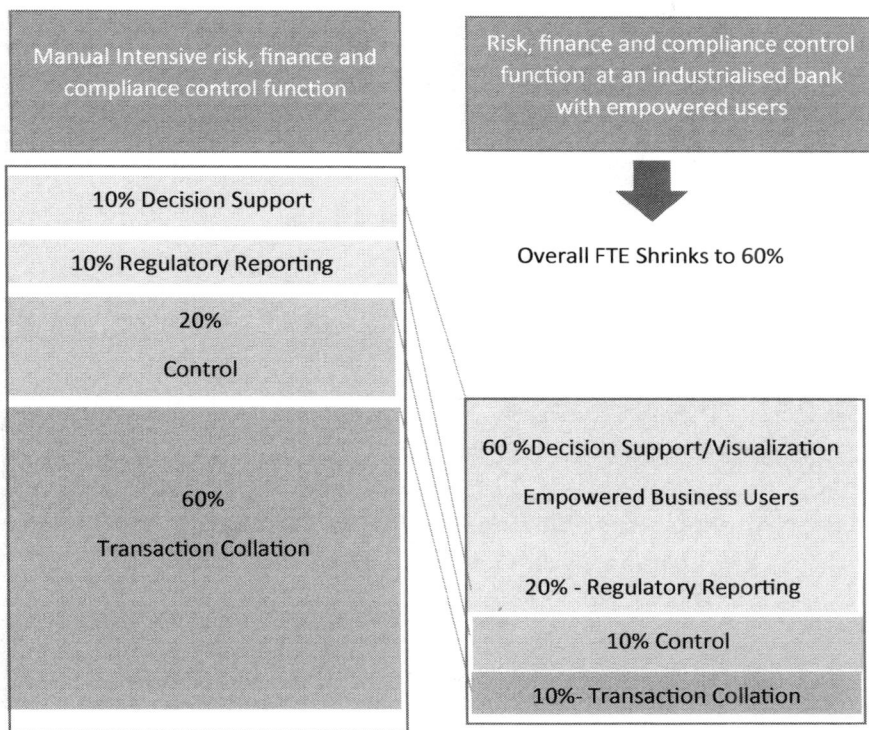

| Manual Intensive risk, finance and compliance control function | Risk, finance and compliance control function at an industrialised bank with empowered users |

| 10% Decision Support |
| 10% Regulatory Reporting |
| 20% Control |
| 60% Transaction Collation |

Overall FTE Shrinks to 60%

| 60 %Decision Support/Visualization |
| Empowered Business Users |
| 20% - Regulatory Reporting |
| 10% Control |
| 10%- Transaction Collation |

7.5 Industrialise to Engage Regulators

7.5.1 Technology Is Breaking Down the Barriers to Collaborate with Regulators

- Through open banking, regulators are mandating technology collaboration with the industry.
- Banks need to integrate with the new market infrastructure being established.

- Banks should be agile to embrace changes in the legal structure, regulations, rules, and standards being set by regulators.
- Regulators have the dream of tracking and monitoring every transaction in the economy.
- Regulators are digitising.

7.5.2   The Regulator Has the Dream of Monitoring Every Transaction in an Economy

The world over, regulators have a dream: to build a monitoring mechanism to track transactions in their economy, and in the global economy, in exchange for assets within and outside their jurisdiction.

I have a dream. It is futuristic but realistic. It involves a Star Trek chair and a bank of monitors. It would involve tracking the global flow of funds in close to real-time, in much the same way as happens with global weather systems and global internet traffic. Its centrepiece would be a global map of financial flows, charting spillovers and correlations. (Andy Haldane, Chief Economist of the Bank of England, 'Managing Global Finance as a System', Speech, Maxwell Fry Annual Global Finance Lecture, Birmingham University, 2014).

7.5.3   Regulators Are Digitising: A Vision Statement on Digitisation by Ravi Menon, MAS MD While Establishing the Data Analytics Group (DAG)

The digitisation of information and the harnessing of data from multiple platforms have created the opportunity to use data analytics to understand the economy and the financial system with a depth that was not possible before. MAS is committed to building strong capabilities in data analytics to seize this opportunity. Our new Data Analytics Group will work with the financial industry to sharpen the surveillance of risks, and with the various departments within MAS to transform the way we do our work.

7.5.4   Build Agility to Incorporate Regulatory Mandates on the Use of Machine Learning Models in Banking

Regulators are likely to mandate rules for:

- The use of new datasets like social media, utility, and public registers;
- The use of data science and analytical techniques;

- Privacy and the responsible and legal use of algorithms;
- Fairness, accountability, transparency, and the responsible usage of AI and ML.

7.6   Industrialise Risk, Finance, and Compliance

Regulators are tracking risk measurement and compliance at a very granular level. They demand data at the transaction level of granularity and additional information on an ongoing basis. According to one estimate, about 20% of risk, finance, and compliance requirement is redefined annually.

The computation of systemic risk at the economic level is being implemented by regulators the world over. To deliver systemic risk measurement, regulatory reporting requirements will grow five to ten times by 2025. To feed data at a very low granularity in near-real-time submission, regulators are rolling out machine-readable regulatory reporting.

7.6.1   Containing Risk, Finance, and Compliance Annual Costs to Within 10–25 Basis Points of Assets

Banks of asset size USD1 trillion spend USD2–3 billion every year on risk, finance, and regulatory compliance technology and processes. To contain the cost, regulators are establishing a new data strategy including digitisation of regulation and machine-readable regulation. Industrialisation means an ability to contain the cost of risk, finance, and compliance functions. It also means an upgraded technology and target operating model within the bank to smoothly migrate to digital regulation without much technical debt.

7.6.2   Building a Banking Ontology, Data Dictionaries, and Data Taxonomies to Manage Voluminous Data Through Semantics and Machine Learning

Data standards are used by banks to build a foundational ontology to deliver semantics and machine learning data management.

7.6.3   The Financial Industry Business Ontology (FIBO)

FIBO is an industry collaborative ontology for use across financial industry firms, created by the EDM Council. FIBO provides a conceptual ontology, which helps in building reusability in the data model and creating contextual nuances. Both these help in:

- Reducing the number of data elements multifolds;
- Creating concepts and concept hierarchies;
- Creating relations and relation hierarchies;
- Building machine learning algorithms.

7.6.4   The ISO 20022 Data Model with Business Concepts

- The existing ISO 20022 vocabulary covers products and services in terms of cards, payments, channels, deposits, securities, trading, forex, investment funds, securities clearing, trading, and settlement.
- The framework can be extended to any additional product or service enabling re-usability.
- The semantics of ISO 20022 provides an internationally agreed vocabulary of more than 6,000 financial industry concepts.
- Vocabulary is standardised at the lowest level of granularity, so it can be re-used to build additional concepts.
- Adoption of ISO 20022 will help in applying consistent definitions and in industrialisation.

7.6.5   Managing and Monitoring Changes in Credit Risk: Credit Risk 3.0

7.6.6   Technology and External Data Is Available Now

With the availability of public datasets, pricing and valuation data for collateral, industry data, adverse news data, and the cognitive reading of documents and unstructured data for better risk management, the following are now available:

- Managing and monitoring credit risk in loan portfolios, i.e. corporate, commercial, SME, and retail:

  - High-frequency early warning signals and alerts;
  - Managing non-performing assets;
  - Theme-based actions and alerts.

- Monitor drivers of credit risk:

  - Financial risk of customer:

      Increase in financial leverage;
      Increase in operational leverage.

- Indicators of integrity and trust in financial statements:

  Failure on commitments;
  Failure on covenants;
  Integrity of documents;
  The integrity of managers and owners;
  Audit report.

- Estimation and valuation of structure of financial statements of customer:

  Estimates of cash inflow and outflow;
  Valuation of assets;
  Estimation of assets;
  Valuation of collaterals;
  Estimation of collaterals;
  Valuation of liabilities;
  Estimation of liabilities.

- Structure of financial statements:

  Financial leverage;
  Operational leverage.

- Incidents and events:

  Operational risk events: failure of people, process, and technology in customer's business.

7.6.7 Monitoring High-Frequency Indicators of Change in Credit Risk

- Continuously measure the impact of change in integrity and trust in management and financial statements:

  - Failure on commitments;
  - Failure on covenants;
  - Integrity of documents;
  - The integrity of managers and owners;
  - Audit.

- Continuously measure the impact of changes in the estimation and valuation of the financials of customers:

  - Changes in the estimates of cash inflow and outflow;
  - Changes in the valuation of assets;
  - Changes in the estimation of assets;
  - Changes in the valuation of collaterals;
  - Changes in the estimation of collaterals;

- Changes in the valuation of liabilities;
- Changes in the estimation of liabilities.

- Continuously measure the impact of incidents and events during the period:

  - Operational risk events, failure of people, process, and technology at customer's business.

- Monitor changes in credit risk of customer and generate alerts:

  - Changes in financial and operational leverages due to:

    Transactions in the account and transactions in the group accounts;
    Transactions with the group's companies;
    Discrepancy with financial statements sourced from public data and websites;
    Changes in integrity and trust in management and financial statements;
    Changes in estimation and valuation.

  - Compare financial and operational leverages with history, peers, and thresholds.
  - Thresholds for changes in financial and operational leverages.
  - Generate high-frequency alerts for changes in the credit risk beyond the threshold.

- Disposal of alerts:

  - L1 alerts to be actioned by credit administration by obtaining additional and compensating documents or reducing limits or recalling credit:

    Adverse events;
    Adverse valuation of collaterals;
    Failure on commitments;
    Failure on covenants;
    Negative news from government sources, stock exchanges, and documents submitted.

  - L2 alerts to be actioned by credit underwriter by reassessing credit risk:

    Adverse valuation of assets and liabilities;
    Adverse findings or comments on integrity of documents;
    Increase in estimated financial leverage;
    Increase in estimated operational leverage;
    Reduction in estimated assets, collaterals, and cash inflow;
    Increase in estimated liabilities and cash outflow.

  - L3 alerts to be actioned by credit risk officer:

    Status of L1 and L2 alerts and their relations with L3 alerts;
    Status of theme-based actionables based on the prioritized risk management themes;

Status of NPA actionable.

7.6.8   Monitoring Theme-Based Actionables and Alerts

- Monitor and estimate the impact of external events on the assets, financials, and collateral of borrowers. Identify all borrowers likely to be impacted, and estimate likely impact, and generate alerts beyond a threshold for:

  - Physical events: flood, earthquake, fire, war, disease;
  - Technology events: cyber attack, accidents, technology failure.

- Monitor and estimate impact of industry stress:

  - An adverse change in market demand for products and services of the borrower, of a supplier to the borrower, and to the customer of the borrower;
  - An adverse change in supply;
  - Adverse collateral valuation;
  - Collateral concentration;

- Bankruptcy in the industry:

    Insurance provider;
    Customer and group companies of customer or customer of the customer;
    Banks, NBFC, and other financial intermediaries;
    Payment network, clearing, settlement, and stock exchange.

- Monitor and estimate impact of fraud scenarios:

  - Impact of the title of collateral and integrity of documents submitted on the collateral estimates and valuation;
  - Credit risk of the customer.

- Monitor and estimate impact of change in:

  - Ageing threshold of L1 and L2 alerts;
  - Financial risks across customers;
  - Collaterals valuation and loan to asset value;
  - Covenant compliance;
  - Performance and NPA
  - Collection and DPD;
  - Account provisioning;
  - Concentration risk;
  - Stress testing results.

- Monitor and estimate impact of the use of fund:

- Capability to analyse and classify transactions in a customer's bank account into different categories based on alerts and provide suggestive/corrective/preventive measures.
- The solution should be capable of storing corporate history with whom the borrower is transacting to identify the relationship between linked accounts, customers, companies, directors, etc.
- Large transactions.
- Fund transfer to the group companies and analysis of the group of transactions (transaction with the same counterparty).

- Cash transactions:

  Single transaction;
  Total transaction: accumulated transactions over the past so many days as a percentage;
  Transaction since last deposit;
  Amount of time coverage;
  Credit transaction type for the cash withdrawal.

- Change in the structure of balance sheet, cash flow, and income statement.
- Monitor relationship and changes in the relationship of the customer with group companies:

  - Changes in the assets liability structure:
  - Changes in the financial strength of guarantor;
  - Changes in the financial strength of the guaranteed organisation;
  - Changes in the revenue and revenue source;
  - Analysis of all debits to the account;
  - The total net worth of group companies.

- Monitor news and sentiment scoring (legal, site visit, social media):

  - Negative news about directors;
  - Managers;
  - Group;
  - Guarantor;
  - Industry;
  - Supplier;
  - Purchaser;
  - Defaulter list.

7.6.9   Operational Risk Management 3.0

With more than 90% of transactions moving to real time, banks are upgrading their operational risk systems from a record of historical losses, control, and risk assessment to a monitoring tool for forward-looking control assessment and risk indicators.

7.6.10   Elevated Regulatory Mandates to Manage Non-financial Risks Need ORM 3.0

According to most of the regulators, non-financial risks—conduct, compliance, and operational risk (CCOR)—have surged at financial institutions. Banks need to upgrade their technology and target operating models for non-financial risks. Operational risk & compliance risks remain elevated and it is recommended that banks focus on cybersecurity, third parties, fraud, and compliance risk. Regulators have also mandated the protection of consumers/customers of financial institutions.

Banks are upgrading their non-financial risk systems to build forward-looking non-financial risk and control monitoring and assessment. This is called Operational Risk Management 3.0.

Functionality	ORM 3.0 Components	Pain point addressed
Well defined risk taxonomy	Hierarchical library of risk, control, and processes, mapped to Basel event types	Defining hierarchies of risk and control indicators to represent integrated and common processes and aggregating mechanisms
Configurable business and process hierarchies	360-degree view of business units, processes and risks, controls, and regulatory requirements	Defining business hierarchies for aggregation of risk and control impact and action items
Automated risk and control assessment	Automated assessments, scenario views, aggregation, and dashboard view	360-degree view of risk, controls, and processes across all business lines
Intelligent risk and control monitoring	API integration for continuous, near-real-time forward-looking, predictive monitoring of thresholds	Intelligent technology with AI/ML and cognitive computing
Configurable risk and control assessment and monitoring models	Model calibration, configuration, validation, governance, and model deployment	Better predictive power of risk models
Developing and calibrating and machine learning based predictive models deploying ML models	Calibrated models—using AI and ML—for the batch process as well as near-real-time streamlining data Deployment of ML models	

(continued)

(continued)

Functionality	ORM 3.0 Components	Pain point addressed
Integrating with sources providing data for the exception, anomalies, errors, losses, failure, and events	Integration with risk data stores, marts and lakes in near-real-time for structured and unstructured data	Integration of risk data stores: handling large volumes, formats, varying latency, and storing technology
Orchestratable ML pipeline and process to generate alerts and action items Orchestrate process for compliance, control, and operational risk processes	Extendable to all non-financial risks with the capability of delegating the process	Process orchestration and delegation for meeting BU and non-financial risk process-specific requirements
Configurable architecture	Integration at varying levels of granularity and delegation	

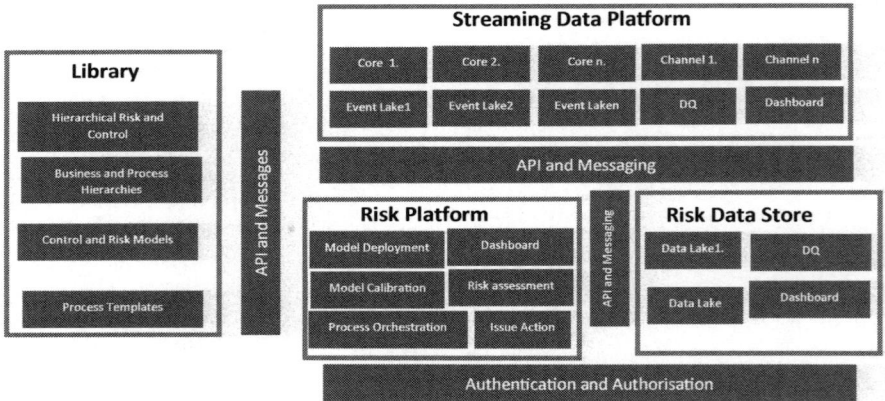

7.6.11   Forward-Looking Automated Risk and Control Assessment

The following is an illustrative list of automated risk and control assessment. Control and risks for which a threshold cannot be defined or where due to a higher true negative, the bank assesses the impact and actions items manually. Risk visualisation and simulation plays an important role.

An illustrative list of control assessment coverage is:

- Business process risk;
- IT and cyber risk;

- Digital risk;
- Compliance risk;
- Legal risk;
- Reputation risk;
- Regulatory risk.

An illustrative list of risk assessment coverage is:

- Business and compliance process;
- Assessment, audit, investigation;
- CCOR risk vectors;
- Infrastructure, network, data, application, and users;
- Fraud, IS security, cyber;
- eDiscovery and forensics.

7.6.12   An Illustrative List of Forward-Looking Risk and Control Monitoring

The following is an illustrative list. Control and risks for which a threshold can be defined, where automated monitoring is required, where the bank is satisfied with dealing with false positives and true negatives, can be monitored in an automated way.

Forward-looking control monitoring:

- Identified control indicators for products and BU, customers, locations, IT system, employees, and business and financial processes;
- Forward-looking and predictive control indicators;
- Behaviour indicators of machines, applications, processes, employees, customers, and partners;
- Resiliency indicator of machines, applications, systems, liquidity, market-predicting stress, and recovery.

Forward-looking risk monitoring:

- Monitoring key control, behaviour, and risk indicators;
- Actionable metrics;
- Control weakness;
- Intrusive and non-intrusive monitoring.

Banks are implementing these best practices to comply with elevated regulatory requirements for increased exposure from real-time transactions and a digital way of working.

7.6.13   Capability of Monitoring, Preventing, and Recovering from a Cyber Attack

Banks are under almost constant cyber attack. They need to build an ability to collaborate with industry and regulators to share attack signatures to monitor newer signatures on the bank's network with faster time to market. They need the ability to recover faster and employ a resilient technology infrastructure.

7.7   Conclusion: Banks Need to Industrialise to Manage and Exploit the Changes in the External Environment

The industrialisation of banks is not an option or choice any more. Even delaying the industrialisation decision to the future is not a choice.

To address the high cost, fees, and interest being charged to the consumers of financial services, regulators have established a regime to encourage the establishment of fintech to provide competition to the established players and disrupt the cost of financial services to consumers. Regulators have established a sandbox to engage fintech firms, to guide and understand their business model. This has brought hundreds of small fintech players and tens of Bigtech players with billions of dollars of investment and capital.

The provision of most banking services is no longer the monopoly of banks. Fintech and Big Tech (GAFAM) with no technical debt burdens are disrupting the banking business model at all levels—the delivery of digital customer experience, real-time services, customer journey coverage, and better risk management, and at a low cost to the consumer.

Digitisation with the industrialisation of technology is no longer confined to fintech firms. In the past five years, disruption has moved to the mainstream banks. Tier II and tier III banks with an agile organisation started the industrialisation initiatives. Soon tier I banks also joined the race.

Every bank has to digitise and industrialise. Not digitising and industrialising is not a choice. If the competition to a bank is providing a better customer experience, better pricing, and faster decisions, the bank will lose its market share if it does not upgrade its capabilities.

The choices a bank has is to upgrade from the third generation to the fourth generation business model or acquire fintech and integrate their technology or license third-party products or the white label technology of a leading bank. If none of this is opted for, this leaves the bank with only one option, which is to be acquired by a leading bank or merge with it. And this merger will be the migration of customers to the industrialised acquiring bank. Ultimately customers want to be serviced by an industrialised bank.

Chapter 8
Platform Banking Business

8.1 Introduction

Banks are building platforms to industrialise Front Office and Back Office technology so that they can provide financial and non-financial services to their customers.

8.1.1 Banking Customers and Partners Have Shifted Their Residence to the Cloud and the Marketplace

All individual customers are already on the cloud, be it Facebook or YouTube or Google or WhatsApp or a mobile or smart device or Alexa. Most firms have plans to make the cloud their permanent home and have a platform business on their strategic roadmap. All banking customers deal with the marketplace. So, the banks have to engage customers who reside in the cloud and marketplace.

8.1.2 Industrialisation Enables a Bank to Reach Its Customers and Partners in the Cloud and Marketplace

Industrialisation makes a huge difference to the banking business. It moves business from a shortage of technical resources to the flexible availability of technical resources, from fragmented to unified technology, from managing a supply chain to managing outcomes, from customisation to standardisation, from personal resources to community resources. The purpose of industrialisation is to enable scalability, reduce latency, leverage technology, and leverage business partners so that banks are with their customers and partners.

© Springer Nature Singapore Pte Ltd. 2022
M. Bhatia, *Banking 4.0*,
https://doi.org/10.1007/978-981-16-6069-6_8

Industrialisation enables a presence on the web ecosystem, improves business/technology co-working, and maximises the data used for decisions and automation. Leader banks have completely redesigned their Front Office and Back Office by creating a strong machine interface to service residents of the cloud and marketplace in real time and with very high resiliency.

8.1.3 Platform Banking Helps Participation in the Marketplace

The bank is one of the most trusted firms in any economy. Banks are experts in producing and distributing financial products of their own and that of a third party. In addition to dealing in financial products, it facilitates business transactions by leveraging its customer authentication services and issues and authenticates digital IDs, fiduciary and trust services, bank guarantees, letters of credit, and payment services.

Marketplaces are evolving with newer structures. The marketplace is redefining the economics of business. The industrialised banking business model facilitates the completion of business transactions electronically for third parties and customers. Industrialised business embeds banks and their services in every economic transaction of a customer.

8.1.4 Platform Banking Helps Banks to Become Technology Firms

Banks are redefining themselves as technology firms that do banking. Banks are becoming (financial) service and technology firms in a true sense. At fourth-generation banks, the change driver is technology and technology differentiated products, rather than the availability of capital.

8.1.5 Case Study: Capital One Has Created a Vision and Implemented a Strategy to Become a Technology Firm

In the 2018 Annual Report, Capital One CEO, Richard D. Fairbank, outlined the vision:

Build a technology company that does banking, and compete against banks that use technology.

For years, we have been building a leading technology company that can thrive in a world being revolutionised by software and data. We are transforming our infrastructure, data and technology tools, and we are now considered one of the most cloud forward companies in the world.

8.1.6 Case Study: DBS Aspires to Be in the League of Big Tech Players like Google and Facebook

To compete effectively, DBS has overhauled its existing technology platform to become digital to the core. It has re-engineered deep into its core tech infrastructure to emulate tech giants like Google, Amazon, Netflix, Apple, LinkedIn, and Facebook (GANALF). DBS aspired to be the D in GANDALF. That aspiration made a real difference in breaking the historical trajectory of technology adoption and business growth. Aspiration to be a technology firm makes the future very different for a bank.

8.2 Platform Banking Is the New Capital for Banks

In a low and negative interest rate environment, capital intensive traditional banking business does not provide the returns expected by the bank's investors.

The market structure of economies is being disrupted every day with technological innovations. In the new market structures emerging, highly successful firms will be the ones who can build trust with customers and stakeholders. Banks are in a very advantageous position here as they are the most trusted firms in any economy.

Digital transformation and innovation opens up growth opportunities for banks in areas beyond traditional banking business into areas of low capital requirement. In the new market structure, technology and innovation drive the competitive landscape, change, products, and operations.

Platform banking institutionalises the speed, scale, security, transparency, and precision that new technologies offer, thus enabling banks to create new services and experiences for clients and disrupt the marketplace with a low capital-efficient business model and earn higher returns for the bank's investors and owners.

8.2.1 Develop a Strategy to Build Platforms and not Implement Projects

Banks cannot pay off technical debt unless they pursue a big picture strategy of attaining the escape velocity of technical debt.

The most important challenge every bank faces is building a business case for its industrialisation. This is almost impossible if the bank and its technology are managed through the business model for projects.

A strategy for platform banking, a vision of empowering business, a strategy of disrupting cost and revenue, a strategy of high performing agile teams, a vision of automating everything, and a strategy to modernise applications can propel a bank out of a vicious cycle of technical debt.

We have covered in detail how to develop a strategy to propel a bank out of the technical debt trap in different chapters of this book.

8.2.2 Innovative Banking Technology Is Disrupting Marketplaces

Platform banking offers an opportunity for banks to stake their claims in the marketplace. This marketplace is becoming a profitable business for banks due to the trust they enjoy with their customers and, as a result, banks can steer their customers to the marketplace. Banks with stronger success in redirection earn better margins and secure exclusivity.

Fourth-generation banks are equipped to reap this opportunity if they can participate, orchestrate, and build marketplaces required by their customers.

There are three business models of participation in the marketplace:

- Participate in the marketplace along with other banks. This role is an entry-level role and provides the lowest financial opportunity overall. It helps banks monetise their product portfolios with minimal additional investments, provided the bank has built a flexible banking platform with APIs for the services offered to the marketplace. With this, the bank gets an opportunity and access to service a large customer base. The bank has to build a business model operationally suitable for the marketplace to encash the opportunity.
- Orchestrate a marketplace along with other financial services firms. A group of financial service firms can become the primary and exclusive orchestrator of the marketplace. Blockchain-based platforms fall under this category. JPMC has established a blockchain-based platform to execute intraday repo transactions. It has also established JPM Coin, a cross-border digital currency or remittance platform. The current repo market is the market for secured financing. However, current operational limitations (of completing the settlement of both security and cash twice within the same day) prevent the meaningful use of such financing to meet intraday liquidity needs. Blockchain technology enables shorter-term, intraday, repo transactions in real time, with simultaneous transaction settlements, creating new ways to access intraday liquidity. Both collateral legs are settled on the repo platform and the cash leg on the JPM Coin. Both platforms are blockchain-based.

- Invest and build a marketplace singularly by a bank. This role provides better financial and non-financial benefits to the bank. However, it is the hardest to implement and has a larger gestation period. Also, slowly the competition catches up with the idea.

8.3 Platform Banking Business

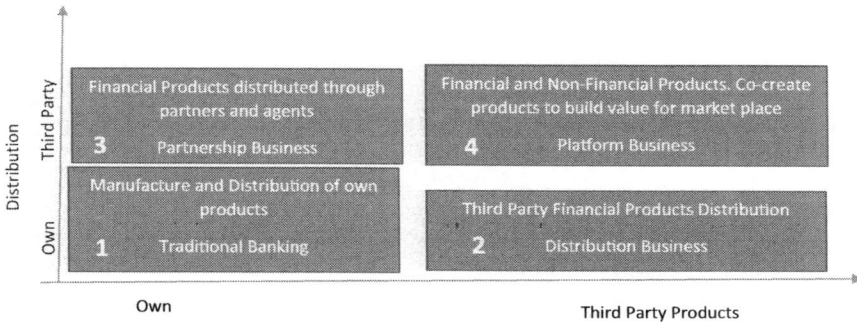

The banking business model is evolving in two dimensions:

1. The first is to deal with third-party products. The business model is evolving from dealing with products of third-party financial service firms to products of third-party non-financial firms.
2. The second is the use of partner distribution and sales channels. This is evolving from sales and distribution to partner's and agent's sales and distribution channels.

The platform banking business is the business of third-party products and business conducted on third-party channels. Platform banking business provides banking and non-banking services in partnership with other financial services and non-financial service firms.

- Manufacturing and distribution of own products. A traditional bank has a regulatory franchisee to distribute its financial product and services. At a basic level, it distributes its products on its channels, through its sales and marketing, and branch services; all financial products are manufactured by the bank itself. This can be called a traditional banking approach. This model is a highly capital intensive model. Revenue is earned by way of net interest income. Capital is required based on the risk exposure of assets and revenue.
- Distribution of third-party financial products by a bank. Traditional banks also have a regulatory franchisee to distribute third-party financial products through their distribution facilities. In this process, the bank earns commission and fees.

In a low income environment, as is prevalent today, non-interest income is a very important source for banks. This is also called the distribution business.

Bancassurance is a good example of this model. Innovative banks can earn non-income revenue by leveraging their franchisee, brand, and technology platforms.

8.3.1 Case Study: DBS Distributes Manulife Products

DBS Bank and Manulife Financial Asia Limited entered into a partnership to provide Bancassurance solutions to DBS customers. Manulife paid SGD1.2 billion for this partnership. As a part of it, DBS and Manulife are planning to invest SGD100 million in digital technology and innovation enhancements for the distribution business. Through this partnership, Manulife gets access to 6 million DBS retail, wealth, and SME customers for its suite of life and health solutions, across the DBS's extensive network of over 200 branches and its sales force of over 2000 professionals, as well as DBS Internet and mobile banking platforms.

A partnership business is where the distribution of financial products of the bank happens through partners and agents. The bank as a producer can market its products through a third party, who can sell, market, and promote its products. As a producer, the bank grows assets, income, and fees. Co-branded cards and mortgages through agents is a good example of this model.

8.3.2 Case Study: Citi Launches IKEA Family Credit Card in Partnership with Ikea

The IKEA Family Credit Card by Citi is available to IKEA family members at a 'zero joining fee and zero annual fees' and can be used for purchases made on IKEA's online and offline stores, or anywhere in the world that accepts credit cards. Together with Citi, IKEA has secured an affordable EMI option for customers that runs from 3 to 48 months, allowing even more flexibility. The IKEA Family Credit Card provides instant in-store card bookings, direct payments via Bharat QR, accelerated reward points, and attractive EMIs. Furthermore, the card also offers reward points on all purchases with instant reward redemption at IKEA. Citi has completely digitised the in-store card application process with instant verification and immediate usage, a first for any co-branded card in India.

Platform banking is where banks are trusted institutions with the ability to transfer funds for a transaction. Banks create substantial value through their participation, ownership, and management of the marketplace, which fully leverages the bank's products and distribution might. Based on the closeness in the relationship with the marketplace, the bank provides tailor-made products and services. There are two models: the bank as an exclusive banking solution provider, and the bank as a participant with other banks in the marketplace.

8.3.3 Platform Business Case Studies

1. Case Study: A Banking Platform for Digital Natives

   The platform can be a channel for products (e.g. loan, wealth management), for a process (onboarding, trade financing), and for a control function (collateral management), with digitization.

   The State Bank of India has implemented a comprehensive online mobile platform that integrates data across third-party products and streamlines the customer experience. It has four pillars:

   a. A digital bank for convenience;
   b. A financial superstore offering investments and other financial services;
   c. An online marketplace with lifestyle products from partners;
   d. An overall digital transformation with analytics that connect these options end to end.

2. Case Study: A Marketplace Owned and Serviced by DBS

   DBS Singapore Marketplace is a bank which is a sole owner and solution provider of the marketplace platform.

   DBS provides a marketplace to buy property, book flights and hotel, for travel, buy and sell cars, and compare and switch desired electricity and telecommunication utilities. It provides tools to help customers search, plan, and learn; to help sellers it provides tools for promotion. It extends its banking services in terms of financing and payment to both sellers and buyers. Ownership provides exclusivity to the bank and an ability to provide tailor-made differentiated solutions to businesses.

3. Case Study: A Government-owned Marketplace Serviced by Multiple Banks

   Government e-Marketplace in India (GeM) provides an end-to-end online marketplace for central and state government ministries/departments, central and state public undertakings, and autonomous institutions and local bodies, for the procurement of common use goods and services transparently and efficiently. The marketplace has more than 20 banks as a solution provider to the marketplace, resulting in a very similar banking solution for buyers and sellers for e-procurement on the government marketplace platform. The bank guarantees and payments are integrated with the marketplace or portal. Banks generally serve only their customers as a supplier on the portal.

4. Case Study: Energy Trading Platform Promoted by Banks in Partnership with Energy Trading Firms

Three of the European banks—Societe Generale, ABN AMRO, and ING—along with top energy traders globally have promoted a blockchain-based, smart contracts, and machine-learning-empowered global commodities trading platform by creating a secured and trusted ecosystem. The platform focuses on contracts, all aspects of logistics, invoicing data, and settlements. Energy producers and traders like BP, Total, Chevron, and Saudi Aramco are also promoters.

Deal recap and confirmation:

- Creating a way to master agreements at the industry level: immutable agreements and contracts.

Trade finance:

- Integrated with trade finance banks and platforms for easier, faster, and cost-effective access to trade finance.

Logistics:

- Transparency, security, and efficiency for the nomination of trading parties, surveyors, and terminals, with actualised figures and time stamps.

Invoice data:

- Blockchain-powered invoicing with dates, quantities, specifications, and escalators.

5. Case Study: The Digital Platform and Marketplace as a Separate Business Unit in UBS

    UBS Personal & Corporate BU has established UBS Atrium, a mortgage platform for corporate and institutional clients. UBS has built a mobile payment platform called Swatch Pay for smartphones and a wide array of wearables. It has established a platform called Twint to pay parking fees and has more than 1.5 million users in Switzerland. The bank has established 'we.trade,' a blockchain-based trade finance platform.

    The bank has launched UBS Start Business, which includes digital accounting, mentoring for business planning, and many other services in addition to the banking services UBS offers. The attractive offering aims to assist young entrepreneurs in every stage of their business's journey.

    UBS Digital Business has bundled digital offerings for small companies which provides the convenience and leading digital solutions that small companies look for. The bank has introduced a vendor leasing solution, an online tool that allows vendors to provide leasing proposals directly to their clients (based on online credit decisions) and to generate contracts.

    UBS Payment Tracking service (SWIFT global payments innovation) is offered to corporate clients.

6. Case Study: Industry-wide Scalable Post-trade Services Platform in Collaboration with the Market Infrastructure Provider

Exclusive platforms beyond an e-commerce platform may not scale.

In platform banking, participation by the industry players in the platform ownership creates wider acceptability, scale, breadth of offerings, and develops businesses in the competitive marketplace and grows the revenue of, and transactions on, the platform.

For better industry participation, in 2020 UBS sold a majority stake (51.2%) in UBS Fondcenter to Clearstream, a Deutsche Börse Group post-trade services provider. The platform creates a leading global B2B fund distribution platform with approximately USD230 billion in assets under administration (AuA).

The platform provides scale and breadth of capabilities and extends a local presence as a compelling proposition for distributors and fund providers.

7. Case Study: Scaling Internal Services to Build a Bank-wide Platform

Banks service a customer through various business and product units and technology and applications. Every unit of a bank may serve a different part of the customer business process. A bank may be present in some part of servicing a customer, with a competitor servicing another. To capture a larger share of the customer's wallet, the bank should collaborate internally to accelerate business growth for the entire bank. To do this UBS fully leverages the expertise and resources within the wider UBS Group. UBS transferred UBS Partner, the highly innovative white-label technology solution, to the Corporate & Institutional Clients International business within the Personal & Corporate Banking business division. UBS Partner is now part of UBS's 'The Bank for Banks' client offering. The UBS Partner solution supports the financial service customers of UBS in giving investment advice to their clients. The UBS platform has built-in wealth management expertise and technology. It is a modular, cloud-based solution to increase efficiency and revenues for the customer whilst also lowering operational risks; it can be configured to serve the specific requirements of customers.

8. Case Study: White-label Fintech Technology for a Wealth Management Platform

UBS is building a 'Wealth Management Americas' platform in collaboration with a wealth management application provider: Broadridge. This is a next-generation platform for digital native customers that aims to solve a key financial services challenge by creating a modern, industry level, best in class technology solution. It mutualises investments in technology, innovation, and security.

The platform aims to improve financial advisor productivity, enhance customer experience, and digitise the wealth management process. Being a platform, it has adopted industry-wide standards, open for integration through APIs, with real-time data fabric, open to adapting to ongoing innovation and regulatory changes. It addresses the challenges of fragmented solutions used by industry by providing: a unified solution for performance reporting, managed accounts support, and sleeve accounting; multi-market order management and trade routing; and full back-office functionality that handles multi-currency, global clearance and settlements, asset servicing, and integrated workflow across the entire enterprise to accelerate client on-boarding and other key service tasks. It has built cyber-security requirements. It leverages analytics and machine learning to support advisor functions.

8.4   Replicate the Big Tech Business Model

The platform banking business model is an attempt to replicate the key differentiators of a technology firm in a banking business model. The three key differentiators of the technology firm's business model are:

1. Build a business model on a very strong foundation of innovation. Embed innovation in the BAU and culture of the firm.
2. Technology firms are data companies: build a value proposition for a customer through the provision of innovative and alternative data.
3. The strong value proposition to embed itself in every customer journey.

8.4.1   Innovation Is the New Oxygen for Banks

Digital transformation aims to harness technology to deliver superior and differentiated services. To roll out the digital transformation strategy, banks are establishing innovation labs to facilitate the adoption of best in class technology and ideas, through data-driven outcomes, ease of doing transactions, enhanced product and service portfolios, improved customer experience, risk management, pricing, and liquidity management. The aim of banks is to speed up innovation by facilitating proofs of concept, and creating alternative data and capabilities to serve clients.

8.4.2   Innovate to Disrupt Cost and Build Non-interest Revenue Streams

FS firms have financial and operating levers to grow net income or accretion to capital:

- Financial leverage: backed by capital, takes asset and risk exposures against deposits and borrowings to earn net interest margins and net interest income.
- Operating leverage: earn fees and non-interest income for low capital intensive and non-funded services. Also, invest in technology to reduce operating expenses.

In the low-interest rate regime, as it prevails the world over, the net interest margin is shrinking and has reached less than 1% for many banks. The impact of a low-interest regime is directly visible in a very high cost-to-income ratio. The purpose of the platform banking business model is to build an additional revenue stream of fees and other income from the low capital intensive services of the bank.

8.4.3 Cost to Income Ratio as an Indicator of How Far the Bank Is from Becoming a Tech Firm

Interest rate regime (%)	Net interest margin (%)	Cost to income ratio (%)
0–2	<1	>80
0–2	<2	>75
2–3	<2	>80
3–6	<3	40–80
>6	3–4	35–60

Banks with a >3% interest rate regime and a >45% cost-to-income ratio, or in a <3% interest rate regime and a >60% cost-to-income ratio, may imply one or more of the following:

- The bank has not yet started industrialisation;
- The bank has very high technical debt and is still in the paying off phase;
- The bank is not reaping the benefits of industrialisation;
- The bank has yet not matured its platform banking business model.

8.4.4 An Illustrative List of Innovations Being Pursued by Banks

Some of the initiatives to uplift revenue and reduce costs are given below with a special focus on automation and non-interest income.

Uplift Revenue			Automate to Reduce Costs and Losses		
Prospect Marketing	Customer Sales	Services to grow revenue sources	Automation BOTs, workflow and API	Self Service	Better Risk Measures
Customer Similarity Segment	Auto approved products and limits	APIs	Auto data collection	Customer channel affinity	Collection Dashboard
Feedback and Social Network Funnel – Sentiments	Customer Product affinity	Tax and Accounting Services	Data extraction	Hyper personalization	Early Warning for Credit
Customer counterparty's affinity	Customer Portfolio dashboard	Participation in Marketplace	Auto fill of application	Differentiated pricing	Fraud Prevention
Recommendation Engine	360 degree view of customer	Value added services for fees based products	Auto verify and reconcile	Digital Onboarding	Customer counterparty Delinquency Signals
Lead Generated	Hyper personalization Engine	ID and authentication service	Process analysis	Digital non financial transactions	Customer Delinquency Signals
Prospect Segments	Recommendation Engine		NLG to complete report		Better Underwriting
	Low capital intensive product dashboard		Conversational BOTs		Monitoring Correspondent Banks
	Daily Relationship performance dashboard		Chatbots		Account Activities and Fund Diversion
	Simulation for RMs		Q&A BOTs		Capital Simulator
	Relationship pricing inputs		Automated Underwriting		RAROC Dashboard
	Customer Persona		Extract and Write- Narration		Liquidity Monitoring
	Revenue Leakages		Partner / Vendor Fees paid / services consumed dashboard		

8.4.5   Banks Are Discovering Data Is the New Oil

8.4.6   Case Study: Digital Investment Bank of the Future as Data Provider to the Customer

At the Investment Banking Division of UBS, the bank is striving to develop new products and solutions that are consistent with the capital-efficient business model:

- The bank has set up the UBS Investment Bank Innovation Lab to help connect business teams to leverage best practice, build and test proofs of concept safely and quickly, and inspire a culture of innovation.
- The bank provides investment banking clients with financial and other datasets that they can incorporate into their models. UBS has established Data Solutions to meet those needs through a centralized robust data processing and distribution platform.
- The bank provides FX spot and STIR tree e-pricing, which supplies client-tailored pricing streams and hedging optimization:

  - Sales of currency and other trade asset data integrated with rate data;
  - Superior client outcomes based on collaboration, technology, and data-driven client intelligence.
  - The client portal of UBS Evidence Lab Innovations expands value propositions in the alternative data space, which relates to innovative ways to capture data critical for investment decisions.

8.4.7 Embedding the Bank in the Customer Journey

Financial service is not a separate activity or service. It is a seamless part of the everyday life of customers. To be a part of customer life every single day, an FS firm has to maintain a relentless focus on customers' real 'jobs-to-be-done'. To become more customer-centric, an FS firm has to invest in and prioritize embedding itself in its customer's every journey. This means working with the ecosystem of partners and embedding the bank's services into the marketplace or launching such marketplaces.

An FS firm embeds itself in the non-financial marketplace for cars, property, electricity, transport, and so on. It also embeds itself in a financial marketplace, the list of which can be very long. The primary services provided by a bank to the financial and non-financial marketplace are payment and credit.

However, participation and provision of the following services to the marketplace greatly enhance the value proposition of the bank:

- Credit rating and credit scoring of participants and customers;
- Sharing banking transaction information with account aggregators and authorized third parties;
- Aggregating banking transactions for parties;
- Authenticating participants and customers;
- Providing digital ID;
- Providing hyper-personalised services for the participants and customers based on the confidential information it holds, providing immutability to transactions by leveraging blockchain and other technologies;
- Promoting financial marketplaces.

The idea is to embed the bank in the everyday life of the customer. Over the past three years, the participation of banks has grown into hundreds of marketplaces. During the same period, banks have promoted tens of marketplaces globally. Leader banks have kick-started significant non-interest revenue streams from platform banking pursuits. Partnership strength and not the degree of participation drives the quantum and quality of the revenue stream.

8.4.8 Case Study: Innovative and Differentiated Value Propositions for SME and Commercial Customers

Digitising SMEs by Democratising API banking		
Non-banking services	Process	Banks
Relationship	Transaction categorisation and scoring	Wells Fargo

(continued)

(continued)

Digitising SMEs by Democratising API banking		
Non-banking services	Process	Banks
Document management	OCR image processing invoice processing	UBS
Collection management	Engaging debtors, providing analytics	PNC, RBS, JPMC
Payroll services	Payroll analytics and cashflow management	HDFC Bank, Bank of America
Salaries to employees	Payment services world over	Uber has partnered with payment services firms globally to pay salaries to drivers
Tax management: indirect	GST automation: integration with PoS	Davo and Avalara Fintechs
All non-banking services	Manage SME businesses: offering a comprehensive set of services that assists in setting up and managing a new business including regulatory filing	Royal Bank of Canada
Inventory management	Centralised inventory analytics and status across channels	TradeGecko Stitch Labs Fintechs
Trade finance online	The financial health of trading partners	Citi
Integrated ERP	Includes CRM, invoicing, payroll, HR, point of sale, reporting, financial services, and debtor tracking	Xero Marketplace in New Zealand

8.4.9 Number of Banking Platforms as an Indicator of the Industrialisation of a Bank

Number of banking platforms	As a measure of industrialisation of the bank
Up to 5	Very initial focus on industrialisation and digital transformation
5–12	Initial and ad hoc focus on industrialisation. Some product and business units have industrialised technology. Bank has started focusing on digital transformation
12–20	Repeatable but intuitive focus on industrialisation. A unified focus on industrialisation is still missing or the bank is still busy paying off technical debt

(continued)

(continued)

Number of banking platforms	As a measure of industrialisation of the bank
20–30	Managed and measurable focus on the industrialisation of bank and digital transformation. Every business unit is focusing on industrialisation; however, it is either still a work in progress or investment in some areas of digital transformation is still lacking: a reasonable achievement of Digital First
More than 30	Every business unit has industrialised technology and undertakes digital transformation. At the existing rate of returns, investment in digital transformation is optimised

8.5 APIs Are the Building Blocks of the Platform Banking Business Model

Banks are building platform banking for the digital enablement of the bank's technology and business model.

In Chap. 9 we cover in detail the working of API technology. In this section, we will cover their role in the platform banking business model.

8.5.1 A Platform Banking Business Model Runs on a Low Latency Agile Technology

The platform is built on microservices, containers, orchestration, and a low latency data infrastructure. This helps FS firms to achieve low latency, agility, scalability, and resiliency. API works as an integration layer in banking as a platform and is autonomous, easily discoverable, stateless, and loosely coupled.

8.5.2 Platform Banking Services Marketplaces Through Published APIs

API works both ways. The bank provides APIs to consume its services. The bank consumes the APIs of the third party to participate in the marketplace. It integrates third-party APIs with its services for consumption by its customers.

The banking platform provides and consumes APIs. It enables banking customers to consume third-party services on the banking platform along with the banking services. Banking as a service provides third parties with access to bank functionality so that non-bank companies can connect users outside of the bank's existing footprint to banking services.

8.5.3   Closed or Internal APIs Industrialise Integration of the Front Office with the Back Office

Closed APIs can only be accessed within the boundaries of the bank. An internal/closed API is an interface that provides a means of accessing data based on a private standard, also known as internal API. Internal APIs industrialise the integration of the Front Office with the Back Office. They industrialise the bank business model for employees.

8.5.4   Open APIs: Banks Provide Four Types of APIs

Open APIs (often referred to as public APIs) are publicly available APIs outside the bank providing access to the bank's internal applications or certain functions of an internal application. Open APIs are made available to developers outside the bank. They may also provide access to data. An open API, however, does not mean anyone can access it. There is always restriction and control to protect security, access control, contractual requirements, and privacy.

The level of openness varies, based on the business model around APIs and the sensitivity of information shared by APIs.

APIs share sensitive information about customers and customer transactions, customer authentication, customer account details, and the regulatory reporting of the bank, which is sensitive and needs stronger agreements, authentication, and discipline from the partner seeking such information.

Some information a bank is keen to distribute, such as information about its products and branches, may not need stronger authentication and agreements from partners seeking such information.

8.5.5   Typical Open APIs Provided by a Mature Bank's API Hub

Functions	Service Channel: Distribution and customer experience							
	Retrieve	Create	Confirm	Update	Calculate	Block	Unblock	Activate
Accounts, prospect, prospect contact details, opportunity, opportunity details	X	X	X					
Transaction	X	X	X					
Internal fund transfer		X	X					
External fund transfer Transactions, settlements, clearing, trade confirmations		X	X					
Payee details and payee list	X							
Rewards	X				X			
Loan amount and loan tenor					X			
Unsecured loan application, standing instructions, fixed deposit, debit card application, mortgage loan application, property and collateral details	X	X	X	X				
Matching conditions: branches, ATM, service, deposit machines, offers, countries	X							
Rates	X				X			

(continued)

(continued)

Functions	Service Channel: Distribution and customer experience							
	Retrieve	Create	Confirm	Update	Calculate	Block	Unblock	Activate
Account information: servicing customer profile/account details, and customer queries/feedback	X	X						
Education loan, home loan, retirement, renovation loan					X			
Details of credit cards, credit card promotions, car insurance policies, Endowment Insurance Policies, SB Accounts, Current Accounts, Home Mortgage Insurance, Maternity Insurance Policies, Travel Insurance Policies, Securities Bond Investments, Listed Securities, Treasury Products, Car Loans, Cash Loans, Property Loans, Secured Overdraft, SME Loans, Mortgage Loan Applications,	X							
Debit Card, Credit Card						X	X	X

8.5.6 Partner APIs Open only to the pre-selected partner

An API can be created with strategic partners who create applications and add-ons, on top of integration with the bank's API. APIs are available only to the pre-selected partners with whom a bank has entered into bilateral contracts. APIs are accessible only at the discretion of the bank and the bank has back-to-back consent from the customer for sharing.

The best example of a partner API is the bank's partnership with accounting software which provides accounting services to the bank's customer, based on the transactional information sent by the bank through APIs.

These APIs contains sensitive client data, therefore stronger user/partner authentication is required.

8.5.7 Case Study: Integration with Accounting Software

Tens of banks are providing transactional information APIs for integration with pre-determined accounting software. Citi Bank, HDFC Bank, and DBS are a few examples of such banks. Citi Bank's API can integrate with Xero, an accounting software. Citi has a partnership with Xero. APIs provide transactional information feeds of the customer to Xero, without the login and password of the account holder. For this, the customer has to grant Xero access to their Citi account information.

8.5.8 APIs Open to Authorised Members of a Pre-selected Organisation or Community

The bank provides API access to authorised members. Membership compliance is ensured and managed by another organisation or third party. European PSD2 and UK open banking mandated account information are two good examples, mostly driven by the regulator in a country.

The purpose of the API, the information content of the API, the format of the API, and the contracts for information sharing are all standardised. Mostly they operate within a country (the UK for example) or jurisdiction (the EU for example). These relate to customer profile/account details and are sensitive, needing customer and partner authentication. In an open banking jurisdiction, exposing such APIs is mandatory.

8.5.9   APIs Are Made Available by Registering with the Organisation Subject to Certain Conditions

The API portal of a bank distributes this type of API. There is a standardised agreement with API consumers, which can be a two-party or three-party agreement. Marketplace APIs and merchant access to PoS APIs are two good examples.

8.5.10   APIs Are Made Available to the Authenticated Parties by Registering with the Organisation

Here, APIs can typically be accessed using some pre-registration, identification, and authentication, though they are not completely freely accessible. Mostly these APIs have general information only. They provide static information like a bank's product details, rates, and branch/ATM locations.

8.5.11   APIs Are 24/7 Invitations to Customers and Partners to Consume the Bank's Services

Banks are expanding their business model by being present throughout the entire customer journey. A bank's digital strategy includes collaborate, build, promote, and participate in networks and digital platforms as partners provide banking services in the entire value chain. Banks, being trusted by customers and market participants, add tremendous value to the ecosystem, network, and digital platforms. An API drastically reduces time to market and makes the bank agile, and enables working with partners. APIs enable faster and efficient customer onboarding, creation of products, completion of internal processes and decisions, and integration into the marketplace:

- The success measurement metrics for APIs are the impact created on customers, employees, and partner experience.
- Design APIs drive user experience.
- Best practice is assessing whether the user is an employee or customer or partner; the experience should be similar.
- Design APIs to create a value proposition for both the API producer and consumers.
- To enable easier access to partners, the publication of APIs through self-service subscription, the API portal is designed to be slick and convenient to develop and test subscription and use. Market leader banks provide a developer portal to partners.
- APIs are designed to be consistent, simple, and efficient.

8.5.12   Regulatory Mandated Open Banking Versus API Banking

To provide competition to existing banks for the betterment of price and service standards, regulators have made the sharing of data using APIs mandatory in the EU and Australia. In Australia, the sharing of product and service information including bank charges and customer information is mandatory, and in the EU, the sharing of account information and providing fund transfer is mandatory. Some regimes like Singapore and Japan have only provided a framework to standardise APIs, while China and the USA have not yet provided any framework. On the business front, this is a way to secure a better deal from the customer. It empowers the customer to obtain better information on financials. It enables comparison across firms.

Regulatory mandated open banking APIs aim to provide transparency, customer choice, and customer control over personal data. Open banking is the mandatory sharing of bank-held customer-permission data with third parties. It allows a banking customer to access their profile and financial data more easily and securely.

8.5.13   Open Banking Is Driven by Regulatory Mandate

Open banking is a type of open API. It is mandated by a regulator, therefore service patterns, coverage, service level, and contracts are determined by regulatory mandate. It is mandatory to provide APIs for open banking. Mandatory coverage of open banking is limited as compared to the coverage of open APIs. Open banking APIs are used to provide faster and easier payments, greater financial transparency, options to account holders, new and improved account services, and marketing and cross-selling opportunities. Open banking covers API-based data sharing of banking products, services, fees, account information of customers, and fund transfers.

8.5.14   Open Banking Coverage Varies Widely Across the Jurisdiction

Coverage of the open banking regulatory framework varies widely across jurisdictions.

Open banking is at a different level of maturity and development in a different jurisdiction.

It disrupts on both the business and technical fronts.

8.5.15   Open Banking APIs May not Be an Indicator of the Industrialisation of the Bank

On the technical front, being a regulatory requirement, banks must publish the mandated APIs. Banks generally take a tactical approach when publishing open banking APIs. The publication of open banking APIs may not be an indicator of the industrialisation of a bank's technology or business model.

8.5.16   API Banking

Provision of services beyond regulatory mandating is called API banking.

8.5.17   Mutual Contracts Drive API Banking

Open APIs are based on the relationship of the bank with its partners, therefore service patterns, coverage, service level, and contracts are determined by mutual agreement.

8.5.18   Case Study: BBVA Open Platforms Provide API Banking

This is a development platform that can be white-labelled for use by the marketplace. Banking services will be provided by BBVA. It provides access to the best in class APIs and the secure infrastructure and regulatory support of BBVA to integrate APIs into the customer's marketplace.

The platform provides the following banking services:

- Verify the identity of the customer;
- Verify the business and its ownership;
- Move money with business logic and different payment types and simplified endpoints;
- Create deposit accounts for the customers of the firm;
- Design, issue, and manage co-branded debit cards;
- Receive near real-time information.

8.5.19   Open APIs Are not Standardised

Banks provide open APIs with varying degrees of openness. Since the degree of openness varies, it is very difficult to achieve standardisation across the jurisdiction for the purpose of APIs, the information content of the APIs, the format of the APIs, and the contracts for information sharing.

Attempts are being made to standardise all four. Due to regulatory mandating, open banking APIs have probably achieved standardisation within a regulatory jurisdiction. For others, attempts are being made to define standards. However, the industry is still far away from the standardisation of open APIs across a jurisdiction, and this is likely to continue.

8.5.20   Currently, Banks Use Disparate, Bank-Specific Formats, and Definitions for APIs

In 2016 banks started publishing APIs, and as of the end of 2020, more than 2000 banks and financial services firms have published more than 20,000 APIs. Unless banks adopt API standards soon, it will be difficult for marketplaces to be managed. The adoption of standards helps to jump-start the API strategy. Currently, banks use disparate, bank-specific formats and definitions to share information through their APIs. Without standardisation, the consumption of APIs will be custom made. Non-standardisation substantially increases TCO and creates inefficiencies across the ecosystem. BIAN has started publishing standard banking APIs. It has published 140 downloadable swaggers to cover 1,800 unique business components and 900 business capabilities.

8.5.21   Case Study: The Working of the API Register of the Monetary Authority of Singapore

APIs are registered to build a single repository of APIs exposed by all financial services firms in a regulatory jurisdiction. The Monetary Authority of Singapore maintains one such register for Singapore based on financial services firms for faster discovery and as a stop-gap arrangement until APIs converge to the standards. The Authority maintains a register of all APIs published by financial services firms. It registers all four types of open APIs. The MAS Register aims to help consumers discover APIs. It classifies APIs into the functional categories of transaction, servicing, information, authentication, reporting, and regulatory.

1.   Transaction APIs:

     a.   Create, confirm, and retrieve accounts and transactions;

    b.   Create and confirm internal and external fund transfers;

    c.   Retrieve payee details and list;

    d.   Create and confirm bill payments retrieved, redeemed, and computed rewards.

2.   Servicing:

    a.   Account information: servicing of customer profiles/account details and customer queries/feedback;

    b.   Fund transfer-transactions, settlements, clearing, and trade confirmations.

3.   Product and service information: products, sign-ups, sales/cross-sales, lead generation, and information on financial product details, rates, and branch/ATM locations.

4.   Other: authentication and reporting—authentication, authorization, reporting, market data, and compliance.

5.   Regulatory APIs: extract datasets related to the financial industry as a whole.

The register classifies APIs into transactional and informational. As of October 2020, the register had more than 500 APIs and more than 125 transactional APIs. MAS itself provides more than 50 APIs to retrieve information.

Almost all APIs registered are from only three financial services firms, that is OCBC, DBS, and Citi.

8.5.22 Risks in Open API

Banks share customer data with third parties by exposing APIs for consumption. Contracts with partners drive data usage. The framework is evolving to manage technology risks in API banking.

8.5.23 Regulatory Framework to Manage Data Shared Through APIs

The regulatory framework stipulates how the third party will manage and control the customer data shared with them:

- Placing restrictions on screen scraping and reverse engineering practices.
- Implementing data privacy, disclosure, and consent requirements.
- Provisions related to whether third parties can share and/or resell data onward to 'fourth parties'.
- Use the data for purposes beyond the customer's original consent and whether banks or third parties could be remunerated for sharing data.

- Scope of the jurisdiction and requirement for bilateral contracts between a third party and a bank.
- In some jurisdictions, like the EU, data-sharing requirements are imposed on banks and third parties. Banks are obliged to share certain types of data with the third parties
- A complaint and alternative dispute resolution mechanism.
- Data privacy laws.
- Disclosure and consent.

8.5.24 Open API Regulatory Technical Standards for Stronger Customer Authentication and Secured Sharing

- Open APIs provide third parties with access to a financial institution's customer data with the customer's permission or the financial institution's service offerings and their functionality. This empowers the customer to control data and provides the third party with the ability to create value-added services for customers. Countries like Singapore, HK, and the EU have published open API standards.
- Regulatory technical standards for strong customer authentication and common and secure open standards of communication.

8.5.25 Increased Cyber Risk Management Due to API Provision at Banks

- Open API exposes banks' applications, which results in a bigger surface area for cyber attacks. Third parties consume the bank's APIs and data and collect other data. Data with third parties can be stolen or compromised.
- This includes data breaches, misuse, falsification, denial of service attacks, and unencrypted logins. Other risks include infrastructure malfunction, speed of execution and operations, man-in-the-middle attack, token compromises, and IP address spoofing. An API gateway could also be a single point of failure if not designed to be resilient.
- As more data is shared and more parties are added, the possibility of a data breach increases and therefore effective data and cybersecurity management becomes more crucial.
- Mechanisms used by some banks to mitigate these risks include stricter access privileges, authorised end-to-end encryption, authentication mechanisms, vulnerability testing, establishing an audit trail, setting expiration times for tokens, IP whitelisting, firewalls, and monitoring cyber incidents related to APIs as part of the overall cyber incident monitoring program.

- There can be wide variation in third-party contracts and contract enforcement. Some of the third parties may not have a contractual relationship with the bank. There is a risk that third parties may share data with fourth parties without the bank's knowledge. The liability for data leakage or assignment of the event of financial loss is very complex under open banking. Some of these risks are managed through contracts, insurance and third-party audit, control, and control testing.

8.6 Blockchain Platforms Are Disrupting the Revenue Model of Banks

8.6.1 Blockchain is an Emerging Technology for Building Immutability and Trust

Blockchain leverages digital signatures and biometric signatures to conclusively prove the immutability, integrity, and validity of the record and customer.

Blockchain enables and supports the creation of trust among participants. Blockchain technology makes the violation of integrity very difficult and ensures accuracy through smart contracts. Blockchain-based immutability and trust disrupt the existing business models of clearing, settlement, authentication, and trade finance.

8.6.2 Players in the Blockchain Business Model

- Blockchain relies heavily on cryptography and data security, especially in terms of message authentication for tampered-evidence and tamper-resilience.
- Distributed ledger or data: ownership and/or custodianship of electronic data with more than one person.
- Immutable distributed data: immutability in data is authentic (original), reliable (tamper-free), and from a credible source (known origin). This ensures the long term integrity of data. This is achieved through the creation of a cryptographic hash function—which is one way—it is practically impossible to generate input from a hashtag.
- Public key infrastructure: this is a security method to implement strong authentication, data encryption, and digital signatures to ensure immutability and integrity of data, often implemented along with biometric authentication.
- Smart contracts: a computer program to implement business processes to ensure accuracy and minimise exceptions, both malicious and accidental.

8.6.3 Blockchain Business Model

The immutability of distributed data is the single most important requirement driving blockchain adoption. Any process which requires immutability is a good use case for blockchain. Some examples are:

Identity and KYC	Financial services	Auditing and finance	Contracts and documents	Digital IDs
Digital ID	Industry-level utility and open banking Payments	Assessment of financial statement assertions: existence, occurrence, accuracy, and completeness	Wills and contracts	Aadhar and similar IDs
GDPR: consent management	Trade finance to exchange goods and finance	Continuous assessment	Business and all other registration	Driving licence
Visa, tourism, immigration clearance	Loans	Verification of transactions and balances between parties	Property and immovable registration and titles	Sharing of data-smart cities
Customer reporting	Treasury: trading, clearing, settlement	Document management	Regulatory reporting	Health records

8.6.4 Case Study: Trade Finance Platforms on Blockchain

Several banks globally have promoted and are participating in trade finance platforms on blockchain:

- Data and documents provided are visible to all and verified by all.
- Platforms standardise trade finance and trade credit insurance processes, data, flows, and documents. This unlocks opportunities for the participating banks in new markets and new underlying trades across the globe.
- The solution supports and integrates liquidity pools built as a part of the trade finance process. This opens up a new opportunity for financing.
- Smart contracts allow the legal representation of trade documents for the execution of global trade transactions. This fastens up the entire process and builds efficiency.
- Real-time auditing of the entire process flow is established. This helps in compliance with regulatory requirements.

- Banks, traders, carriers, freight forwarders, inspection agents, chambers of commerce, and other trade facilitators are members of the trade finance on a blockchain platform.
- Globally trade finance on the blockchain platform is promoted by a bank or a group of banks. Some examples are: www.contour.network; https://tradeix.com/; www.cryptoblk.io/en/products/atlas-elite.

8.7 Conclusion: Platform Banking for New Revenue Streams

Platform banking enables access to customers who have shifted their residence and changed their shopping habits.

Banks are building platform banking to reach out to customers on the cloud (WhatsApp, Facebook, Twitter, etc.) and service them at the marketplace where they shop. Platform banking enhances technology and business models to address the technology limitations of third-generation banks.

Platform banking delivers non-banking services, differentiated value-added service, and data services. It helps the bank to deliver low capital intensive business to overall improve the returns on the capital.

API banking and blockchain platforms are the differentiated offerings of banks. API banking is widely used by banks to disrupt the banking business. Even regulators are promoting open banking to provide choices to the banking customer. Blockchain builds immutability and trust in the marketplace and is disrupting cross-border banking business.

APIs and blockchain are being embraced to build a platform banking business model.

Chapter 9
APIs Are the Public Persona of an Industrialised Bank

9.1 Introduction:—APIs Industrialise Integration and Collaboration with Customers and Partners

Existing data and application deployment and integration technology at third-generation banks are not sufficient to handle the expected data volume, data variety coverage, process latency, and agility requirements. What prevents the existing technology from achieving business outcomes is its ability to integrate in an agile way. Agility can be achieved only when integration capabilities are industrialised.

To industrialise integration and achieve agile integration, banks are building microservices and API-based architectures to interconnect digital solutions on a cloud with on-premise applications and millions of smart devices with new tech and fintech and start-ups. Banks are modernising capabilities to integrate new data sources available from external data providers into business processes to create competitive differentiation. Banks are integrating AI capabilities into almost every application to improve their response to business events.

Industrialised integration is not a re-platforming exercise. Industrialised integration technology can process a very large volume of data in various formats, streaming, and batch processing at very low latency. It is a business transformation exercise to build in the technology and ability to support business outcomes. Agility, scalability, and resilience provided by microservices and APIs enable the achievement of business outcomes.

APIs as an integration industrialisation tool provide a capability to integrate processes and information sources by making them accessible synchronously, propagated in near real time by event streams and by using a multitude of other mechanisms. Since APIs work at a micro level, as the number of APIs balloon increasing exponentially the complexity of managing APIs. The complexity of managing thousands of APIs orchestrated to deliver in real time can only be managed if integration and management are industrialised.

In this chapter, we will be discussing industrialising the management of API integration to ultimately industrialise the bank.

© Springer Nature Singapore Pte Ltd. 2022
M. Bhatia, *Banking 4.0*,
https://doi.org/10.1007/978-981-16-6069-6_9

9.2   Designing APIs

The chapter "BIAN Framework to Build Semantic APIs" covers API design in detail.

9.2.1   API Business Model Drives the API Design

Application programming interface (API) is a standardised way for software to communicate with each other. It is the standard used to expose digital assets to customers and partners and APIs are the invitations to engage. They invite functions and units internally and other firms, customers, partners, suppliers, providers, and consumers externally to do business with the API provider.

APIs are valuable assets in a business environment. An API helps define the business model, which thus drives the API design.

9.2.2   API Monetisation Strategy Drives the API Design

API strategy help banks to create new revenue streams from consumption of their APIs. A bank's API strategy covers the delivery of own and third party products and services through own channels, third party channels, and marketplaces. Banks are implementing API strategy that consists of both public and private APIs to embed the bank in every customer journey.

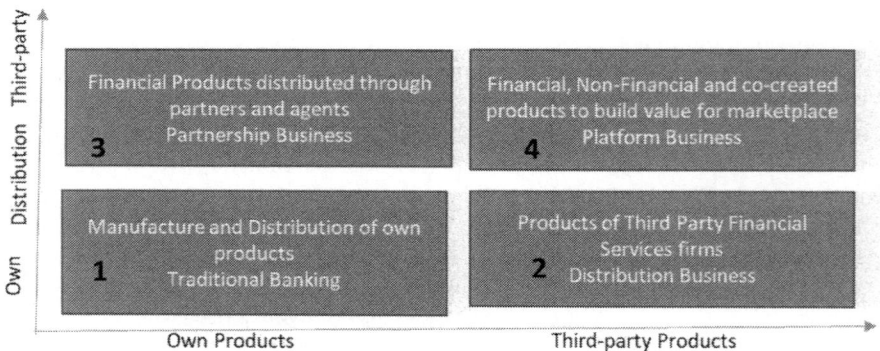

Sensitivity: Internal & Restricted

9.2.2.1 API Design Components

The primary differentiator of APIs is to abstract the complexity of the backend system and drastically reduce the skills and depth required to understand the complexity of the backend. APIs are the tool to democratise access to digital assets.

The API modelling process specifies the data needed for the API endpoints visually or programmatically. The modelling process identifies the participants, or actors, who will interact with the API provided by the bank. It identifies the activities that participants wish to achieve.

API orchestration is a process to combine or normalise data from multiple sources. It is the act of integrating two or more applications or services to deliver a business outcome. Typically it merges multiple API calls into a single process.

Design	API technical formats and standards
Data access	Two types of standards are used to manage data access for APIs. XML-based framework called SAML—this is largely used in business-to-business access control. OAuth is used for consumers and individuals
Data transmission	Almost all banks use HTTP/HTTPS for securely transmitting data. HTTPS secures connections to API, preserves user privacy, ensures data integrity, and authenticates the server providing the API
Data exchange	XML and JSON are the two widely used formats for data exchange. Most banks offer APIs data exchange in both formats
API design	REST (Representational State Transfer) provides the requisite performance, scalability, modifiability, portability, and reliability

APIs should be scalable, re-usable, and secure while offering ease of use for developers through self-service.

9.2.2.2 Three-Layer API Architecture

Third- and second- generation banking were designed to streamline and automate highly structured banking processes. Over time, these systems were augmented with incremental process automation. This has resulted in fragmented and overlapping application portfolios as new process-oriented solutions have simply been superimposed on existing processing facilities.

APIs Published	Process APIs for internal consumptions Processing Layer APIs	Platform Banking / API Banking/ Open Banking Experience APIs
Monolithic Process-oriented	Product Processors Legacy Application Wrapper APIs	Self Service at Channels Experience APIs
	Back office Product Delivery- Managing Finance and resources	Front Office- Customer Interaction- Distribution Delivery

Sensitivity: Internal & Restricted

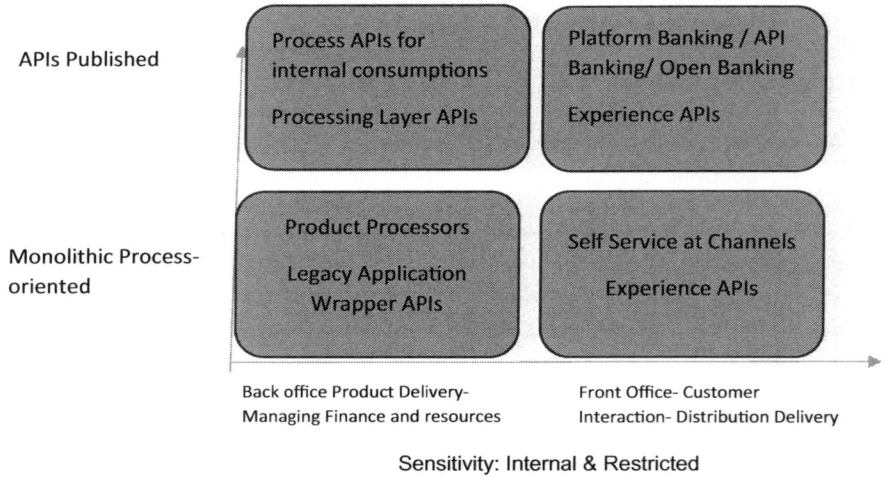

9.2.3   Legacy Application Wrapper APIs

To build agility into third- and second-generation technology, banks need to build a componentised model of banking business. This will help the bank to define discrete functional building blocks that can be flexibly assembled. Banks repurpose legacy applications to build agility.

Product processors, channels, GL and financial applications built as a part of second- and third-generation banks are not easily accessible since they are monolithic applications. The granular level functionality required for the processing and experience layers is made accessible by wrapping second- and third-generation legacy application with system layer API. System APIs hide the complexity of the underlying systems. These APIs are managed as a centralised layer that change less frequently.

9.2.4   Process APIs

Underlying business processes which shape the back-office data are encapsulated in microservices independent of the source system providing the data. The business logic, transformation, orchestration, and enrichment are encapsulated in the process APIs, which interact with systems APIs for functionality and data. Process APIs also interact with experience APIs to deliver processing for them.

9.2.5   Experience APIs

Data is consumed across channels. Microservice has access to the same data in a variety of forms. For example, a retail branch, a POS system, or a mobile application accesses the same customer information fields, in different formats.

Experience APIs enable reconfiguration of data in the consumable format by the intended audience, device, and application. This is to avoid separate point-to-point integrations for each channel.

9.3   Developing APIs

9.3.1   Deliver integration with a very large number of endpoints

On a scale, the number of endpoints to be integrated for a fourth-generation bank could be 100–500 times the endpoint integration capability of the legacy systems at third-generation banks. APIs are built to integrate a very large set of endpoints with the consumers of the banking services internally and externally. APIs manage access control and security architecture built for a high volume of endpoints.

9.3.2   Agile Integration

APIs are fine-grained. API-based applications take a short business-led iteration from requirements to implementation. This makes it possible to deliver business outcomes in a timely manner. Agile internal integration provides near real-time integration across the bank using scalable and resilient applications and services. Agile external integration through service discovery and standardised interfaces provides scalable access control and security architecture.

9.3.3   Stateless API to make Integration Scalable

REST APIs are stateless which makes API integration horizontally scalable through allocation of on-demand resources. Statelessness reduces environment configuration divergence across the implementation. The component becomes stateful only if it were, for example, to cache the data in the backend database within the component so that future requests can respond more quickly by not needing to go all the way to the backend system. Not all APIs can be stateless, some will be stateful.

9.3.4   Deployment in Seconds

API integration is fine-grained and takes less time to start. Deploying APIs in an event-driven architecture is an asynchronous pattern that helps to reduce the response time and latency.

9.3.5   Continuous Integration

APIs in the production environment can be retired and replaced through automation of development, testing, and deployment of APIs to the environments. This improves the consistency of code and testing and reduces deployment risk.

9.3.6   Easier Retirement

APIs are deployed in a lightweight container technology—this enables changes, redeploying amended images rather than by nurturing a running server.

9.3.7   Minimum Interdependencies

APIs grouped on functional and operational characteristics. Related APIs are deployed in the same container. Unrelated integrations are not grouped.

9.3.8   Decentralised API Development Teams

For agile development, banks are decentralising the design and development teams to empower businesses to innovate in real time. Decentralised development team does not necessarily mean a fragmented API development, deployment, or publishing.

The level of decentralisation in the development may not be uniform across the various types of APIs. Decentralisation is a function of agility and agility drives the quantum of decentralisation. The changes in legacy applications wrapper API are less frequent and hence more centralised. Experience APIs need to be highly agile and are therefore decentralised. Process API development is somewhere in between.

The most important challenge decentralised teams face is to build consistency across the team, so to overcome this, banks are using automation tools and enforcing a standardised design and architecture governance framework.

Re-usable semantics APIs are discussed in a separate chapter.

9.3.9   Leveraging Automated Development Tools

The teams leverage the automated development tools to build consistency and automation in the design, development, testing, and deployment of APIs and pipelines.

- Automated development
- Automated testing
- Automated deployment.

An automated development environment also enables the adoption of open standards for DevOps.

9.3.10   Consistent and Standardised API Design and Architecture Framework

To empower business users, banks are building decentralised API design and architecture.

An architect is introduced into the decentralised agile team and adheres to re-usability and bank-wide governance framework. Adherence will be better if the development environment is automated. Besides this, the complex documentation and review processes are avoided through the following:

- Use of templates to build the appropriate level of granularity, identify ownership of control record, and identify delegated service.
- Automated code review.
- Standardised and compliant deployment topologies.
- Automated testing of adherence to re-usability and standards.

9.3.10.1   Build Technology Artefacts for API Development

- For an industrialised bank, technology management should be minimal.
- Instead of technology management, the agile team should develop artefacts to deliver business results.

9.3.11   Deployment of APIs

Build delivery-focused integration architecture by using architectural and design practices for API, microservices, and event-driven application integration.

9.3.12 Discoverable REST APIs

- OpenAPI specification is standardised on RESTful APIs. This standardisation allows both humans and computers to discover and understand the capabilities of the service without access to source code, documentation, or through network-specific traffic analysis.
- The banking industry BIAN framework which helps analyse existing application landscape to build semantic REST APIs is adopted.
- Re-use business outcome-driven architectural patterns where change can be released in a production environment at a high velocity.
- Business outcome drives the granularity of APIs to meet the business consumption requirements. Business consumption of API granularity drives APIs at the process and legacy application wrapper levels.

9.3.13 Agile API Operationalisation

Build cloud portable integration infrastructure to improve operational agility by using a platform-neutral, cloud-native approach to integration infrastructure.

- Securely expose IT assets and make them discoverable to enable the bank to always stay agile, build real-time integration, and respond to the new requirements, new data feeds, and manage performance.
- API-based integration makes the entire IT operations agile:
  - Every API can be changed, rebuilt, and deployed independently of other APIs. This enables safer change and maximises the speed of change to production.
  - Every API can be scaled on its own. This, along with elastic scaling of cloud infrastructures, makes every part of the application scalable.

Build discrete resilience by deploying non-related APIs in separate containers so that none can affect another by stealing shared resources, such as memory, connections, or processors.

9.4   APIs Are the Public Persona of the Bank

Application programming interfaces (APIs) are the information highways of the fourth-generation bank. The ultimate aim is that all the bank's services—internal and external—are enabled by APIs.

APIs enable banks and their customers to harness the power of different systems quickly, safely, and in a standardised manner. APIs provide a set of rules and specifications for software programs to communicate with each other that forms an interface between different programmes to facilitate their interaction.

9.4.1   APIs Across the Two Banks Are Different

APIs across the two banks are different. Two banks can never have similar software programs nor a similar business strategy. Thus, two banks can never have similar APIs.

API portfolio of the bank is a fair representation of the state of the industrialisation of the bank. The API portfolio is also a fair measure of the bank's focus on the digitisation and platform offerings. It is also a fair indicator of paying off of the technical debt. API portfolio is the public persona of the bank.

Due to changing business models, banks are interested in joining every customer journey. This leads to the proliferation of endpoints through which banks' services might be consumed to provide every customer with a personalised experience unless the underlying services are standardised and re-used, which will lead to an exponential increase in services almost impossible to manage. APIs provide standardisation, re-usability, and discoverability. Furthermore, the data at the endpoint consumption are decoupled and made independent from the source data in the system of record.

9.4.2   Establish API Gateway to Manage APIs

As an increasing number of APIs are created by a bank, it becomes a challenge to manage the API lifecycle (discover, build, publish, retire). To effectively manage the API lifecycle, the bank needs a robust and feature-rich API platform. An API platform facilitates interactions between both API producers and consumers and it also provides insights into how those APIs are being consumed.

API platforms should be designed to keep internal integration separate from external integration. Such a separation helps in better management of security threats such as denial of service, payload-based attacks, and XML threats.

An API gateway works as a separation layer between internal and external integration, making it easier, faster, and configurable at a lower cost.

The gateway maintains an API catalogue for consumers to discover microservices and APIs. Externally, the API catalogue is called the API developer portal. The API portal is a mirror image of an API gateway. APIs are published to the API gateway and are available on the API developer portal. API gateways and portals are always synchronised.

An API gateway transforms integration of the bank's IT assets with the external world. It works as a gateway for the external world to access the bank's APIs. The gateway provides a single unified entry point across a group of APIs and secures communication with consumers.

APIs are discoverable on the API developer portal. Consumers search the developer portal to identify APIs which are relevant for them. APIs are subscribed to on a developer portal. The entire process of subscribing to new services should be automated so that new users can be onboarded with minimal impact and within the policies.

9.4.3   Functions of an API Gateway

- Retire API: It implements the integration logic. It aggregates and merges data from multiple sources.
- Manage API version, that is, deciding which version of API is to be retired.
- Manage throughput as per agreed SLAs with the consumer.
- Manage security: implement authentication and authorisation mechanism based on the rights of subscribers.
- Manage format: conversion of different API formats.

An API gateway makes banking services as autonomous as possible:

- Discover and access APIs: rules with supported contracts about who can discover, subscribe to, and access the API available on the bank's API gateway.
- Subscription policy administration: based on the type of subscription, implement policies for throughput, access, and security models.
- Usage analytics: during run time, the gateway captures events relating to its usage which are then interpreted and placed in an analytics store. Usage analytics can be retrieved for diagnostics, planning, and charging.

9.4.4   API Gateway Enables Internal Multi-Tenancy and Decentralised Ownership

In every bank, multiple teams spread across businesses—corporate, institutional, commercial, retail, and wealth management units build, publish, and retire APIs daily. Most banks begin with a centralised API team, but soon, this becomes a bottleneck. Banks have established decentralised teams to write their APIs, by giving them tools that abstract away complexities for designing, building, deploying, and publishing APIs.

A good API management capability should provide strong multi-tenant capabilities so that it can expose APIs from multiple separate implementations and provide good isolation. The primary motivation to having multi-tenancy is to go faster and service decentralised API teams.

To help in API discovery an API gateway should have centralised management across the gateways.

For centralised management, ideally, an API gateway should be on a centralised infrastructure with decentralised ownership or management. In case some of the BUs set up separate physical infrastructure for gateways, those gateways should be federated architecturally and managed centrally as multi-tenancy.

Multi-tenancy enables an API manager to administer own APIs without referring to a central team. Multi-tenancy architecture enables the management of heavy traffic of one API without affecting the performance of other APIs, even though traffic may be passing through the gateway concurrently. There should not be any chance of leakage of runtime data between APIs on the portal, gateways, and components. Users with one set of access should not be able to gain access to another set of APIs.

9.4.5 Federated API Gateway to Build Consistency Across the Business Units of the Bank

An API gateway aims to industrialise API integration with external partners. API industrialisation helps the bank to embed itself in the customer journey and extend services beyond banking.

To comply with the data privacy requirements, banks store data locally within the country. An API's gateway location is decided on to comply with the privacy regulations.

Banks may have multiple API gateways. Different product and customer units within the bank may establish their own API gateway.

Banks also build a product or customer-specific API gateway. A federated API gateway management platform manages multiple API gateways with a consistent security and business policy. An API platform helps to decentralise API provision and centralise discovery and subscription.

9.4.6 Building API Security Blocks

API gateways are built to create APIs at a scale without the need to manage servers. They handle all of the heavy lifting needed including traffic management, security, monitoring, and version/environment management. There are two types of API end users: consumers and publishers.

API publishers design, develop, and publish APIs. They also monitor and manage access to their published APIs.

API consumers discover and request access to the published API.

API Gateway		API Portal		Service Cosumers

```
API Gateway              API Portal                  Service
                    ┌───────────────────────┐        Cosumers
┌──────────┐        │  APIs Published       │
│          │        │  Discover APIs        │       ┌──────────┐
│Functions │        │  Consume APIs    ◄────┼───►   │ Partner  │
│  .....   │        └───────────────────────┘       │ Customer │
│   ...    │        ┌───────────────────────┐       │ Developer│
│          │        │  Request Access       │       └──────────┘
│          │        │  Manage Access        │       ┌──────────┐
│          │        └───────────────────────┘       │ Busienss │
│          │        ┌───────────────────────┐       │ Manager  │
│ APIs     │        │  Publish APIs         │       │ Portal   │
│ Published│◄──────►│  Retire APIs          │       │ Manager  │
└──────────┘        │  Monitor APIs         │       └──────────┘
                    └───────────────────────┘
```

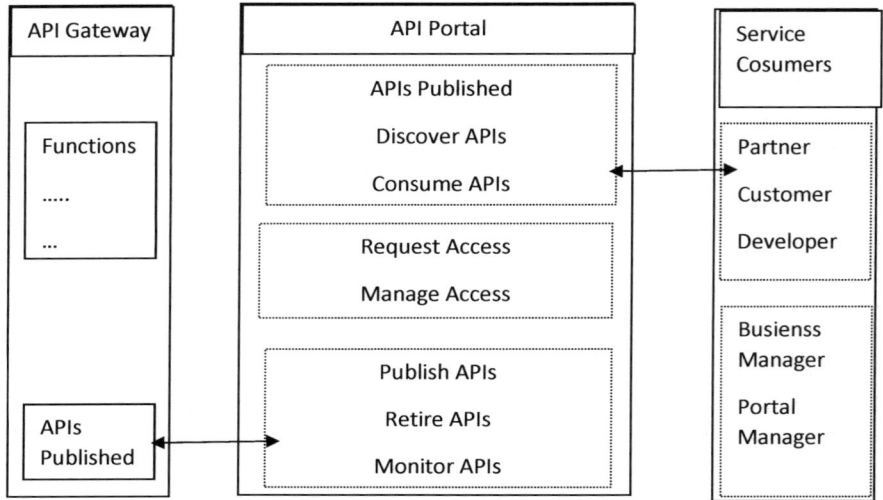

9.5 Publish APIs

An API developer portal helps co-create niche products and services along with partners and customers. API portals provide keys and API usage quota to developers (bank's own, partner, customer, and third party). The portal provides Swagger with a set of open-source tools to design, build, document, and consume RESTful APIs.

The primary functions of the API developer portal are outlined below.

Search and discover APIs
APIs published on the API gateway are also published in the API Catalogue on the API developer portal. The portal provides the search capability to discover APIs within the access rights of the consumer. Authorised API consumers search the developer portal for APIs that are related to particular data resources, and explore documentation before committing to integrate APIs in applications. APIs access control is appropriate for the role and underlying contracts.

API subscription
With centralised discovery and subscription, the bank controls the use and behaviour of API consumers and this provides consumers with confidence about the security of APIs. External firms who consume bank's APIs can easily find a bank's published APIs. The platform enables easier discovery and use. It empowers with finer level controls implemented by the API platform and it is possible to create a fine-grained application.

Self-service to authorised consumers
Authorised consumers use the API developer portal to subscribe to APIs. On the portal, the consumer receives keys and secret codes that are necessary to call the API. The entire consumer authentication and authorisation process is automated so that new users can be onboarded with minimal impact or delay.

API usage analytics
Once authorised on the API the usages invoked are tracked and controlled. API portal provides API consumption statistics to bank and consumers.

Sandbox environment
API portal provides a sandbox environment to build, test, and learn about a bank's APIs and test data.

9.5.1 Case Study–APIs as a Tool to Deliver Digital Experience at DBS

DBS bank started a technology revamp in 2009 and over the next six years completely revamped technology infrastructure. This was done independently of a business case. One of the key transformations the bank achieved was to build service-based or microservices-based architecture or API-based internal and external integration.

DBS invested to build industrialised API fabric for integration both internally and externally. The investment assessed for the business case was used to start integration of existing APIs and not for upgrading technology infrastructure for building API fabric.

A loosely coupled API-based system cannot be managed unless strong preventive and proactive controls are built and the predicted behaviour of every device, server, network, application, user, and customer is managed. To build microservices architecture, the bank built resiliency into the hardware, network, and applications thereby enhancing substantial certainty into technology—a must for microservices architecture.

9.5.1.1 Number of APIs Published as a Measure of Industrialisation of the Bank

An API is a bank's public persona. APIs expose business capabilities and services and form a bridge for interactions between services, such as mainframe and databases, and customer-facing services. The key indicator of the industrialisation and digitisation of a bank is the API portfolio of a bank. APIs allow a bank to expose some functions of a programme or service in a managed and secured environment. Using APIs, a bank can expose a certain portion of code with developers to develop new applications and services. This way, the bank can build differentiated products, services, and customer experiences and construct a new business model.

The implementation of API is not a single IT project phenomenon at a bank. API means a substantial improvement in the entire technology value chain; it is a portfolio level phenomenon. API means a change in the target operating model of the bank and also means the bank is moving towards low latency. API means the bank is industrialised and the value derived from API is further accelerated if the bank has a developer portal and is engaged with the ecosystem to renew continuously. It requires a change in mindset, competence, culture, discipline, and a cross-project, across line-of-business collaboration to build a coherent business portfolio of APIs.

Number of APIs	As a measure of industrialisation of the bank
Up to 100	No focus on the industrialisation of the bank
100–250	Initial and ad hoc focus on industrialisation and digital transformation of the bank. Some products have invested in digital transformation
250–500	Repeatable but intuitive focus on industrialisation and digital transformation. Some business units have made a unified focus on digital transformation. Bank-wide focus on industrialisation is still not achieved
500–1000	Managed and measurable focus on industrialisation and digital transformation. Every product and business unit is focused on industrialisation. However, it is still a work in progress as some technical debt has to be paid before bank-wide impact is created
> 1000	Every product and business unit has undertaken industrialisation and digital transformation and at the existing rate of returns, investment in digital transformation is optimised

9.5.1.2   Case Study: API Developer Portal of National Australia Bank

National Australia Bank has published 1200 APIs under ten categories, namely, FX, locations, authentication, accounts, products, account service, account balances, transactions, discovery, customer.

The NAB Developer portal is open to any developer or partner.

9.5.2   The Cost of Building APIs is the Major Challenge for Smaller Banks

APIs are still custom made by the banks, that is, very specific to the needs and therefore not standardised at the technical or process levels. Unless APIs are standardised, a third-party productised API will be very difficult. The time and cost to build and maintain APIs on a bilateral basis with multiple organisations is a costly affair. Smaller banks do not have sufficient resources and this dampens the business case for API implementation in smaller banks.

9.6 Conclusion: APIs Are the Tool to Disrupt the Business Model of the Bank

Application programming interfaces (APIs) are the information highways in the connected world. Over the past few years, banks have started building APIs. As is the case with a highway, it takes a few years to a decade to build. Once built, it has a paradigm impact on connectivity with customers and partners and also on the business model of the bank.

Chapter 10
BIAN Framework to Build Banking AI and Semantic APIs

10.1 Introduction: Developing Banking AI

We will discuss in Chap. 12 that generic AI platforms provided by several vendors have developed suites of APIs and microservices covering a wide range of AI/ML capabilities. However, the existing generic platforms are limited to the technology enablement of AI with a focus on enhancing data preparation, packaging a broad array of ML libraries, and integration capabilities to augment open-source libraries with third-party libraries.

10.1.1 Existing AI Platforms Are Incapable of Learning Banking Processes

Fundamentally AI is learning for problem-solving. Whilst the existing AI platforms can deliver solutions geared to problem-solving they are not mature enough for automated learning for the banking process.

The primary reasons why existing algorithms are not mature enough to automate banking process learning are:

1. AI learns from historical data. However, the privacy of the contract requirements of a bank's relationship with the customer is far more restraining than regulations like GDPR. This means there are severe restrictions on data usage to enable learning from historical experience.
2. Almost every process and task are regulated and regulations vary widely across a jurisdiction. Regulatory compliance is not learnt but applied upfront. This means banking AI needs to develop a regulatory compliant persona. And this persona has to be very specific to the regulatory regime. Regulators are updating 10–20% of their regulations every year. This also means machines should be able to unlearn the older regulations and learn the current ones in force.

© Springer Nature Singapore Pte Ltd. 2022
M. Bhatia, *Banking 4.0*,
https://doi.org/10.1007/978-981-16-6069-6_10

10.1.2   Develop Banking AI to Enhance the Accuracy of AI Systems

The accuracy of generic AI platforms may be in the range of 30–40%. And this may be sufficient. When you are running a Google query, a 30% hit rate is a very good rate.

Banking is a financial contract. Any compromise on accuracy means financial losses, non-compliance to regulation, and inconvenience to customers. To achieve 100% accuracy banks implement four eye, six eye, and eight eye principles, that is maker-checker, maker-checker-approver, and maker-checker-approver-reconciliation processes. On top of the maker and checker process, the bank also implements quality assurance, an internal audit, and an external audit to cumulatively achieve 100% accuracy. Manual maker process accuracy starts at 83% with iterative checking, approvals, quality checks, and reconciliation accuracy at an enhanced 100%.

To achieve greater accuracy, maker and checkers with financial education and banking experience are employed. Makers and checkers are further trained and certified on the particular banking processes they are going to work on.

In machines, makers, checkers, approvers, control testers, and auditors are the control personas. Each persona has a different role with the same purpose of improving accuracy.

Banks need to build context-awareness, namely banking knowledge, banking concepts, banking computation, specific processes, and specific control personas, in banking machines and AI. Banking machines are trained frequently on a specific process with the availability of newer samples and learning. A different set of personas needs to be developed to ensure business outcomes are achieved.

10.1.3   BIAN Service Domain Structure is a Template to Build Banking AI

A BIAN service domain is a template to identify unique and exclusive processes and help in analysing and defining banking processes exclusively and uniquely. BIAN service domains are the templates to build context-aware learning. Without templates it would be difficult to build the information model required for creating context-aware learning for banking knowledge on machines and banking AI.

BIAN is a conceptual and extendable framework with rich artefacts that can be used as a template and benchmark for the analysis of banking processes and creating context awareness.

10.2   BIAN Artefacts Are Benchmarks for Building Banking AI

BIAN is a conceptual architecture, which aims to establish a semantic framework to identify and define IT services in the banking industry. The underlying architecture pattern originates from Service Oriented Architecture (SOA).

BIAN has released BIAN 9.0, the service landscape, as an architectural framework for banks. This simplifies and standardises banking architecture across the financial services ecosystem.

10.2.1   Leverage BIAN Artefacts to Build Banking AI Machines

BIAN is a conceptual architecture. A bank can extend BIAN artefacts if there are any gaps. Following design, artefacts are published by BIAN:

- BIAN service landscape.
- BIAN service domain:

  - Control record;
  - Functional patterns;
  - Asset types;
  - Action items.

- Examples of business scenarios.
- Examples of wireframe diagrams.
- BIAN semantic APIs.

10.2.2   Business Context is the Key to Industrialise Banks

Banking process machines are built on the foundation of banking concepts, banking process templates, and banking knowledge. BIAN artefacts with embedded ISO 20022 dictionaries are the benchmark of banking concepts, templates, and knowledge.

BIAN is a conceptual architecture to define components, unique banking services to address duplicity, identify unique processes, and untangle process complexity and application portfolios at banks.

10.2.3   BIAN Metamodels as a Benchmark of Banking Process Hierarchies and Process Aggregation

To identify the non-overlapping and elemental business function, the BIAN meta-model has three elements that capture the design of the BIAN service landscape:

1. There are five business areas—the bank-wide division of capabilities—at the highest area of classification.
2. There are 40 business domains at the next level, defined as the coherent collection of capabilities within the broader business area.
3. There are 183 service domains at the finest level of process or functional partitioning, which are unique and exclusive.
4. There are 345 elemental level business capabilities.

The BIAN metamodel is extensible. Any process or product or capability not covered by BIAN V 9.0 can be added, bottom up. Process hierarchies up to business capability is a benchmark to build context-awareness in banking machine learning. It also helps in creating semantic processes and APIs.

10.2.4   BIAN Service Domain Represents a Unique and Exclusive Business Context

Since BIAN is a service-oriented architecture, each artefact is a design template for banking AI.

BIAN identifies discrete, non-overlapping, and elemental business functions called a 'service domain'. A discrete business function is assignable in its entirety. Each service domain is responsible for handling the full lifecycle of a business function.

Each service domain exclusively owns the control record or key information required for that domain and applies functional patterns to the business assets. The control record can be modified by other service domains using delegated services or service operations using action terms.

A BIAN service domain along with BIAN artefacts help in the design and granularise microservices, semantic APIs, and data ownership of control records. Non-overlapping and discreteness helps in creating a banking context.

Each service domain uses re-usable artefacts like functional patterns, asset types, and action terms. Re-usable artefacts help in implementing consistent learning and actions, the creation of a persona, and semantic learning in the business context.

10.3 ISO 20022 Dictionaries Are Benchmarks for Banking Definition, Processes, and Concepts

10.3.1 BIAN is the Benchmark of Business Definition

BIAN functional patterns and action terms are used to build semantic APIs within the business context of changes made to business assets and modification made to the control record. Re-used functional patterns and action terms are the benchmarks of business meaning.

10.3.2 BIAN Leverages a Standardised ISO 20022 Data Model for Products and Processes and Computation

The default version of ISO 20022 covers the following products and processes:

- Credit card debts.
- Revolving credit other than overdrafts and credit card debt.
- Credit lines other than revolving credit.
- Reverse repurchase agreements.
- Trade receivables.
- Financial leases.
- Other loans.
- Assets:

  - Security;
  - Security lending;
  - Securities financing;
  - Money;
  - Letters of credit;
  - Derivatives and swaps;
  - Credit cards.

- Settlements.
- Interest.
- Risk management.
- Trade reporting.

Data and process covered by ISO 20022:

- Instrument data.
- Financial data.
- Accounting data.
- Counterparty:

- – Counterparty instrument data;
- – Counterparty reference data;
- – Counterparty risk data;
- – Joint liability data;
- – Instrument protection received data.

- • Collateral management:

  - – Agreement;
  - – Margin;
  - – Valuation;
  - – Risk evaluation;
  - – Adjustment;
  - – Dispute;
  - – Administration;
  - – Movement;
  - – Balance;
  - – Collateral parties.

The reporting data model of ISO 20022 has.

- • more than 100 data attributes for: The reportable instrument;
- • The collateral or guarantee securing the instrument;
- • The counterparty using the instrument or providing the collateral or guarantee.

10.3.3 ISO 20022 Business Object Model is Extensible

BIAN provides a framework to re-use and enhance the ISO 20022 business object model. This helps in building a semantic data model for the entire bank, which is a foundation for automating and industrialising banking technology. ISO 20022 has emerged as a standard for the interoperability of products and services: the entire bank can be standardised on ISO 20022.

ISO 20022 Business Vocabulary is the Foundation to Build Semantics and Banking AI

- • Existing vocabulary covers products and services in terms of cards, payments, channels, deposits, securities, trading, forex, investment funds, securities clearing, trading, and settlement.
- • The framework can be extended to any additional product or services enabling re-usability.

10.3.4   BIAN and ISO 20022 Are Extendible

Banks need not wait for the release of the next version. BIAN artefacts and ISO 20022 templates are extendable by the bank:

- The semantics of ISO 20022 provides an internationally agreed common vocabulary of financial industry concepts.
- Vocabulary is standardised at the lowest level of granularity, so it can be re-used to build additional concepts.
- The existing release covers more than 6,000 financial industry concepts.

ISO 20022 Business Vocabulary Framework is Extendable

- Extends the framework to non-covered products and functions at a bank level.
- An industry-level extension may take many years and the industry may not find investments for it.
- The purpose is to build semantic data models and functions.

ISO 20022 Business Vocabulary is Extendible for Both Banking Products and Banking Services

- Extends it beyond the existing coverage of services like payments, clearing, settlement, trading, reporting, account, and onboarding.
- Supplements it with industry standards like open banking.

10.4   BIAN Service Domain as a Template for Identifying Data Ownership of Microservices and APIs

We know that at present similar data is instantiated in multiple records across different databases and applications within a bank. As we have noted in other chapters, legacy applications at banks have 90% duplicate data records. Unless we identify data ownership at a granular functional level, with the transformation of legacy applications to microservices and APIs, data duplicity may shoot to 99 or 99.9%.

BIAN Service Landscape V9.0 Matrix View- Business Capabilities

REFERENCE DATA

PARTY
- Legal Entity Directory
- Customer Profile

EXTERNAL AGENCY
- Information Provider Administrator
- Syndicate Management
- Interbank Relationship Management
- Correspondent Bank Relationship Management
- Correspondent Bank Data Management
- Sub Custodian Agreement
- Product Service Agency
- Product Broker Agreement
- Contractor/ Supplier Agreement

MARKET DATA
- Information Provider Operation
- Market Information Management
- Financial Market Analysis
- Financial Market Research
- Quant Model
- Market Data Switch Administration
- Market Data Switch Operation
- Financial Instrument Reference Data Management
- Counterparty Administration
- Public Reference Data Management
- Location Data Management

PRODUCT MANAGEMENT
- Product Design
- Product Deployment
- Product Training
- Product Quality Assurance
- Product Directory
- Special Pricing Conditions
- Discount Pricing

SALES AND SERVICE

CHANNEL SPECIFIC
- Branch Location Management
- Contact Centre Management
- Branch Network Management
- E-Branch Management
- Advanced Voice Services Management
- ATM Network Management
- Contact Centre Operations
- Branch Location Operations
- E-Branch Operations
- Advanced Voice Services Operations
- ATM Network Operations
- Branch Currency Management
- Branch Currency Distribution
- Product Inventory Item Management
- Product Inventory Distribution
- Card Terminal Administration
- Card Terminal Operation

CROSS CHANNEL
- Party Authentication
- Transaction Authorization
- Point of Service
- Servicing Event History
- Contact Routing
- Session Dialogue
- Interactive Help
- Contact Handler
- Customer Workbench
- Servicing Activity Analysis

CUSTOMER MANAGEMENT
- Customer Relationship Management
- Customer Product & Service Eligibility
- Customer Agreement
- Sales Product Agreement
- Customer Access Entitlement
- Customer Behavioral Insights
- Customer Credit Rating
- Account Recovery
- Customer Event History
- Party Reference Data Directory
- Customer Proposition
- Customer Products and Services

SERVICING
- Servicing Issue
- Customer Case management
- Case Root Cause Analysis
- Customer Case
- Card Case
- Servicing Order
- Servicing Mandate
- Payment Initiation

MARKETING
- Business Development
- Brand Management
- Advertising
- Promotional Events
- Prospect Campaign Management
- Prospect Campaign Design
- Customer Campaign Management
- Customer Campaign Design
- Customer Surveys

SALES
- Prospect Campaign Execution
- Party Lifecycle Management
- Lead/Opportunity Management
- Customer Campaign Execution
- Customer Offer
- Sales Planning
- Underwriting
- Commission Agreement
- Commissions
- Product Matching
- Product Expert Sales Support
- Product Sales Support
- Sales Product

OPERATIONS AND EXECUTION

PRODUCT SPECIFIC FULFILLMENT

CUSTOMER MANAGEMENT
- Loan
- Leasing
- Current Account
- Deposit Account
- Corporate Current Account
- Consumer Loan
- Corporate Loan
- Corporate Deposits
- Corporate Lease
- Merchandising Loan
- Mortgage Loan
- Fiduciary Agreement
- Savings Account
- Standing Order

CARDS
- Credit Card
- Card Authorization
- Card Capture
- Card Billing & Payments
- Merchant Relations
- Merchant Acquiring Facility
- Card Network Participant Facility
- Credit Card Transaction
- Credit Card Transaction Execution

CORPORATE FINANCING & ADVISORY SERVICES
- Corporate Finance
- M&A Advisory
- Corporate Tax Advisory
- Public Offering
- Private Placement

PAYMENTS
- Payment Execution
- Financial Message Analysis
- Financial Gateway
- Correspondent Bank
- Payment Order
- Cheque Processing
- Central Cash Handling
- ACH Fulfillment
- Card e-Commerce Gateway
- Card Financial Settlement

COLLATERAL ADMINISTRATION
- Collateral Allocation Management
- Collateral Asset Administration
- Collections

INVESTMENT MANAGEMENT
- Investment Portfolio Planning
- Investment Portfolio Analysis
- Investment Portfolio Management
- E-Trading Workbench
- Investment Account

WHOLESALE TRADING
- Trading Book Oversight
- Trading Models
- Dealer Workbench
- Quote Management
- Suitability Checking
- Credit Risk Operations
- Market Making
- ECM/DCM
- Program Trading
- Traded Position Management
- Market Order
- Market Order Execution

CONSUMER SERVICES
- Corporate Trust Services
- Currency Exchange
- Bank Drafts & Traveler's Checks
- Brokered Product
- Consumer Investments
- Customer Tax Handling
- Consumer Advisory Services
- Trust Services
- Service Product

TRADE BANKING
- Letter of Credit
- Bank Guarantee
- Trade Finance
- Credit Management
- Credit Facility
- Project Finance
- Limit & Exposure Management
- Syndicated Loans
- Cash Management Account Services
- Direct Debit Mandate
- Direct Debit
- Cheque Lock Box
- Factoring

MARKET OPERATIONS
- Mutual Fund Administration
- Hedge Fund Administration
- Unit Trust Administration
- Trade Confirmation Matching
- Order Allocation
- Settlement Obligation Management
- Securities Delivery & Receipt Management
- Securities Fails Processing
- Travel/Price Reporting
- Custody Administration
- Corporate Events
- Financial Instrument Valuation
- Account Balance Sweeping
- Netting/Clearing

CROSS PRODUCT OPERATIONS

ACCOUNT MANAGEMENT
- Position Keeping
- Position Reconciliation
- Customer Position
- Securities Position Keeping
- Reward Points Account
- Accounts Receivable
- Account Reconciliation
- Counterparty Risk
- Transaction Engine
- Product Combination
- Fraud Diagnosis
- Fraud Evaluation

OPERATIONAL SERVICES
- Issued Device Administration
- Issued Device Tracking
- Disbursement
- Operations Risk Management
- Leasing Item Administration
- Customer Billing
- Rewards Point Awards & Redemption
- Channel Activity Analysis
- Channel Activity History
- Card Transaction Switch
- Delinquent Account Handling
- Card Collections
- Internal Bank Account

RISK AND COMPLIANCE

BANK PORTFOLIO & TREASURY
- Corporate Treasury Analysis
- Corporate Treasury
- Asset Securitization
- Asset and Liability Management
- Bank Portfolio Analysis
- Bank Portfolio Administration
- Stock Lending/Repo

MODELS
- Market Risk Models
- Financial Instrument Valuation Models
- Gap Analysis
- Credit Risk Models
- Liquidity Risk Models
- Economic Capital
- Business Risk Models
- Credit/Allergen Behaviour Models
- Fraud Model
- Production Risk Models
- Operation Risk Models
- Contribution Models
- Customer Behaviour Models

BUSINESS ANALYSIS
- Segment Direction
- Product Portfolio
- Customer Portfolio
- Brand Portfolio
- Channel Portfolio
- Competitor Analysis
- Market Research
- Market Analysis
- Contribution Analysis

REGULATIONS & COMPLIANCE
- Guideline Compliance
- Regulatory Compliance
- Compliance Reporting
- Regulatory Reporting
- Fraud Resolution
- Financial Accounting

BUSINESS SUPPORT

IT MANAGEMENT
- IT Systems Directions
- IT Standards & Guidelines
- Systems Administrations
- Development Environment
- System Development
- Production Release
- Systems Deployment
- Systems Operations
- Platform Operations
- Systems Help Desk
- Systems Assurance
- Internal Network Operation

NON-IT & NON-HR ENTERPRISE SERVICES
- Legal Compliance
- Internal Audit
- Security Advisory
- Security Assurance
- Approved Supplier Directory
- Procurement
- Company Billing & Payments
- Fixed Assets Register

BUILDINGS EQUIPMENT AND FACILITIES
- Property Portfolio
- Site Operations
- Site Administrations
- Equipment Maintenance
- Equipment Administrations
- Utilities Administrations
- Building Maintenance

BUSINESS COMMAND AND CONTROL
- Corporate Strategy
- Corporate Policies
- Products & Services Direction
- Business Architecture
- Continuity Planning

FINANCE
- Financial Statements
- Financial Control
- Financial Compliance
- Enterprise Tax Administration

HR MANAGEMENT
- Human Resources Direction
- Employee Assignment
- Employee Data Management
- Employee Help Desk
- Systems Assurance
- Employee Evaluation
- Employee Certification
- Employee/Contractor Contract
- Employee Payroll & Incentives

KNOWLEDGE & INTELLECTUAL PROPERTY
- Management Manual
- Intellectual Property Portfolio
- Knowledge Exchange

CORPORATE RELATIONS
- Corporate Communications
- Corporate Alliance/Stake Holder
- Regulatory & Legal Authority Relations
- Investor Relations

BUSINESS DIRECTION
- Organization Direction
- Business Unit Financial Analysis
- Business Unit Financial Operations
- Business Unit Accounting
- Business Unit Direction
- Business Unit Management

DOCUMENT MANAGEMENT & ARCHIVE
- Document Library
- Archive Services
- Correspondence
- Document Services

10.4.1 How to Identify Original Data from a Set of Electronic Data?

All data are electronic and not a paper document. How do we identify duplicate data? What are the criteria for labelling data as original?

The BIAN concept of control record ownership has solved this problem!

Each service domain is the owner of 'key business information', also called a 'control record' (controlled or owned by a service domain). The control record is referenced and exchanged between service domains.

Deployed system functionality is mapped to the service domains. Mapped service domains are the owners of the underlying data and systems. Since each service domain is unique and exclusive, under one-to-one mapping all underlying data and systems should also be unique and exclusive. Many (database and applications) to one (service domain) is identified as duplicate. Control record ownership helps in the identification of 'delegated' or 'externalized' services. Delegated services are the BIAN artefacts which non-owner service domains apply to a control record.

10.4.2 Role of a BIAN Service Domain for the Owned Control Record

A BIAN service domain owns the control record database. Other service domains can update the control record or database through delegated services. A BIAN service domain bounds the scope of business activity and type of updates that the owner service domain and other service domains can make to the control record.

A BIAN service domain provides a business context to the control record, microservices, and APIs. Because the service domain provides a business context, the APIs built by leveraging the BIAN service domain are the meaning benchmarks and are rightly called semantic APIs.

A BIAN service domain defines the governance of all information exchanged with other service domains.

10.4.3 BIAN Service Domains as a Template to Identify Duplicate Application Functionality in Banks

At the heart of BIAN are the service domains which are unique, exclusive, and elemental. All service domains put together represent an entire bank.

The BIAN service domain landscape is a template to consistently identify service operations and functional patterns. It is also a template to consistently identify the control record for each service domain and map it to the underlying database. The service domain helps in mapping the functionality of the underlying applications to the service domain.

BIAN artefacts help in mapping the underlying database and application functionality to the mutually exclusive, elemental level, business service domains or business components. They map the underlying control record to databases and systems under each of the service domains.

The service domain owner becomes the owner of the underlying systems and control records mapped to his or her service domain. Identification of control records, underlying databases, and applications consistently across service domains helps in identifying 'delegated services' and delegated control records (duplicate underlying applications and data).

This helps in the identification of systems and data duplicity within the bank. Duplicity identification also helps in planning to switch off applications and data.

10.4.4   Template to Identify Duplicate Data in the Bank

For every control record or database owned by a service domain, BIAN helps in identifying and segregating delegated services consumed by other service domains. Any database other than the control record used by the delegated service is a duplicate control record or database.

Identification of duplicate data helps in building a blueprint to switch off the underlying database.

10.5   BIAN Templates

BIAN service operation artefacts are action terms and functional patterns. The service domain uses functional patterns to sub-partition the control record.

BIAN has a standardised service operation definition in terms of functional patterns and action terms. This helps in standardising service operations within a service domain (say across products in the product fulfilment service domain) and across service domains.

Standardising granular level service operations and defining mutually exclusive services at the service domain level helps in creating re-usable services across product delivery and distribution delivery.

10.5.1   BIAN Templates Are Applied to the Deployment

BIAN is a canonical model or a framework to map underlying systems to service domains. BIAN service domains are generic functional building blocks that make up any bank. Each one is a framework to interpret the service domain consistently to build a deployment blueprint.

10.5.2 BIAN Functional Patterns

The service domain applies functional patterns to business assets. It offers service operations to other service domains on its control record through delegated services.

To deliver products, distribution, sales, and marketing or manage enterprise resources, finance, or fixed assets

	Functional patterns	Deliver or manage	Information profile
Create, make plan, design solutions	Direct	A plan to achieve goals	A collection of goals and objectives at various level of aggregation
	Manage	Tasks or duties for results	A collection of tasks or duties or responsibilities
	Administer	Routine work	A collection of one or more clerical routines
	Design	Templates or requirements	A collection of operational services
	Develop	Deliverables	A collection of one or more deliverables that may be further defined
Initiate process or work or operate tooling for support and product use	Process	Procedure: work step to deliver or manage	Work steps to be followed in the execution of a procedure
	Operate	Equipment or automated facility	Operate intranet
	Maintain	A service to provide maintenance	A collection of tasks to support maintenance tasks
	Fulfil	Fulfilment of financial facility	Product features or facility available with the financial facility
	Transact	Execution of the financial transaction	Sub-tasks in the execution of the financial transaction
	Advise	Special advice or ongoing support	Provision of tasks with a purpose to achieve outcomes

(continued)

(continued)

To deliver products, distribution, sales, and marketing or manage enterprise resources, finance, or fixed assets

	Functional patterns	Deliver or manage	Information profile
	Monitor	A mechanism to track and report on the state or dynamic property of some term or activity	A collection of information feeds/measures that can be used to track the status of one or more items/entities
	Track	Log	A collection of the events/transactions recorded by the log
Register	Catalogue	Capture reference information	Catalogue metadata
	Enrol	Maintain a membership	A collection of clauses that govern membership
Evaluate	Assess	Test compliance	A collection of one or more tests to certify a subject
	Agree to terms	Govern activity	A collection of terms (within some jurisdiction) that can be selected and configured to define a contract/agreement
Provide	Allocate	Track and allocate business resources	A collection of different allocation types and states

Source BIAN functional patterns adopted from BIAN Semantic API Practitioner Guide V8.1

10.5.3 BIAN Service Operations

Every service domain offers a collection of service operations and it usually consumes or 'delegates' by calling the service operations of other service domains as needed to complete the work.

10.5.4 BIAN Action Terms that Characterize the Purpose of an Offered Service

The action term determines the access and updates to the attributes referenced by the sub-partitioned control record instance.

	Action terms	Explanation	Examples
Establish control record	Initiate	Initiate a new task	Initiate interest charging
	Create	Create and distribute	Create an ML model
	Activate	Commencement of operational or administrative service	Activate internet banking network Activate salary preparation
	Configure	Change operating parameters for ongoing service	Configure PoS machines
Update or access control record	Update	Update the control record	Update the merchant's reference details
	Register	Register new record	Register new merchant's details
	Record	Record the transaction or event	Record the time spent by an employee
	Execute	Execute a task	Apply incoming debit payment to an account
	Evaluate	Check, trial, or evaluate	Evaluate customer creditworthiness
	Provide	Assessor allocates resource or facility	Allocate cash to the branch
	Authorise	Allow the execution of a transaction	Authorise publication of balance sheet
	Request	Request provision of service	Request credit approval
	Grant	Seek authority to use resource	Grant credit approval
Extract details and subscribe	Notify	Provide details	Notify new data
	Retrieve	Return information	Retrieve report

10.5.5 BIAN Action Terms Are the Foundation to Build Semantic APIs

Semantic APIs are the service operations or application of one or more action terms within the context of the service domain.

10.5.6   BIAN Action Terms as a Template for Granularity-Level Decision Making

BIAN defines action terms at a very granular level to build semantic APIs for a service domain and a control record at a different level of granularity across system, process, and customer experience.

Action terms are the finest level of service operation and functional pattern, which helps in identifying the finest level of control record or data attributes.

The action term determines the access to and updates the attributes referenced by the sub-partitioned service record instance.

Based on the action term, attributes of the sub-partitioned control record is filtered to select those required for input and output messages.

This concept of sub-partitioning helps in building APIs at a different level of granularity. For legacy applications, it also helps in combining a few service domains to identify a larger control record covering all the service domains.

10.5.7   An Indicative Proportionality Level of API Granularity

As we have discussed in the chapter APIs Are the Public Persona of an Industrialised Bank, we have identified three types of APIs: legacy repurposed, process, and user experience.

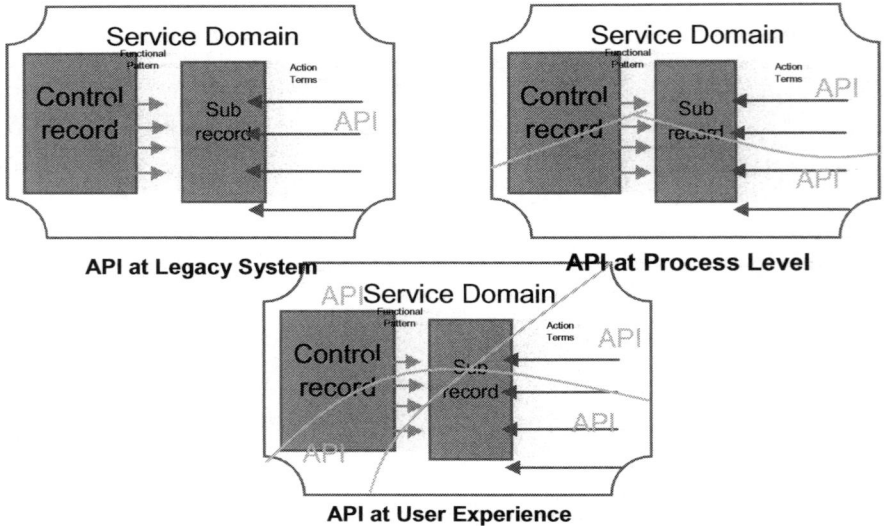

API at Legacy System   API at Process Level

API at User Experience

An indicative proportionality level of API granularity for different types of APIs	
Legacy systems: Wrapped	One per service domain
Process level	Two per service domain
User experience	Four per service domain

In Chap. 5 we discussed how banks are investing in building new applications for customer engagement and experience, while for the Back Office they are leveraging existing monolithic applications by building and extracting out an API wrapper.

Monolithic applications across the banks have uneven granularity. The granularity level between Front Office and Back Office applications may have a wider difference. This is also in line with the logical business functions that are 'coarser' in the Back Office as compared to the finer granularity in the Front Office.

At the Back Office, transaction processing and business activities are more repetitive and of a fixed sequence in nature. The component connections tend to be more permanent in the Back Office. Throughput, performance, accuracy, and complexity of orchestration is usually more important in the Back Office.

10.5.8 BIAN is a Benchmark Semantic API and not a Design Standard

Building semantic APIs is driven by managing the conflicting goals of achieving the level of granularity that creates flexibility. However, it should also be noted that granularity introduces significant overheads in terms of service latency and orchestration challenges. For computation-intensive functionality, granularity creates accuracy, testing, and performance challenges. Building new semantic APIs greatly suits the Front Office processes where interactive collaboration needs the flexibility to mix and match internal and external business capabilities.

BIAN service domains provide a benchmark for 'logical business functions'. They work as a granularity benchmark and business meaning benchmark for semantic APIs. A mutual exclusivity template helps in extracting and wrapping functionalities from a monolithic application onto logical business functions to build flexibility into systems.

Note that BIAN is the benchmark and not a design standard. The level of granularity across the service domain may be different and that of the deployed applications may vary from BIAN service domain benchmarks.

Deployed architecture may have a different level of granularity than that of BIAN benchmarks. Deployed application architecture may be more 'BIAN aligned' than 'BIAN mapped'.

10.5.9   Compliance to BIAN Framework Over Iterative Cycles as a Template for IT Governance and Architecture

Templates and benchmarks are to be consistently applied over several cycles of implementation and switching off to eliminate fragmentation, redundancies, and industrialising the bank.

The best practice for using BIAN aligned benchmarks and templates should be built into the IT architecture and design practices. This needs to be reinforced periodically top-down by building incentives and penalties. Banks should provide a separate budget to participate in initiatives like BIAN to build artefacts at the industry level. The bank should also promote and participate in building banking AI libraries and interoperability.

The bank should implement a mechanism to pass on learning using benchmarks and templates and the adoption from one process to another process and from one business unit to another business unit.

10.6   BIAN Semantic APIs as Templates

BIAN artefacts include BIAN semantic APIs. Examples of semantic APIs can work as a benchmark for the level of granularity and REST mapping.

10.6.1   BIAN Template and Attribute Directory for Control Record Help in Creating Semantic APIs

BIAN artefacts include control record templates and attribute directories. Templates and attribute directory templates help in bringing consistency across service domains. Templates and attributes are semantic. Therefore, an attribute directory and template help in creating semantic APIs.

BIAN artefacts define control record archetype patterns. Each pattern has to be consistently applied across APIs:

- Artefacts help in building loosely coupled discrete, specialised, service-enabled business functions that can be re-used in applicable business contexts, leading to very high degrees of operational capability re-use.
- Identification of discreteness helps in the containerisation and re-use of legacy systems.
- A service domain taking responsibility helps in encapsulating the business information and logic; only external information is exchanged.

BIAN is a framework to build consistent semantic APIs. Creating consistency at the sub-elemental level in back-office functions is useful in building a semantic layer between services.

10.6.2   BIAN Framework to Build Wrapped/Repurposed Legacy System APIs

BIAN artefacts are templates for architecture and design. They can be applied to build semantic APIs for wrap/repurposing legacy systems and to integrate containerised micro/microservice solutions into the bank's application portfolio.

BIAN control record mapping and identification of delegated services to the underlying legacy system can be used to map and repurpose legacy systems.

10.6.3   BIAN Framework to Build Distribution and Customer Experience

This considers the approach needed for restructuring the back end transaction-processing systems and also addresses the far more interactive workforce and customer facing systems that cover activities such as customer servicing, new business development, risk management, and product delivery and distribution.

BIAN service domains cover the functionality of an entire bank. BIAN includes process layer APIs for activities not covered by legacy systems and customer servicing, new business development, risk management and product delivery, and distribution delivery under customer experience layer APIs.

10.6.4   BIAN Semantic API Examples as a Benchmark

We know that REST APIs are compatible with SOA. A BIAN framework is also compatible with an SOA. Therefore, a BIAN is compatible with a REST API. However, BIAN artefacts are by choice implementation agnostic.

BIAN semantic API examples are built in the REST API architecture style.

BIAN defines semantic APIs as a collection of service operations offered by a service domain. This has formatted service operation specifications in a manner that is suited for development or enhancement or extension. For example, the format has a placeholder for adding bank implementation-specific reference attributes.

We know the REST API is the widely adopted approach in API development in the banking industry at this time. To support this, BIAN has mapped its definition and

artefacts to the REST architecture style. Since BIAN is based on business components, BIAN service domain partitions and service operations work as a framework
for container-based architectures and the more general use of APIs. BIAN has built
principles to design artefacts for generating semantic API specifications that provide
high-level service operation descriptions.

10.6.5   Defining Semantic APIs: Learning from 180+ Semantic REST APIs Published by BIAN

BIAN has published a REST API endpoint specification for 140 service domains. A
REST API endpoint associated with each BIAN service operation covers the scope
and purpose of the core business function defined by the service domain.

The BIAN semantic endpoint definitions describe a business exchange that can
be consistently implemented using the REST architectural style. To build semantic
APIs, for each BIAN service domain, and to define BIAN semantic APIs, its service
operation is captured in the 'REST API endpoint' description.

A REST API endpoint specification cannot be used directly for the physical implementation of the design and the developer's needs. The following needs to be added
to the REST API endpoint to make it fit for development:

- Error and exception handling;
- Data structure of the host system and applicable message data standards;
- Message header, security handling, message index, etc.

10.6.6   The Purpose of Semantics is to Consistently Interpret the Nature or Purpose of the Service Domain

Where possible BIAN currently maps its semantic attributes to the ISO 20022 model,
but due to gaps and misalignments, it has been necessary for BIAN to maintain
its own intermediate conceptual business object model (the BIAN BOM). The key
information governed by a service domain component is catalogued in the semantic
attribute definitions of its control record. At a fairly high level of detail, the control
records for the collection of the included service domains define the primary governed
information for the application.

10.7 Conclusion: Building Banking AI by Aligning with BIAN Templates and Benchmarks is an Iterative Journey

The objective of discussing the BIAN framework in this chapter is to apply BIAN as a benchmark and template for building intelligent applications, for identifying the level of granularity for services and to identify and build re-usability of data and applications within the bank.

A BIAN framework provides an approach to break up the entire bank's processes into mutually exclusive business service domains or functionalities. A BIAN business component view is a useful template to build mutual exclusivity for granularity, re-usability, and semantic services and APIs.

Adoption of the BIAN framework is an iterative journey. It may take several iterations to align the business areas in a bank to the BIAN framework.

The benchmark and templates are to be consistently applied over several cycles of implementation and switching off to eliminate fragmentation, redundancies, and industrialise the bank. The best practice of benchmarking and template adoption should be built into the IT architecture and design practices.

Chapter 11
Conversational Banking

11.1 Introduction to Conversational Banking

For the past 20 years, banks have attempted to build technology to engage customers in human and human-like conversations. They have been using call centres and IVR as voice channels for the past two decades. However, they have not been able to provide human-like conversation, mainly due to technology limitations. Conversational banking aims to change all this and enable human-like conversation with the machines of the bank, by the customers, employees, and prospective customers.

Conversational banking is about service experience As we have noted in other chapters, for the time being, the focus of the banking process and technology enablement is to deliver banking transactions. Only in the past few years, have they started focusing on services and customer experience. Conversational banking is one of the basic pillars of service experience.

Conversation banking is about the provision of services which banks could not provide previously. Banks may not be providing some services because of the cost. For example, they are not providing investment advice below a certain threshold due to the high cost of manual delivery. They are not able to provide full information about the merchant where the credit card transaction was executed. This may be because all merchant information is not available in one place and the agent at the counter may not be trained to find that information. Since conversational banking is a machine interface, a bank may choose to build such services into its conversational banking.

Conversational banking is about providing greater insight to a customer. It is about empowering the customer. It is about getting answers to the questions a customer asks but banks are not able to give. It is about personalised help and assistance. For example, at present very limited details about transactions are collected and provided by agents to the customer. At present, agents do not handhold a customer to complete the account opening form, do not explain in detail the charging of fees and commission, product features, and so on.

© Springer Nature Singapore Pte Ltd. 2022
M. Bhatia, *Banking 4.0*,
https://doi.org/10.1007/978-981-16-6069-6_11

11.1.1   Conversational Banking is About Addressing the Limitations of Call Centre and IVR Technology

Banks have attempted to improve call centre and IVR services. The biggest challenge is the waiting time to receive a personalised service. To improve this, banks enhance embedded rules to route calls based on language preferences, geography, IP address, mobile number, number called, place of call origination, or line of business of the calling customer. However, being rule-based technology, enhancements have brought limited improvements to creating human-like conversations.

Experience in creating a large business value through voice channels has not been very encouraging in attracting additional investments. At multiple banks, more than 50% of the time, investment in voice technologies have failed to create the expected value in terms of growing revenue or reducing the cost or providing the desired or planned level of customer experience. Being rule-based, the technology provided service creates frustration and other negative impacts. The value created by automation through IVR and call centres must be adjusted downward for negative impacts in terms of the increase in traffic on other channels, customer complaints, additional customer queries, and customer attrition.

Conversational banking must aim to replace rule-based with cognitive and context-based conversational technology.

Conversational banking is about making voice communication intelligent. It aims to make outward communication more intelligent, and enhance and grow customer acceptance of the bank's machine-initiated voice conversation. So far, inbound IVR and call centre calls have better acceptances with customers as compared to outgoing calls and auto-dial out with a pre-recorded message. Conversational banking aims to improve outbound call acceptance. Intelligence in voice technology can be built only on intelligent customer transactions and services or industrialised customer engagement technologies:

- To support an intelligent voice channel, the bank has to build knowledge about customer behaviour, customer expectation, and customer intent. This mean building a knowledge repository about banking customer and banking service fulfilment and this requires:

  - Collection of customer conversational data in electronic form, covering both service requests and service fulfilment;
  - Implementing a system of managing and controlling customer consent to support privacy and access control of conversational data with no repudiation of transactions and service fulfilment;
  - Continuous extraction of learning from customer conversation by building cognitive conversational models for dialogue management, intent, intent extraction, and actionable and service fulfilment supported by financial and other computations;
  - Inculcate a culture to invest, promote, and augment knowledge about customers, customer transactions, and banking service fulfilment; Augment

transaction intelligence and computation capabilities for intelligent and contextual service requests.

- To build a knowledge base to service conversational requests is a long-drawn-out process, a paradigm shift in the way banks design, invest in, and build technology where investment in learning is not RTB (run the bank) but CTB (change the bank) spend. Moreover, this is true for all cognitive applications.

Conversational banking is about leveraging smart devices. Examples are 'smart speakers' like Alexa and Google Home, and 'smartphones' like Apple and Android phones. Smart devices have the in-built capabilities of generic intelligence and contextualisation. Conversational banking rides on these inherent capabilities.

Conversational banking is about embedding banking artificial intelligence in smart devices. All GAFA (Google, Amazon, Facebook, and Apple) applications, products, and devices lack banking context and banking process intelligence. The smart device is smart because of dialogue management, NLP, NLG, and voice recognition capabilities, technology, and software libraries. By default, the smart device is useful only for rule-based voice communication. So, unless each of these is upgraded within the banking context and banking process intelligence, smart devices are far away from the humanlike experience required in this context.

Conversational banking is much more than chatbots. Rather, it is a conversational user interface for banking services. Conversational banking is much more mature, with banking specific intelligence.

Bots	Chatbots	Conversational banking
Microservices or apps	A chatbot is enhanced by bots with a conversational user interface	User and machine interaction: in text or voice in the user's language
Bots work with other bots, apps, applications, or services	The user interfaces with the chatbot similar to human-to-human communication	Informal and bidirectional, these interactions range from simple to complex
Bots respond to event triggers or user requests	Interaction can be via text or voice	Multiple approaches to design and architecture. Depend upon applications and related services

11.1.2 Conversational Banking Requires Establishing Conversational CoE at the Bank

With the widespread availability of smart devices, the foundational capabilities in terms of processing voice and language, providing two-way human-like cognitive experience has come within the technology reach. To realize human experience, banks are augmenting smart devices with the expertise of banking products and computation, banking process, banking regulatory compliance, Banking industry, technology product companies, cloud providers, and smart device makers need to invest in building banking artificial intelligence. Banks need to invest in establishing conversational CoE.

Conversational banking is building conversational technology at a bank-wide scale. This is so that customers access omnichannel conversational banking, for the entire product portfolio of the bank and for the entire life cycle of the customer journey. Positive business outcomes will be visible only when conversational banking is offered for the entire bank. Otherwise, engagement with non-intelligent channels or non-intelligent engagement products or services will create expectation mismatch and a negative impact. Only intelligent conversational banking will create trust, acceptability, and adaptability.

As we have noted in other chapters, technology or automation returns are diminishing in many areas. Voice conversation is one such area. Automation alone no longer creates a substantial/considerable value for stakeholders. Intelligent and cognitive technology is required to create greater value. This also means investment in creating banking services on smart devices may see a better success if it disrupts the banking business model drastically by reducing 40–80% of the cost of services provided by banks that require 'human intelligence'. Humanlike conversation and not a conversation with machines helps in growing customer loyalty and customer experience and therefore revenue.

11.2   Conversational Banking CoE

Case Study: Conversational Banking CoE at Capital One.

Capital One has built banking process expertise into dialogue management, natural language processing and generation, and the voice recognition of Alexa. Capital One has successfully built conversational intents for retail banking and conversational banking services for retail banking products.

Case study: Conversational banking CoE at capital one, USA

Amazon Alexa based text and voice chatbot assistance called Eno
Channels covered
1. Smartphone
2. Browser
3. SMS, messages, and texting
4. Inbox, emails, voice on Alexa
5. Smartwatch
Retail banking products covered:
1. Credit card
2. Checking
3. Savings
4. Auto loan
Customer intents covered:
1. Marketing and generic information about retail banking products for non-customers
2. Account related information and non-financial transactions for customers
3. Simple services on a specific account
4. Financial planning assistance to a customer
5. Low value: known parties transactions
6. Intelligence on account transactions
7. Monitor charges
8. Track spending
9. Fraud alerts
10. Get answers
11. Shop safer
12. Language translation

Case study: Conversational banking CoE at DBS bank India

DBS launched in India as Digibank, a mobile-only bank, with no branches and no call centres. Customer acquisition is assisted by Virtual Assistant Chatbot
• A 90-s paperless account opening for individuals enabled through India's Aadhar biometrics identification system
More than 10,000 customer intents covered:
• VA covers the following intent groups including more than 10,000 intents and actions on
  – Marketing and generic information about retail banking products for non-customers
  – Account related information and non-financial transactions for customers
  – Simple services on a specific account
  – Low value: known parties transactions
  – Intelligence on account transactions
• Retail banking products covered
  – Deposits
  – Investments in mutual funds
  – Insurance: health and auto
  – Loans: personal loan, home loan, loan against property
  – Debit cards
  – International fund transfers
Volumetric: DBS has acquired 2.5 million users in the past three years. A virtual assistant handles 80% of all interactions with consumers. Digibank India runs at 20% of the cost of a traditional bank
https://asianbankingandfinance.net/retail-banking/exclusive/dbs-betting-big-india

11.3   Conversational Banking Design Principles

Based on interviews and information in the public domain, below we have detailed technology features of conversational banking provided by banks, by six big technology firms, and six chatbot companies.

Conversational Banking Design

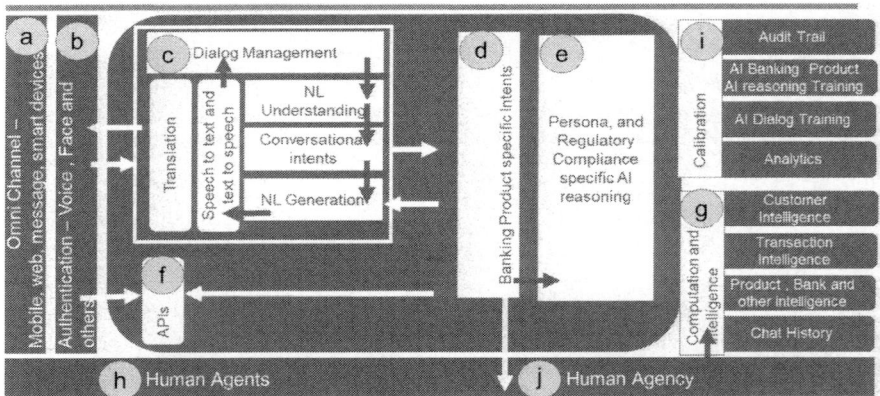

a. Omni Channel: To provide a very similar service experience on both inbound and outbound communication; a very similar conversational experience for banking transactions and services. Voice-based and dialogue-based text communication and voice communication on Omni Channel through:

- Mobiles.
- Web.
- Message.
- Smart devices.
- API to integrate with messenger:

  – Alexa;
  – Facebook Messenger;
  – Slack;
  – Kik Messenger;
  – WeChat;
  – Line;
  – Skype;
  – Twitter;
  – Google Assistant.

- API to integrate with devices:

  Smartphone;

Smartwatch;
Internet banking;
Other devices.

- Intelligence to provide meaningful customer experience across channels or devices. For example, to a customer question "What are my last ten transactions?" provide a summary through voice and send a statement through a mobile application or through messaging.

b. Authentication: Conversational banking is about Omni Channel contactless voice and face authentication. For the past five years or so, banks have implemented voice recognition as a way to authenticate the customer. Voice-based authentication has helped banks to improve overall customer engagement and grow the acceptance of voice channels. However, most banks have not yet integrated voice-based authentication across all channels, for all products, or for all customer types.

Conversational banking aims to expand voice and face authentication. It aims to make voice and face authentication enterprise-wide. Different levels of authentication may be required, based on intent, read vs write, transaction, fulfilment, and so on. Since voice and face authentication is biometric authentication, re-authentication is required for every intent change, for read vs write requests, and the fulfilment of services. Privacy, confidentiality, and non-repudiation require re-authentication.

c. Dialogue manager:

The purpose of dialogue management is service fulfilment. A group of activities accurately captures intents and fulfils service requests. The purpose of a dialogue manager is to enable and enhance interaction with a user and make it more human-like and more accurate and provide an engaging conversational experience in voice and chat.

It manages conversation topics in the context of the banking process and remembering and tracking conversations in the same session and previous sessions.

A generic dialogue manager provided by GAFA is not designed to manage the banking context. Therefore, a new dialogue manager for banking needs to be built or an existing dialogue manager needs to be augmented with a banking context. In our design, we have assumed a generic dialogue manager provided by GAFA and enhanced it with a banking context.

Translation, speech to text, and text to speech providing and enabling voice and text in multiple languages other than English. Industrialisation of the translation capabilities already available commercially may be needed and to be in other major languages like Chinese, Japanese, French, and Spanish. All translation capabilities need to be updated for banking, banking process, and banking computation terms and statements.

A. NL understanding: the purpose of Natural Language Understanding (NLU) is to convert the spoken or written text to one of intent, To identify the dialogue's intent:

1. NLP analysis and classification: identify banking intent, and banking products and services—this should help in determining product persona. NLP involves the analysis of each utterance using:

    - Tokenisation.
    - Parts of speech tagging.
    - A bag of words.
    - Semantic role labelling.
    - Semantic interpretation of inputs:
        - Semantic grammar;
        - Syntax driven semantic analytics.

2. Statistical approach to language understanding:

    - Generative models;
    - Discriminative models;
    - Deep learning for natural and spoken language understanding.

3. The purpose of analysis of content and utterance is the identification of the intent or goal of the conversation:

    - Expert natural language processing and generation: read, write, and parse banking process-related text;
    - Intelligent conversations that can track user goals and intents;
    - Deep-domain expertise is required with the ability to reason and interpret context and intent-based infrastructure with conversational context tracking and switching;
    - It can understand all of the idiosyncratic ways humans communicate and then reason to help users get things done;
    - Answering a question also requires deep domain expertise to get more accuracy in intents and goals.

4. NLP sentiment analysis: investigates and links with chat history and complaints to better understand sentiments:

    - NLP intent parsing: links to product, services, computation, location, and branch intelligence;
    - NLP information retrieval: links to intelligent customer and transaction data.

B. Conversational intents:

    - The purpose of intent is to identify and draft queries to fulfil transactional and non-transactional customer service requests.
    - Intent level utterances:
        i.   The same SQL query may be required to be run hundreds of times for different utterances; however, the structure of response may be different for a group of utterances.
        ii. A slight change in the utterance may completely change the SQL query.

      iii.   To achieve greater accuracy in drafting an SQL query, the structure of historical utterances is analysed and using NLP techniques SQL queries are calibrated. At one of the banks, the historical utterance record showed that the account balance is requested in more than 2000 different ways. The structure of dialogue and utterance was analysed and calibrated for drafting SQL queries and responses.

      iv.   Identification of change in context greatly helps in improving accuracy.

      v.   Accuracy of intent: use a slot or template to make a customer fill and/or confirm correct, complete, and accurate input data for the intent.

C.   NL generation should be in line with:

    a.   Persona;
    b.   Banking product-related processes;
    c.   Based on confirmation of intent;
    d.   Based on a template for computation;
    e.   In sync with translation and speech to text and text to speech library.

d.   Banking product-specific intents:

- Creation of thousands of customer intents for banking services specifically contextualised for banks, customers, products, and location.
- Elicitation of confirmation of intent and action, specifically through written messages or completing a template. Customers and devices may be re-authenticated for reconfirmation.
- Entity resolution—with the ability to relate to group members—of customer group members, bank's group entities, customer transaction parties, and common and well-known groups and their members.
- Retail banking specific intents with specialization in liability products, consumer credits, merchant services, small business banking, mortgages, student loans, and personal business lines.
- Wealth management specific intent with specialization in investment and portfolio management.
- Corporate and commercial banking specific intents with specialization in cash management, trade finance, payments, forex, trading, and lending products.
- Banking contextual engagement—for:
  - Banking regulation: country and regulator;
  - Banks and their policies and processes;
  - Procedures for services;
  - Customer, customer transactions, and information;
  - Historical conversations;
  - Conversations underway;
  - Language, currency, time, device, geography, etc.;
  - Persona.

e.   Persona and regulatory compliance specific AI reasoning: personas with an appropriate discharge of regulatory, fiduciary, and trust responsibilities. Conversational dialogue has to be in compliance with conduct and operational risk requirements. It also has to comply with the legal and contract requirements:

- Intelligent transactions with additional information, regulatory compliant computational logic and methodology, and hand-coded compliant computation libraries;
- Reinforce regulatory compliant learning—the entity resolution technology available needs to be upgraded to be compliant with KYC, related parties, group definition, privacy, and other regulatory requirements.

f.   APIs for:

- Integration with channels for voice and chat conversation;
- Integration with chat, phone, and video for live agent conversation and chat;
- Integration with an authentication system for continuous re-authentication, event-based re-authentication, and additional authentication;
- APIs for connecting internally with customer intelligence, transaction intelligence, chat history, and product and bank intelligence to obtain data required in conversations.

g.   Computation and intelligence:

- Chat history.
- Product, bank, and other intelligence:

  - Enable and empower a customer to adopt self-service;
  - Enhance, catalyse, add, and provide digitised banking services delivery;
  - Minimise the difference in services between paper-based documents and electronic data and documents.

- Transaction intelligence: transaction is to be augmented with details generally asked by the client, details of the merchant, and timings of a transaction.
- Customer intelligence.

h.   Manually override and smooth handover to the human agent.
i.   Calibration
     Audit trail:

- Audit trail of all interactions;
- Accuracy testing;
- Testing live agent hands off;
- Testing customer experience;
- Segment customer cohorts and channels

     AI banking products and AI reasoning training: a mechanism to monitor and correct bots. A bot represents a bank. Every action and statement, including emojis, should be compliant with regulation:

- Actions, series of actions;
- Communication, language, terms;
- Persona;
- Computation, search, results;
- Privacy;
- Choice of interface, a channel to deliver replies, all learning should go through a review, using automated tools before applying it in production.

  AI dialogue training: modularization of dialogue manager architecture and enhancing learning for each of the following modules:

  - Recognition of customer intent and conversational obligations;
  - Dialogue management and context management;
  - Interactive messaging;
  - Conversational dialogue;
  - Task automation and logic;
  - Natural language generation;
  - Content editor;
  - Conversational and messaging experience
    Analytics.

j. Human-agency:

No difference between conversational banking and human-agent banking services with a smooth handover from a conversational banking application to a human agent.

11.4 The State of Conversational Technology

11.4.1 Case Study: A Virtual Assistant on Amazon Lex

The Amazon Lex banking application bot is built on horizontal cognitive capabilities. At present, it supports informational requests or intents in terms of accessing the bank account, triggering small transactions, and technology self-service.

These banking functions are built by leveraging cognitive capabilities:

- Recognition of human speech and natural language understanding is enhanced for banking intents:

  - Accessing bank accounts:

    NLU converts the spoken or written text to the intent;
    SQL queries are run for intents to fulfil the customer requests of providing account balances and account transaction details.

  - Triggering small transactions:

    SQL queries are run for intents:

To fetch tickets details;
To write to the data to purchase a selected ticket.

To trigger payment for the purchased ticket.
To order food or call a cab.

– Self-service:

SQL queries are run for intents:

To fetch the user ID and password;
To write to the data to change the password.

Manage dialogue: the purpose of dialogue management is service fulfilment.
A group of activities accurately captures intents and fulfils service requests.
Manage context:

NLU identifies intent from the utterance or spoken or written text and
converts utterance to the intent.
The conversion should ensure that the intent and resulting dialogue
are compliant with banking regulatory requirements for the product,
conduct, payment, and service and computation method.
Customer and account details, product features, augmented transaction
and balance details, location and device details used for communicating
with the bank, and merchant details all provide context.

Accuracy of intent:

use of slot or template to make a customer fill and/or confirm correctness,
completeness, and accuracy of input data for the intent.

Different levels of authentication may be required based on intent, read vs
write, transaction risk, and technology risk of the fulfilment.

- AWS Lambda calls an internal database of intelligent transactions, customer
  information, prediction, and pre-computed results:

  – Using Amazon Polly, information extracted from an internal database is
    converted into speech;
  – AWS Lambda can be integrated with Alexa for the delivery of voice.

- Messages can be deployed on mobile devices, chat services, and IoT devices.
- Amazon Cognito is used for user management and authentication across channels.

11.4.2   Case Study: Azure Cognitive Services

Azure provides cognitive services to build intelligent applications to see, hear, speak, understand, and interpret customers through natural methods of communication. Azure at present provides 12 modules of cognitive services. All modules are horizontal services. Banking expertise needs to be built:

- Personaliser: this learns from the collective behaviour of users. It uses the information submitted about the user and from every interaction, improving personalization outcomes.
- Speech services: text to speech with customised voice fonts.
- Speaker recognition: identification and verification of speaker.
- Bing entity search.
- Bing spell check.

11.4.3   Case Study: Kasisto

Technology for financial institutions, and providing a humanized digital experience for users, are the two most important differentiating factors of Kasisto. Kasisto Artificial Intelligence (KAI) covers cases for retail banking, wealth management, and corporate banking. Kasisto was recently awarded a patent covering design for securing authentication of conversational intents.

What makes KAI unique and different is that it is trained in banking knowledge. It knows and understands banking. It knows the customer, it knows debits and credits as withdrawals and deposits in the customer's account. It knows that the current account is the same as a checking account; it knows the computation methods for fixed deposits and certificates of deposits. It knows about account opening. And it comes with the infrastructure that allows banks to rapidly deploy these systems.

11.5   Conversational Banking Service Use Cases and Intents

Deployment of conversational banking 'at a scale' requires: an intelligent understanding of context, topic, and change in topic; it is personalised, very specific to the customer's intents, in light of the customer's chat history; and conversation needs to be very specific to banking terms and processes, covering the risk and regulatory compliant persona. At the existing level of development, banking conversation bots are not mature enough to converse like human agents on every area of service or converse on the entire value chain of a service or identify a situation where they need to hand over the conversation smoothly to human agents. Substantial work needs to be done in the banking industry to achieve the required level of maturity.

In the following table, we have identified around ten service use cases with more than a hundred intents for more than ten products, covering banking regulatory compliant personas.

Service use case	Banking conversational intents	Banking product-specific intent	Banking regulation-compliant persona
Marketing and generic information	Marketing and generic enquiries for customers and non-customers • Product enquiries • Generic offers and rewards • Product advices • Financial advice	• Marketing and replies contextualised to product, intent, call details, and other factors • Dialogue contextualised and personalised to engagement or intent history	• Fiduciary responsibilities and conduct risk • Regulatory instructions for guidance and advice services • Customer and bank's rights and responsibilities in EFT, security, privacy, authentication practices
Account assist with non-financial transactions	Customer enquiries: • Find a branch • Find an ATM • Find a merchant	• Replies contextualised according to customer master data	• Fiduciary responsibilities and conduct risk • Regulatory instructions for guidance and advice services • Customer and bank's rights and responsibilities in EFT, security, privacy, authentication practices

(continued)

(continued)

Service use case	Banking conversational intents	Banking product-specific intent	Banking regulation-compliant persona
Opening account	Customer acquisition • Current and saving accounts • Personal loans • Credit cards • Mortgages • SME accounts	• Document extraction • Public data search and extraction • Biometric authentication • Third-party data search and extraction • Information and document submission	• Fiduciary responsibilities and conduct risk • Regulatory instructions for guidance and advice services • Customer and bank's rights and responsibilities in EFT, security, privacy, authentication practices • KYC and client list screening for online account opening guidelines
Managing account	Self-service • Password reset • Cheque book requisition • Application status • Offer status • Key account information • Account balance and transactions • Upcoming bills and instalments • Instalment overdue • Control card spend • Reward points	• Independent verification of sales and account opening with a customer, with public datasets • Augmenting transactions to close AML queries	• Fiduciary responsibilities and conduct risk • Regulatory instructions for guidance and advice services • Customer and bank's rights and responsibilities in EFT, security, privacy, authentication practices • AML and sanction screening • Anti-fraud guidelines and practices • Debt collection: regulatory instructions and customer protection

(continued)

(continued)

Service use case	Banking conversational intents	Banking product-specific intent	Banking regulation-compliant persona
Financial planning and advice	Covers advice on • Investments • Retirement • Protection Mortgages • General insurance • Debt	• Suitability • Risk profiling • Product information • Key information Rules for adviser charging	• Fiduciary responsibilities and conduct risk • Regulatory instructions for guidance and advice services • MiFID and AML and sanction screening

Smaller value fund transfer	• Triggers smaller payments
	  – Bills payments
	  – Subscriptions
	• Smaller fund transfer to known accounts
	  – Transfer to previously known accounts within the bank
	  – Transfer to previously known accounts outside the bank
	  – Track fund transfer and transactions
		• Independent verification of transaction with the customer
		• Verification through OTP, transaction on the screen, sending SMS and getting confirmation, etc
			• Fiduciary responsibilities and conduct risk
			• Customer and bank's rights and responsibilities in EFT, security, privacy, authentication practices
			• Regulatory instructions for guidance and advice services

(continued)

(continued)

Service use case	Banking conversational intents	Banking product-specific intent	Banking regulation-compliant persona
Intelligence and alerts on account and transactions	Intelligence on account transactions • Full merchant name • Payment and servicing intermediaries • Unique identifier for payment and transaction • Sufficiently detailed categorisation of transaction • Location information about transaction, merchant, intermediary, customer • Date and time stamp • Geospatial visualisation • Balances • Deals • Search capabilities • Fees, charges, interest, and debit computation method and explanation • Exceptional transaction, amount, and fraud alert • Track spending	Seamless handing over to human agent—ability of bot to • Identify scenarios that are good for handover • Providing context and conversational history to human agents • Monitoring charges, fees, debits, repayments, instalments—past, present, and future	• Fiduciary responsibilities and conduct risk • Customer and bank's rights and responsibilities in EFT, security, privacy, authentication practices • EFT guidelines and best practices • EFT network provider guidelines • Financial advice • Product advice • Regulation on charges, fees, and debits • Debt collection: regulatory instructions and customer protection
Intelligence to manage complex non-financial transactions	• Manage dialogue • Manage context • Manage topic • Manage intent	• Document submission • Document attestation • Customer authentication	• Fiduciary responsibilities and conduct risk • Legal requirements for a contract in electronic media

(continued)

(continued)

Service use case	Banking conversational intents	Banking product-specific intent	Banking regulation-compliant persona
Manage complex services	Mostly for wealth management and corporate customers for • Portfolio management • Cash management • Trade finance • Fees, interest, and charges • Foreign exchange • Consent and power of attorney	• Build intelligence around computation of fees, charges, interest • Intelligence and expertise in a long process like cash management, portfolio and trade finance	• Fiduciary responsibilities and conduct risk • Guidance vs advice persona • Investment advice • Product advice • Contract and agreements • Clearing and settlement network guidelines
Manage high-value transactions	• Built on the top of expertise of cash management, trade finance, and foreign exchange	• ISDA and similar documentation • Trade documentation • Clearing and settlement	• ISDA master agreement, schedule, and credit support clauses • SEF and other guidelines • EFT guidelines • Conduct risk • Clearing and settlement network guidelines

11.6 Implementing Conversational Banking at a Scale

11.6.1 Understanding Existing Conversation Services in the Bank

a. Identify business processes where a conversation is already happening with customers every year:

    i. Identify every conversational channel a bank is using and gather volumetric data for each:

        1. Customer care centre, call centre, and phones;

        2. Emails;

        3. Mobiles;

        4. The Web;

        5. Social media.

    ii. Identify high friction business processes and conversation-use cases:

1. Identify processes for which conversation takes place daily.
2. Conversation use cases: identify processes for which multiple sessions of conversations are established for the same issue by tens and hundreds of customers and prospects and this could be:

   - Generic information about products and services of the bank by customers and non-customers.
   - Account related information and non-financial transactions: this may be from customers with no financial implications. The same query with the same reply is the criterion to categorise a discussion under this category. However, there may be variation in replies across geography, business lines, time, and other broad attributes. This may be like creating an FAQ on topics discussed by tens of customers and employees. Prioritisation can be done based on several queries, customer vs non-customer, internal vs external.
   - Account opening process for various customer types and products.
   - Simple services on a specific account: the same query from multiple customers but replying with account-specific details are covered under this category. Service volume may be a good indicator of classifying a query as simple or complex. Simple services are high in volume, and complex services are low in volume. A cut off may be decided to classify services as simple; 5000 similar replies per month may be a good cut off. Following queries from a customer are good examples:

     i.   My account balance;
     ii. Next instalment due;
     iii. Details about the last debit transaction.

   - Financial planning.
   - Self-service for financial transactions. Many of the banks provide self-service financial transactions through mobiles, internet banking, IVR, ATM, and other channels. There is a risk that the chatbot will not understand the financial transaction. To mitigate and control the risk of wrong payment (either credit/debit, party, and amount) through chatbots, banks permit credit payment to pre-registered utilities with an upper limit on the amount. For example, bills up to USD100 can only be paid (only credit payments) to a utility from a list of utility providers. To reduce the risk further, a customer may be asked to register through the internet or mobile banking the name of the utility, frequency of bill payments, and the range or upper limit of payments for which the customer would like to use chatbots. A similar approach is taken for transferring funds: that is pre-registering, credit only, and within a small limit. Existing utility and counterparty details,

252 11 Conversational Banking

limits on transfers, and bill payment services can be adapted for chatbots.

- Intelligent and enriched transactional data: banks provide enriched transactions and payment detail feeds (in push mode) ready for use by account aggregators and accounting software companies. Enrichment may include details required for multi-currency, tax, audit, reconciliation, location, address, and industry details of counterparty, budgeting, planning, and management review purposes. At a minimum, these details are required by the chatbot to be able to engage a customer on transactions intelligently.
- Complex non-financial transactions: banking is a highly regulated, complex, legal, and contract-driven process. It needs a banking process, and product and computation-intensive knowledge base to manage communication.
- Complex services on specific accounts: complexity can occur when there are several accounts and contracts of a customer or a long process chain. Discussions about certain types of fees, collection and default, dispute investigation, and fraud investigation may fall under this category. Ultimate beneficiary ownership, trust account details, and discussion about the income and wealth of the customer may fall under this category. High-risk customer discussions for wealth management may also fall under this category.
- High-value transactions or transactions with previously unknown parties.

iii. Volumetric measures about conversations:

Audience: total number of customers, employees, and partners conversing during a period.
Total number of conversations started or completed during the period.
Total time spent by bank's employees, gross and net.
Total time lapsed to close the conversation.
Distribution of all the above: customers divided into cohorts and business processed divided by topic of conversation. Business processes can be further divided into transactional and non-transactional.

iv. Identify the processes helping the bank to achieve the strategic business goals.

11.6.2 Segment Audience Conversing with Bank

b. Segment audience of each conversation type by:

    i.   Preferred channels and platforms for conversation. This is very important if a new platform is being introduced. For example, before introducing WhatsApp Banking.

    ii.   Experience of the audience with messaging, text, and voice.

    iii. Demographic and product engagement level segments.

    iv. Analysis of the historical conversational record to understand the focus of conversations and level of intelligence expected.

    v.   Business process and topic of conversation.

    vi. Tendency to migrate to other channels and platforms.

c.   Keep segmenting the audience on a very regular basis.

11.6.3 Capture Audience Experience in a Database

d.   This is all about experience and not process.

e.   Capture experience of every segment:

    i.   Basic rule for a better experience is no need to change the channel or log into another application.

    ii.   The most difficult part of the experience is that existing applications are created for business processes and not customer experience.

11.6.4 Build Conversational Models

Building conversational AI models from historical conversation is very specific to the industry, products, regulation, and the bank's processes.

f.   Reuse and learn from data collected from the existing conversations through various channels, both voice and text. This is a five-step process:

    i.   Recording and transcription of the customer's voice and text calls.

    ii.   Identifying and linking responses to customer questions, responses on social media, and responses sent to a customer; standardised response template.

    iii. Creating the knowledge base: curate, sample, and filter the content; identify gaps in the content.

    iv. Identify the gaps and data quality issues in the content.

    v.   Keep identifying the gaps.

g.   Hand code and build models for the experience the audience is expecting.

11.6.5   Build Models to Personalise Conversations

Make conversation intelligent by building smaller cohorts and modify the conversation based on the static and non-static data about the client. Conversational tools to upgrade the models built for general learning and acquisition of specific information of customer based on:

h.   Static information like demographics mostly and especially for millennials; demographic attributes drive the conversations, transactions, and activities. Demographics attributes are available with a bank as a part of KYC. Attributes value submitted along with KYC documents are static in the short term and medium term (two to five years) and need to be kept updated.

i.   Semi-static information of investment and borrowing pursued by the client in terms of mortgages, auto loans, business loans, etc.; also includes past transactions with medium-term impact, salary, and other income being received in the account.

j.   Dynamic information: some of the attributes can also be collected from social media and conversations. Social media do provide information about the interests of the customer.

k.   Very dynamic short-term activities:

   i.   Trips being planned, food being ordered, other online activities and transactions;
   ii. The mood of interaction with a bank and on social media;
   iii. History of past transactions within the last six months.

11.6.6   Design Conversations

The purpose of design is to create a natural language dialogue with a customer based on greeting the user, recognising intention, conversational topic, named entities, and the emotions and sentiments of the user.

- There are two types of conversational systems: static and dynamic. Static has a collection of pre-defined responses and looks very artificial. Dynamic may generate appropriate and irrelevant responses.
- The system should have conversational intelligence about:

   i.   Be aware of date and time frame;
   ii. A conversation topic;
   iii. Knows what has been said in the past;
   iv. Has an appropriate level of formality;
   v.   Recovers whenever there is a misunderstanding.

- Learn from every interaction: learn in general and also from a particular customer.

2. Make privacy a part of the design:

   a. A historical conversations corpus is used for training the bots, which should ensure that it is not possible to identify the individual from the conversation samples.
   b. In the case of voice chat, the technology design should know when a customer is using a speaker to manage the privacy of transactions and discussions.

3. Personas in conversational banking:

   a. The persona should be in line with the customer intents.
   b. For an intent with financial implications, a persona should be formal with precise language and maybe with a template to complete a higher level of authentication.
   c. A persona should be consistent with communication and brand.

4. Integrate with real humans whenever required or complexity demands, such as when an analyst is not able to handle a discussion, he or she takes the customer to his manager. However, the handover should be smooth.

11.6.7   Reimagine Customer Journeys

As Albert Einstein said, 'We cannot solve our problems with the same level of thinking that created them.' Conversational banking requires imagining or re-imagining customer journeys in terms of:

- Identifying customer segments based on a different journey. The bank may not even be collecting data to segment customers based on the journey.
- Understanding new generation requirements better: millennials may be a broad term. Generation may change every few years and not over decades.
- With the development of the marketplace, the lifecycle of customer engagement with the bank and its customer (other FS firms, corporate, commercial, and SME firms who are customers of the bank) changes and will continue to change. SME, commercial, and corporate customers are themselves building platforms to deliver their services. Business customers are becoming platform companies.
- Re-imagining the bank's new capabilities, which may help re-imagine customer journeys.
- Some of the paths which can be considered for re-imagination of the customer journey are:

   a. Banks building customer engagement 3.0 platforms: they may no longer be engaging customers with point solutions, channels, and fragmented transaction processing or core banking solutions.
   b. Banks participating in the marketplace with its requirements, information flow models, and business models which are evolving.

In the marketplace eco-system, banks are still the most trusted participants who can be trusted partners for non-transactional services.

c. Leveraging branch network and presence, which is intelligent. Some of the new facilities, which can be leveraged, are:

    i. Smart and intelligent ATMs in the branch.

    ii. Self-service.

    iii. Assisted online banking and remote advisors through video conferencing.

    iv. Intelligent technology infrastructure specially built for better customer and employee experience and efficiency around:

        1. Public data;

        2. Paper documents.

11.7   The Future of Conversational Banking

Banks need to build artificial intelligence relating to their products, their own procedures, banking processes, local regulations, and their customers. Unfortunately, except for one or two products, none has built banking specific processes beyond generic non-customer level enquiries (which are horizontal industry processes). This is a very long drawn out process and needs continuous and substantial investment and creation of a knowledge base and learning.

11.7.1   Challenges in Building Conversational Banking

Challenges in building conversational banking	Important challenges	Primary drivers of challenge	Probable solutions
The legacy system will continue for years	• Quality of the data fields required for conversational banking	• Fragmented customer • Fragmented transactional data	• Build a single source of truth for customer and transactional data

(continued)

(continued)

Challenges in building conversational banking	Important challenges	Primary drivers of challenge	Probable solutions
Building intelligence into transactional data	• Fragmented transactional data • Fragmented channel data	• Building and keeping updated intelligence about: – Geography, devices and networks, transaction types, payment types, merchants and intermediaries – Trends and predictions	• Leveraging public data sources, partner data, purchased data to keep intelligence updated
A knowledge base of communication with the customer	• Manual, voice-based, unstructured, multiple file formats	• Customer engagement and communication will be largely manual with no or very little metadata and historical data	• Customer enthusiasm to engage with machines varies a lot, for the same customer and across customers • It also varies the problem statement • Provide the customer with an option to talk to a human agent at multiple points in conversation • Use cloud technology to manage variation in capacity
The complexity of communication is ever- evolving	• Even experts consult others before replying to a customer	• Regulation and legal requirements are continuously changing	• A full end to end technology-based conversational bank is neither possible nor desirable
Smoothness in handover to a human agent should be the primary goal of every chatbot	• Even in a manual process, customer communication is handed over to an expert and empowered person	• Achieving a smooth handover from a chatbot to a human agent should be a determining criterion for technology design	• Smooth handover to a human agent should be the primary criterion • The bank should focus on smooth handover to the human agent before going to the next level of maturity on the chatbot

11.7.2   Limitation of Conversational Banking Technology

The following is an incomplete list of the limitations for most of the chatbots author-reviewed, based on the publicly available information:

- Language is a significant barrier in a multilingual region.
- Dialogue capabilities and style is limited to the format of the specific questions adopted by the development team. Teams, at most of the chatbots, aim to reduce this limitation by engaging with the cross-cultural team.
- The intelligence of chatbots is still limited to providing information about simple transactions, balances, instalments, and product features.
- Substantial effort has to be invested in building intelligence for banking processes and complex transactions and balances.

11.7.3   Designing Conversational Banking User Interfaces

Entry-level CUI can be designed by building a library of customer self-service scenarios and customer services. Scenarios are to be further updated and refined for customer engagement and experience.

The most important design principle is to optimise the design on how users can utilise the service rather than forcing them to change their behaviour. The primary purpose of the conversational banking user interface should be to:

- Strengthen and enhance customer engagement;
- Enhance, catalyse, add, and provide digitised banking service delivery similar to banking transactions;
- Enhance customer experience and provide a similar experience across all channels for both transactions and services and enable the customer in the adoption of self-service;
- Minimise the difference in customer experience between paper-based documents and electronic data and documents;
- Better management of conduct, compliance, and operational risk.

Product chatbots as of the latter part of 2020 at all leader banks in conversational banking still cover scenarios only relating to transactions and balances. In the next few years, all banks need to improve their conversational banking services in terms of:

- Augmenting the medium of interaction to cover both text and voice;

- Enhancing domain and context understanding;
- Enhancing persona, tone, empathy, and personality;
- Enhancing human handover.

All chatbots including out-of-box chatbots, chatbot platforms (Amazon Lex, Azure Bot Services), and messenger services (Facebook Messenger, Slack, Kik, Skype, Twitter, Google Assistant) need to be provided with a conversational banking user interface to deliver the planned customer experience.

11.7.4 Measuring the Accuracy and Effectiveness of Conversational Banking

Banks need to develop a banking process-specific knowledge repository to improve precision, recall measures, and enhance accuracy to a comparable level of human intelligence.

The approach to precision and recall has to be measured at four levels to make the measures actionable:

1. Operational level: the purpose of operational level accuracy is to manage the accuracy:

   a. Unexpected input: the chatbot should have accuracy in managing unexpected input;
   b. Respond to social cues;
   c. Respond to greetings and personality;
   d. Be entertaining and engaging.

2. Quantitative level:

   a. Provide a path to escalation: in case the customer is not satisfied with the services of a chatbot, it should be able to provide escalation to human agents.
   b. Extract out and maintain the required audit trail.

3. Conceptual level: banking expertise specific to context and subject. The best chatbots may be able to deal with up to 60–80% of the intents on a subject. Chatbots can be enhanced, based on banking process themes. In real life also, we have agents with different type of expertise. Similarly, banks need to develop modules with different types of expertise. The purpose is for themed discussion; the intent coverage should go beyond 90%.

   a. Basing on theme and context is one of the ways to improve intent accuracy. However, this needs a stronger and deeper domain knowledge to manage responses with pre-built templates and slots. Like a human agent, the bot can also ask a customer to fill in the template before responding. However, the customer will complete the template if the customer trusts the machine for accuracy and human-like conversation. Otherwise, the customer may not complete it. Design thinking is a must for building theme-based bots.

   b.   Domain-specific questions: the designer has to decide which domain is based on the customer, historical chat, topic, or intent. The bot should have an approach to verification if a domain is identified correctly.

   c.   Detect meaning and intents in the domain context.

4.   Managing regulatory and compliance risk:

   a.   Regulatory and compliance risk should be the driver for persona. The choice of words should be appropriate to conduct risk, privacy, and other compliance requirements.

   b.   Calibrate all intelligence and information available towards better compliance.

   c.   Creating an audit trail of outcomes and intermediate outcomes for regulatory inspection and engagement with regulators.

11.7.5 Calibrate Customer Intent and Financial Obligation Based on Authentication Strength

Quick and accurate determination of the intent or the purpose of the call is the most important challenge in conversational banking. Once the purpose of the call is discovered, pre-defined journeys for a customer segment or the customer can guide interaction until the time the conversational obligations are determined. If the intent or conversational obligation is related to a financial transaction, it is linked with the account and confirmed or reconfirmed through a secure webpage or internet or mobile banking page. Customer intent or conversational financial obligation is calibrated on the strength of authentication. Re-authentication may be required.

11.7.6 Relative Frequency of Conversational Banking Service Use Cases

Service use cases	Product-wise relative frequency		
	Retail banking (%)	Wealth management (%)	Commercial and corporate banking (%)
Marketing and generic information	30	15	5

(continued)

(continued)

Service use cases	Product-wise relative frequency		
	Retail banking (%)	Wealth management (%)	Commercial and corporate banking (%)
Account related information and non-financial transactions	25	10	5
Account opening	10	10	2
Simple services on a specific account	12	10	8
Financial planning	8	30	0
Low value: known party transactions	5	8	5
Intelligence on account transactions	10	15	50
Engagement on complex non-financial transactions	0	2	10
Complex services on a specific account	0	0	10
High-value transactions	0	0	5

Take home:

- Entry-level, rule-based, generic enquiries and types of solution are good only for the retail segment.
- Unless a good banking onboarding process-related intelligence is embedded, the system may not be able to provide the required customer experience and customer engagement. Substantial work needs to be done internally by the bank to make other systems intelligent before moving account opening to conversational banking. Since account opening is the first interaction of the client with the bank, moving this process to conversational banking may backfire.
- Bot experts in financial planning are needed for successfully offering them to wealth management clients.
- There are not many use cases for marketing and generic bots for commercial and corporate banking. Only intelligent systems can engage commercial and corporate customers.

11.7.7 Success Measures of Conversational Banking

Success Measures (at the existing level of adoption, valid up to 2025)	
Reduction in call centre volume	• Between 35 and 60%
Satisfied intents	• An indicator of cognitive expertise at conversational banking • 60–93% of intents do not need a chat with a live agent • The best cognitive solution provides 93% satisfied intents without engaging a human agent
Expert chatbots can engage accurately on 80% of intents of a product or subject: for an individual human being it may be less than 30%	• Expertise may be around products and services like financial planning, credit card servicing, customer onboarding, transaction information and intelligence, fees and commissions, account information, and complex processes like cash management • Expert chatbots may be able to respond accurately up to 80% of intent type in the area of expertise
Uplift in online customer acquisition	• 100% customer acquisition online may not be feasible • Banks target 25–60% online customer acquisition
Smooth handover to and from a human agent	• Conversational context is provided to the human agent Positive customer experience in handover
Growth in upselling and cross-selling	• Growth in revenue per customer, and growth in total revenue from the customers who were engaged in conversational banking at least once in the past three months
Growth in the number of customers opting for automated chat	• Banks provide one to eight use cases on automated chat • Up to 60% of all customer intents are serviced through interaction via automated chat

11.8 Conclusion: Building Conversational Banking at a Scale

For the past three years or so, banks have started investing in conversational banking. However, except for a few banks, the industry has not seen adoption by customers. The primary reason for this slow adoption is a lower level of accuracy and non-human behaviour of conversational banking UI.

Successful banks have made concerted efforts to improve the accuracy and behaviour of UI by building banking, banking process, and banking product knowledge into UI and augmented transactional data. The banks seeing success in terms of better adoption by their customers are still far away from financial benefits. Successful banks will be able to realise the potential financial benefits only when their customers start trusting conversational banking UI. Building trust is a slow process and will come only when conversational banking UI can serve the majority type of customer and banking product.

Chapter 12
Banking AI as a Service

12.1 Introduction: Banking AI Takes Forward the Industrialisation Agenda

AI helps to process a large volume of data, process unstructured data, simulate human-like communication both as voice and textual, automate decision making, and automate complete banking processes. The existing technology is constrained by extremely limited capabilities in processing large volumes of unstructured data and automating decision making beyond rule engines. Therefore, AI can help to complete the automation of a business process and build a machine interface for customers, partners, and employees.

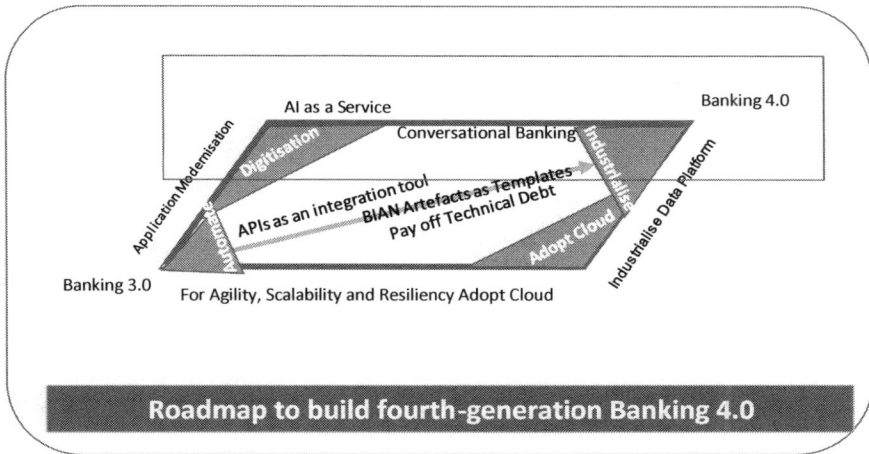

Roadmap to build fourth-generation Banking 4.0

At present, every business process is fragmented and interspersed with manual interventions. AI can increase the number of tasks (steps in a banking process) that can be automated without human intervention. With the growing development

© Springer Nature Singapore Pte Ltd. 2022
M. Bhatia, *Banking 4.0*,
https://doi.org/10.1007/978-981-16-6069-6_12

in banking intelligence, AI is becoming capable of automating a complete business process without human intervention either at the process execution level or the process verification and commit level. This increase in the number of tasks automated together is a basic building block of the industrialisation of a bank.

To disrupt cost structures and create a competitive advantage in engaging customers, banks are industrialising processes.

A consistent, standardised, automated AI platform plays a significant role in the adoption of AI as a service. As compared to point solutions, a machine learning or AI platform provides:

- Managed services for hassle-free development;
- Faster time to production with better completeness in tool and library coverage;
- Code-based and no-code-based tools and library;
- API based AI services that can be embedded in existing applications;
- Capabilities to integrate banking specific libraries, either provided by the platform or by a third party or built by the bank;
- Robust model governance, model building, model deployment, model updating, model validation, and MLOps capabilities as a part of the platform.

12.1.1 *Banking AI as a Service is a Basic Building Block in the Industrialisation Agenda*

- AI takes forward the digitisation process and supplements and complements the digitisation process.
- AI supports conversational banking. Many a time both are synonymous.
- It leverages and is built on API as an integration tool infrastructure.
- AIaaS leverages and catalyses the process of paying off technical debt.
- It is built on an industrialised data platform and is built on the cloud foundation.
- It leverages agility, scalability, and resiliency.

12.2 Establish Banking AI CoE

Banks are upgrading technology strategies and capabilities. Leveraging an AI platform will help a bank to create a Centre of Excellence of Innovation, pursue and execute industrialisation, and digitise customer engagement and conversational banking. An AI platform will help the bank to manage the requirements of a high volume, low latency data infrastructure.

At most banks, AI is not an outgrowth of an analytics team; it is an entirely new group. The primary reason banks are setting up a new group is that they do not have the expertise and experience in managing unstructured data. AI CoE is primarily being established at most banks to manage NoSQL data better, to manage conversational data better, and to manage documents better.

Some of the activities AI CoE is recommended to pursue are developing AI models and systems, building the bank's knowledge and AI functional libraries, engaging AI platform providers to build banking process-related narrow AI, and collaborating at an industry level.

The primary responsibility of an AI CoE is to implement AI as a service.

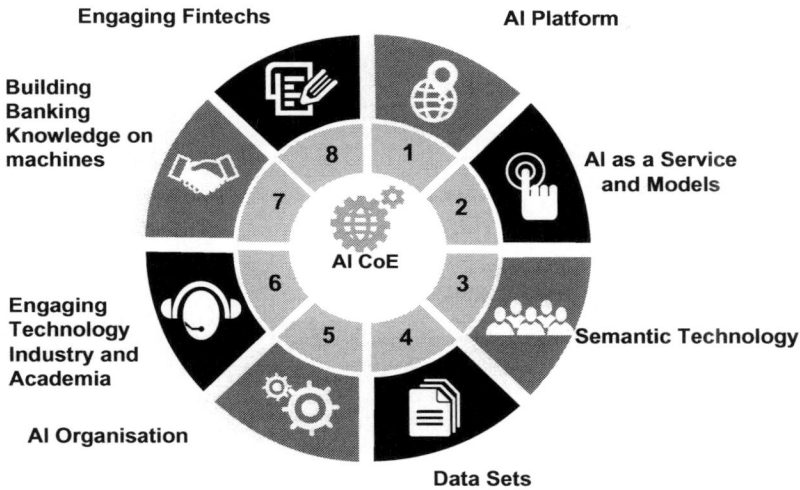

To enable the bank to leverage AI as a service fully, banks are establishing data science, AI/ML, and the visualisation CoEs. Banks are appointing Chief AI Officers and Chief Data Scientists. They are integrating a public cloud-provided AI platform into their technology and strategy.

12.3 Establish Banking AI Organisation

12.3.1 Banks Are Appointing Chief AI Officers

The Chief Technology Officer or Information Officer or Data Officer is largely an engineering role, but AI needs deep expertise in the banking process, regulation, and computations. AI needs deep expertise in AI techniques and their application to banking problems.

In short, a Chief AI Officer is someone with strong business acumen who can solve business problems with strong expertise in technology and AI techniques. Chief AI Officers, in addition to being experienced in data science and ML, need to be experts in industry problems and should be able to define a bank's problem in terms of ML algorithms, data requirements, and data integration requirements.

Banks are appointing a Chief AI Officer to help them industrialise. He or she works closely with Data Scientists, Data Engineers, and Machine Learning Experts.

A Data Scientist is skilled in statistics and mathematics. He or she has several years of experience in managing data and is comfortable with managing big data.

A Data Engineer is a skilled software engineer in languages that are used for ML. He or she is comfortable in integrating applications and data with the existing software systems. He or she is principally focused on big data and ML applications.

An ML expert can write original ML algorithms, understand and customise widely available ML libraries and frameworks. He or she is an expert on the ML algorithms to be used for any given application.

12.3.2   Case Study: Chief AI Officer at JPMC

There is an acute shortage of AI talent. It is almost impossible to find a single person with deep expertise in AI techniques, technology, and banking applications. Talent is still available only within academia. Therefore, banks are collaborating with academia and appointing AI and ML professors in AI teams and as Chief AI Officers.

JPMC created an AI Research Team in 2017 to accelerate the adoption of AI within the firm. The Research Team also collaborates with leading faculty around the world on areas of mutual interest. JPMC appointed Professor Manuela Veloso from Carnegie Mellon University as head of AI Research in areas of core relevance for financial services including data mining and cryptography, machine learning, explainability, and human–AI interaction.

12.3.3   Availability of AI Skills is a Major Area of Constraint

Banks with an AI-first strategy are collaborating and funding academia and innovation, setting up innovation labs, funding AI platforms and fintech, acquiring fintech, funding and acquiring consulting firms and AI start-up service firms, and collaborating with academia to train students in AI and ML.

12.3.4   Case Study: Augmenting AI Capabilities Through the Acquisition of an AI Consulting Firm

TD Bank in Canada acquired Layer 6, an AI consulting firm, to deliver responsive, personalised, and insight-driven experience for the financial services industry.

Bharat Masrani, Group President and CEO, TD Bank Group, says: Anticipating and meeting customer needs are at the heart of our promise, and we are excited to further accelerate our innovation agenda to deliver well into the future. As we deploy new solutions, we will extend our deep relationship with customers across all of our platforms and offer personalized, connected and legendary experiences for our customers in the digital age (Adapted from TD Bank Press release).

12.3.5 Case Study: Augmenting AI Capabilities Through Partnerships with Academia

This case study is about leveraging the available public datasets.

In 2018, TD acquired Layer 6, a world-renowned artificial intelligence company to help deploy new solutions and deepen the bank's relationship with customers. TD bank is getting the benefits and value to the community. The bank announced that Layer 6 would collaborate with University of Toronto medical researchers on developing deep learning models for population health data. Healthcare is one of the next frontiers for artificial intelligence to make a meaningful and positive impact on the lives of people across North America (Adapted from TD Bank Annual Report).

12.3.6 Case Study: Augmenting AI Capabilities Through Investment in AI Startups

Capital One Bank is an investor in H_2O.ai. It uses H_2O for mobile transaction forecasting and anomaly detection.

Capital One Bank strongly believes in innovation. The bank highly values the power of information and technology to be able to bring highly customised financial products to consumers and business customers.

With up to 5000 customers logging into the bank's mobile platform every minute, the bank needed a solution to improve diagnostics and resolution times for outage and other technical issues. The bank needed a forecasting and alert generation tool using machine learning techniques to manage technology catering to such a high volume of traffic.

To deliver a scalable solution, Capital One's data scientists are using Sparkling Water from H_2O.ai to allow them to rapidly test and deploy machine learning algorithms to manage mobile banking platforms. The solution combines Sparkling Water with the H_2O flow UI, Scala, and Python, with the capabilities of Apache Spark.

H_2O's advanced capabilities for in-memory processing have proved to be an excellent match for big data environment needs; and its ability to support Python, Spark, and Scala enabled a unified coding pipeline for the bank's many data experts. The platform has enabled the bank to accurately calibrate spikes and seasonality into the time series to take care of spikes in user activity for better and more accurate ML models.

The Business Analytics Graduate Immersion Programme of DBS.

12.3.7   Augmenting the AI Team Through a Training Partnership with Academia

The Business Analytics Graduate Immersion Programme (BAGIP) is a leading training programme in business analytics for DBS, Singapore to train candidates with a passion for data and who enjoy using analytics to solve business problems.

DBS provides an accelerated programme over 12 months to focus on building core analytical skills essential to business growth.

Students are trained on the state-of-the-art techniques to conquer real challenges in the industry, using technical and business analytics knowledge, ranging from Python and SAS programming to big data computation, machine learning, and statistical analysis.

Senior data scientists and analysts from DBS provide mentoring along with on-the-job training and hands-on involvement in big-data projects. The programme helps in mastering skills in data extraction, reporting, and business advisory.

12.3.8   Banks Are Collaborating with Cloud Service Providers on AI Initiatives

We know that each of the cloud players has announced AI-first as a mission statement. Google announced an AI-first strategy in 2017. Thanks to advances in AI, Google has been moving beyond its core mission of 'organising the world's information' to AI-first. Similarly, Microsoft aims to create 'best-in-class' platforms and productivity services for an intelligent cloud and an intelligent edge infused with AI.

DBS Bank is looking to arm 3000 of its employees with basic skillsets in AI and ML. To remain ahead on the technology curve and to continue focusing on customer expectations, DBS is democratising technology skillsets amongst all employees to help advance DBS's digital transformation.

Citi bank plans to replace 10,000 call centre agents with machines. Call centres at present provide more than 100 customer journeys. Citi plans to replace the 30 most common customer journeys. For example, ordering a replacement of a bank card or requesting a bank statement.

12.3.9 Case Study: HSBC Partners with Element AI

HSBC partnered with Canadian software company Element AI to deliver new products powered by insights from a newly collated data lake.

It is building an AI-powered Client Intelligence Utility (CIU) built on 10 petabytes of corporate and institutional client data from 1.6 million clients. The utility will be underpinned by the largest aggregation of corporate and institutional client data HSBC has ever put together: 22,000 + physical tables of information.

12.4 Banking AI as a Service (BAIaaS) on a Cloud Data AI Platform

The existing technology does not have machine-readable, machine-executable, machine-stored knowledge and intelligence of banking processes, banking products, banking computation, banking contracts, banking documents, and banking services.

12.4.1 The Development of AI as a Service (AiaaS) for Banks Will Be a Very Long Journey

The development of AI as a service for banks will be a very long journey requiring a substantial amount of investment and focus to embed banking intelligence into machines. The banking industry, cloud providers, the technology industry, banks, and fintech are investing in machine extraction knowledge and the machine storage of knowledge process execution with AI tools specific to banks.

12.4.2 General Purpose AI Platform Capabilities Have Matured in the Past Three Years or so

Public cloud players like GAMI (Google, Amazon, Microsoft Azure, and IBM) along with their acquisitions and analytics and machine learning players like SAS, Tableau have developed strong libraries, toolsets, and workflows as a general-purpose AI platform for statistical, text, machine learning, AI algorithms, and functions as a service.

12.4.3   Case Study: GCP AI Platform—A Platform to Provide AI as a Service

The GCP AI platform provides AI as a service to:

- Define and upload a dataset;
- Train an ML model on a bank's data;
- Train models on other data;
- Evaluate model accuracy;
- Tune the hyperparameters of the model;
- Upload and store models in AI platforms;
- Deploy a trained model as a service through the integration of endpoints for serving predictions;
- Consume AI as a service by sending prediction requests to the endpoint;
- Specify a prediction traffic split in an endpoint;
- Manage models and endpoints.

GCP product	Function
AI explanations	To understand how each feature in input data contributed to the model's outputs
AutoML	To develop high-quality custom machine learning models without writing training routines
Continuous evaluation	Helps to obtain metrics about the performance of models in production. It helps to compare predictions with ground truth labels to gain continual feedback and optimize model performance over time
Data labeling service	Labelling for better machine learning models
Deep learning containers	Quickly builds and deploys models in a portable and consistent environment for AI applications
Neural architecture search	Building application-specific models and improving existing model architectures with an automated service
Notebooks	JupyterLab is the standard data scientist workbench
Pipelines	Helps implement MLOps by orchestrating the steps in ML workflow as a pipeline
Prediction	Easily deploys models to manageable, scalable endpoints for online or batch predictions
TensorFlow Enterprise	Easily develops and deploys TensorFlow models
Training	Helps train any model
Vizier	Helps to optimise a model's output by intelligently tuning hyperparameters
What-if tool	Helps to visualise datasets and probe models to better understand their behaviour with an interactive visual interface

12.4.4 Case Study: General Purpose AI Platform

A general-purpose AI platform helps to automate, build, and train models and continuously keep detecting drift. The AI platform helps in building mission-critical solutions that can analyse images, comprehend speech, make predictions using data, and imitate other intelligent human behaviour. The platform helps in getting models to production at lower cost and effort. The platform provides the pre-built capabilities of:

- Algorithms and models;
- Debug models and profile training runs;
- Capture, organize, and search;
- A human review of model predictions;
- Optimising parameters.

AI platform vendors have also developed tools and frameworks that allow developers to collect and integrate data, perform analysis, perform experimentation, develop models, and then test and deploy them in production. The technology components of AI software platforms include:

- Algorithms;
- Computer vision;
- NLP;
- Speech recognition;
- Image recognition;
- Text analytics;
- Managing unstructured data;
- Audio analytics;
- Tagging, searching;
- Machine learning;
- Categorisation, clustering;
- Hypothesis generation;
- Questioning, answering;
- Visualisation;
- Filtering, alerting, navigation.

12.4.5 AI Services on a General Purpose AI Platform

General-purpose AI software platforms typically include knowledge representation tools such as knowledge graphs, triple stores, or other types of NoSQL data stores. They provide knowledge curation and continuous automatic learning based on tracking past experiences. When these individual technology components are sold as standalone, they are accounted for in other software functional markets such as content analytics and search, advanced and predictive analytics, and non-relational database management systems. In summary, the general-purpose AI platform provides the following five types of services along with their combination:

- Analytics;
- Interactive;
- Text analytics;
- Visual analytics;
- Functional.

12.4.6 Managing Cloud AI Platforms

An AI platform is focused on data management for machine learning models and machine learning model management for faster deployment and accuracy:

- Data wrangling is a process of gathering, selecting, and transforming or cleaning data for use in ML, data science, analytics, and other AI requirements. It is different from ETL functionality. Here the purpose of transformation is to fit data for ML; 80% of the data science effort is data preparation and data cleaning. Data wrangling prepares data for consumption by AI or ML or data science or analytics or visualisation. Four areas where data wrangling is required are:
  - Visualisation;
  - Data aggregation;
  - Training statistical model;
  - Data used for algorithms.
- Feature engineering: data labelling and pre-processing for feeding into ML models are a part of feature engineering. Data labelling is required for unstructured data and categorical data. A large part of feature engineering is manual or machine-assisted.
- Algorithm designing: solves specific FS business problems, ML model creation for a specific business problem, information and technology design, and selection, and building an approach to enhance the accuracy of the model, as acceptable in the FS world. This includes result testing and debugging, deployment in production of ML models in inference mode, and monitoring results for any drift and periodically retraining the model.

12.4.6.1 AI Platforms Industrialise AI Model Building, Validation, and Deployment

An AI platform integrated with cloud products provides:

- The capability of handling large datasets along with inexpensive on-demand computing resources;

- Accelerators to build ML and AI models;
- Libraries of advanced techniques in computer vision, natural language understanding, and recommended AI systems;
- MLOps for automation and monitoring of every step of ML model integration, testing, releasing, deployment, and infrastructure management.

Prepare	Build	Validate	Deploy
Data labeling Big data with SQL and NoSQL capabilities to datasets Cloud storage	A kit to embed ML models into applications Tool and functionality to build ML Models Training models Deep learning	Performance and accuracy to achieve business results Evaluate metrics AI explanation What if capabilities	Predictive engines or ML models AI services for search and conversation

12.4.6.2   The Development of Banking AI as a Service is Very Different from a Technology Project

- An AiaaS team requires data scientists, banking processes, and communication and computation experts. The team needs to focus on exploratory data analysis, model development, and experimentation.
- Model development is experimental. Different features, algorithms, modelling techniques, and parameter configurations are tried to find what works best for the problem as quickly as possible.
- The challenge in AiaaS development is tracking what works and what does not.
- Testing an ML system is more involved than testing a software system. Performance and accuracy should be acceptable in a customer engagement, it should be commercially viable, and it should build AiaaS whose accuracy is of an acceptable level. In addition to typical unit and integration tests, testing means data validation, trained model quality evaluation, and model validation.
- Banking AiaaS isn't simply the deployment of an offline-trained ML model as a prediction service. ML systems require a multi-step pipeline to automate, retrain, and deploy a model. The provision of a pipeline adds complexity to deployment. Complexity shoots up multiple times if there are intervening manual steps in data provision or model deployment.
- ML model performance is driven by constantly evolving data profiles. Model performance decays in more ways than conventional software systems.
- The model needs to be closely monitored for the early identification of performance degradation. This also needs the monitoring of input data and their summary statistics.

12.4.6.3   Deployment of Banking AI as a Service

- Latency: The latency of model predictions is largely a function of the cloud computing resources available for model execution. The type of model drives the amount of processing required. Model execution and model training are significantly different. For example, for building a decision tree, an algorithm considers many instances and features. When the decision tree is used to make predictions, the model makes a series of evaluations using data passed into the model. The number of evaluations is a function of the depth of the tree, but it is significantly less work than building the decision tree.
- Latency is also due to the travel of input data and results on the network. Some of the applications like algorithmic trading and cyber risk applications are time-sensitive to the extent of nanoseconds. Therefore, models should be deployed near to where they are consumed by changing the server location or deploying it in edge computing or on an IoT device.
- Scalability: Models need to scale to meet the workloads. Compute Engine and Kubernetes Engine can be scaled to more workloads.
- Version management: An AI platform can deploy multiple models. Different versions are released in production to measure the performance of the version. This can help in implementing different deployment strategies.
- Online versus batch prediction.

12.4.7   Banks Need to Develop Narrow AI Very Specific to the Banking Process

Generic AI platforms are provided by several vendors who have developed suites of APIs and microservices covering a wide range of AI/ML capabilities and have made available AI platforms on premises, the public cloud, and hybrid cloud offerings.

However, the existing generic platforms are still good only for the technology enablement of AI. At present, the focus of platform providers is to enhance data preparation, package as wide as possible ML libraries into the platform, and provide an integration facility to augment open-source library with a third-party library.

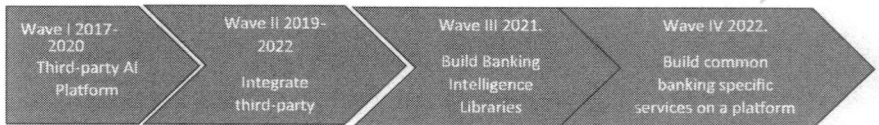

The two most important elements of intelligence are learning and problem-solving. At present, AI solutions focus only on problem-solving, and existing algorithms are still not matured for automated learning. Banking knowledge required by

AI system and common banking services may be initially built by experts manually. To industrialise a bank, an AI platform should be able to solve banking related problems and learn banking knowledge. Banks have started addressing the issue of making machines learn or solve a problem for banks, based on learning and taking the decision which is at a commercially viable accuracy level. However, this may prove to be a very long journey. Very few banking specific services are becoming available as third-party services on some AI platforms. This may be accelerated as the fintech wave starts maturing and makes available some of its services for white labelling on AI platforms.

12.5   Build a Semantic Technology Foundation for Banking AI

Semantic technology leverages artificial intelligence to simulate how people understand language and process information. By automating the understanding of meanings about the banking process, concepts, and computations, semantic technology overcomes the limits of other technologies.

12.5.1   ISO 20022 Has Published a Banking Semantic Dictionary

ISO 20022 has defined consistent products and business processes. Being an open standard, it is adaptable even for a product and process not defined in out-of-the-box ISO 20022 standards. Worldwide 95% of banking transactions should be on ISO 20022 by 2022.

Common Business Concept and Processes								
	Type of Adjustments	Charges	Penalty	Period	Discount	Commission	Allowance	
Adjustment	Adjustments to	Currency Exchange	Payment	Security Order	Collateral	Line Item	Tax	
	Computation of Adjustments	Interest Computation	Cash Account Service	Investment Fund Transaction	Corporate Fees	Securities related fees		
	Interest computed for	Net Assets calculations	Balances	Asset Holding	Tax	Deposit		
Interest	Variable Interest Computation	Security	Life Calculation	Yield Calculation	Duration Calculation	Index		
	Computation method	Charges	Spread	Amount				
	Reporting Trade	Trade Identification	Trade Leg	Clearing System	Master Agreement	Trade Obligation	Trade System Identification	
Trade and Transaction Regulatory Reporting	Reporting Assets	Assets Classification	Asset Classification Scheme					
	Reporting Derivative Asset	Securities Pricing	Securities Pricing Yield Calculation	Securities Pricing Index Calculation	Option Calculations			
	Reporting Securities Tade	Trade Identification	Securities Identification	Securities Quantity				

Banking and Trading Products:

- Out-of-the-box vocabulary covers products in terms of cards, deposits, securities, forex, and investment funds;
- The framework is consistently applied across all five products;
- The framework covers both banking books (cards and deposits) and trading books.

Business processes:

- Covers business processes of payments, channels, forex and securities clearing, trading and settlement, and cards;
- Process framework is consistently applied across all the products;
- Covers all aspects including fulfilment, accounting, computation, and account management.

Consistency in an internal and external process:

- Covers both internal and external leg, so making both incoming and outgoing services and data models consistent.

Re-usability at a physical, logical, and semantic level:

- Re-usability and standardisation across business processes and concepts;
- Re-usability and standardisation across logical structures;
- Re-usability and standardisation across syntax and data;
- Example postal address data structure, logical structure, and meaning are re-used across all products, services, and concepts.

12.5.2   ISO 20022 Dictionary for Banks is at Three-Level—Semantic, Logical and Physical

Consistent and future proof reference data structures:

- International characters in narrative fields, long identifiers, long references, very large monetary amounts, very precise interest rates, and exchange rates;
- Consistent reference data structures.

Consistent logical data and processes:

- Balances, ratings, parties, computation methods, adjustments, assets, collaterals, accounts, transactions, and entries are consistently defined by the standards.

An approach to adopt logical data in a piecemeal way:

- Overall strategic picture of standard adoption, towards which bank migrates piecemeal, responding to business drivers, but with each implementation smoothing the way for those that follow.

Banking industry dictionary of semantics:

- Out-of-the-box dictionary provides internationally agreed, more than 6000 common vocabularies of financial industry concepts;
- Vocabulary is standardised at the lowest level of granularity so it can be re-used to build additional concepts.

12.5.3 Further, Augment ISO 20022

ISO 20022 is a semantic dictionary for banking transactions. No dictionary can be complete. ISO 20022 has an in-built capability to adopt a dictionary, taxonomy, and ontology. ISO 20022 needs to be augmented with a dictionary of reference data, accounting, reporting, and other processes. Adopt, enrich, and extend are the keys to building a global financial industry semantics:

- Financial Instrument Global Identifier (FIGI): a global framework that standardises the way that financial securities are identified.
- Accounting taxonomies:

  – IFRS/FASB/IASB and other accounting boards publish accounting taxonomies;
  – For all financial reconciliation, accounting, general ledger, performance reporting, financial reporting, and regulatory reporting.

- Financial Industry Regulatory Ontology (FIRO):

  – A semantic (word and meaning) map of different regulatory terms that covers several regulatory jurisdictions;
  – Banks Integrated Reporting Dictionary (BIRD) is emerging as a harmonised data model for regulatory reporting.

- Financial Industry Business Ontology (FIBO):

  FIBO references other standards such as FpML, FIX, ISO, MISMO, MDDL, and XBRL.

12.5.4 Context Discovery Drives the Approach to Building Semantic Technology

A semantic layer maps complex data to familiar business terms such as product, processes, and reports. The semantic layer is to add contextual meaning to data. Adding contextual meaning helps in improving searching, sharing of data, and drawing inferences and actions. The accuracy and precision levels are low for contexts discovered from samples vs contexts adopted from a dictionary.

For unstructured data, context is discovered from samples:

- Unstructured data:

- Documents;
- Webpages;
- Document metadata.

- Using NLP and weblink analysis, context is discovered and added.

For structured data, context is adopted from a semantic dictionary:

- Semantic dictionaries ISO 20022, FIBO, FIRO, and IFRS provide industry-wide adopted concepts, dictionaries, definitions, and structures.
- Standards also provide industry accepted computation methods,
- Standards also provide industry accepted tags, annotations, approaches, and process methodologies.

Preparation for building a semantic layer for structured data:
Identification of sub-domain concepts and underlying data and metadata is the key. The same data may be used by different concepts in a different context. The meaning of a given term depends on the context and syntax and could have many different meanings across different domain subsets.
Recommended technology standards:

- SPARQL as a semantic query language;
- Resource Description Framework (RDF) to build a semantic relationship over a relational database;
- Ontology Web Language (OWL) to build ontology;
- The semantics of Business Vocabulary and Rules Specification (SBVR) as a framework to define business concepts.

Identify the subdomain and data model:

- Identification of all concepts within the domain sub-sets;
- Identification of domain sub-sets and relevant data model, logical data model, and semantic data model;
- Leverage metadata and logical data layer;
- Identify all application metadata;
- Map to semantic metadata layer.

Document concept within the sub-domain:

- Concepts mapped to the data models to identify data requirements.
- For each concept, document ontology in terms of:

  - Classes and their hierarchies;
  - Properties and their hierarchies;
  - Supporting loading of data to semantic data network.

- User-defined inferencing rules and queries:

  - to write SPARQL queries for building and drawing inferences on RDF triples— subject, predicate, and object.

12.5.4.1 Building Semantic Layer for Structured Data Using Semantic Dictionary

This goes through transform and load and infers and visualises the process. RDF is a model to establish semantic relationships between different data so that machines can interpret them. The data relationships are presented as a graphical database. The meaning of a given term depends on the context and syntax and could have many different meanings across different domain subsets.

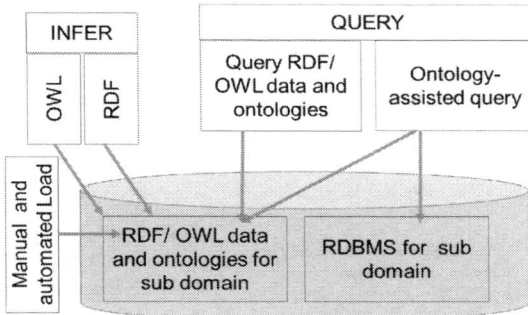

Transforming data: manual and semi-automated:

- Map metadata of RDBMS tables to the semantic metadata;
- Map data to the ontology concepts;
- Semi-automated mapping using R2RML may also be used at table level with mapping driven by domain definitions;
- Fully automated may not give the requisite level of required precision and accuracy.

Load data for knowledge graphs:

- RDF/OWL data management;
- Semantic indexing.

Knowledge network:

- Semantic rules and logic.
- Inferences and prediction:

  - Inference rules and logic;
  - Predicate rules and logic.

- Audit trail.
- Ontology assisted queries.

  Visualise and analyse:
  SQL and SPARQL queries and results for:

- Metadata registry;
- Graphical visualisation;
- Creates scenarios;
- BI and analytics;
- Search.

12.5.4.2 Managing Huge Data Volumes in Real Time is a Primary Reason for Building Semantic Technology

Across all use cases, the semantic layer helps in drastically simplifying and automating the establishment of lineage, identification of anomalies, and verification of accuracy across the physical systems.

The separation of meaning from the structure of data and the linking of concepts without having to reconfigure columns and rows would facilitate scenario-based analysis in response to changing circumstances. Use cases of establishing lineage, verify accuracy and detect anomalies in:

- Predictive analytics;
- Conduct risk;
- Regulatory reporting;
- Financial crime management.

12.5.4.3 The State of Banking AI as a Service

To be successful in delivering AIaaS, banks need to ensure that they do not boil the ocean but adopt a use-case-based approach with full dedication to making the project a success. Banks should also adopt a very different project failure/success criterion which must be much beyond the immediate cost reduction or revenue growth.

12.5.4.4 Case Study: AI Services at Banks

Banks are leveraging AI and ML technologies and have built services to receive input data of various types. They have built context-aware logic. However, as noted elsewhere, learning from input and actions is still weaker and banks need to invent algorithms. Banks have progressed well in task execution. Some of the fintechs have developed good conversational banking. A blank space in the following table is an indicator of what needs to be done.

Problem-solving scenarios at banks
where some work has happened

Receive input data	Context-aware logic	Learning from inputs and actions	Execute actions
Computer vision • Integration with input devices • High-level understanding of images and videos • Visual classification and extraction of actionable signals			**Chatbot** • Two-way communication both voice and text • Based on language, behaviour, and data • Very specific to banking process
Cognitive computing (CPA) • Realisation of cognitive tasks and decision making • Interactive, iterative, and evidence based systems • The adaptability of systems to changes in information or objectives • Context-aware computing			
NLP • Attributing meaning and purpose to the language • Speech recognition and text to speech			**Dialogue** • Textual interaction • With preset question, answers, and logic
Augmented analytics • Context-aware computing • Integration with IoT, geo-spatial, biometrics, big data • Predictive analysis and simulations • Rule-based automatic actions • Recommendation engines			
	Large scale machine learning • Pattern recognition algorithms on ever-expanding datasets • Implementation of machine learning approaches like decision trees, K-means clustering, and estimation methods		
	Supervised and Reinforced Learning • Moving the focus of machine learning from pattern recognition to a process of sequential and experience-driven decision making		

Source Adopted from https://www.ebf.eu/wp-content/uploads/2020/03/EBF-AI-paper-_final-.pdf; EBF position paper on AI in the banking industry

12.5.4.5 Banking AI as a Service Pattern

Based on the personal experience of the author and based on various discussions the author had with global banks, the following is an incomplete list of 15 model and service patterns used by banks. We have compared models or analytical patterns based on eight attributes. A model is different from others by at least one attribute. Accuracy or predictability of model, execution response, and several users are the key drivers for model selection. These three attributes are also drivers for technology and algorithm selection.

Model type	Input data type	Input data pull/push frequency	Transformation execution frequency	Execution response	Accuracy or predictability of output	Validation methods	Output data delivery	Users
Report	Structure and semi-structure	Pull entire/incremental data in batch mode daily or frequently	Daily or pre-set frequency batches	Overnight, daily	Very high	Automated and manual reconciliation of output	Largely pre-set visualisation—limited self-serviced computation	< 100 for each report
Dashboard	Structure and semi-structure	Pull entire/incremental data in frequent batches	Daily or pre-set frequency batches	Overnight daily	Very high	Automated and manual reconciliation of output	Self-serviced visualisation—user can create computed fields with audit trail	< 1000 for each dashboard
Dashboard near real time	Structure and semi-structure	Near real-time incremental data-pushed	Near real time frequency or on-demand	On preset publication time or within 3 min of on-demand	High	Automated and manual reconciliation of output	Visualisation—user can create computed fields + delivery on smart devices	< 100 for each dashboard
Score dashboard	Structure and semi-structure	Push data	Daily or periodic batches	On preset publication time	Low to medium to high	Automated and manual reconciliation	Visualisation—user can create computed fields	< 1 k–10 K for each dashboard
Computation bot	Structure and semi-structure	Pull data in frequent batches	Pre-set frequency or on-demand	< 1 h	High	Automated and manual reconciliation of output	Deployed for serving other applications	> 1 million for each bot
Chatbot	Structure and unstructured text	Push incremental data in real time	On-demand	< 5 s	High	Periodic manual validation and updation	On smart devices and social networks	> 1 million for each bot
NLG	Structure and unstructured	Push incremental data in batch	On-demand	< 3 min	High	Periodic manual validation and updation	Deployed for serving other applications	< 100 K for each bot
Conversational bot	Structure and unstructured text + voice	Push incremental data	On-demand	< 5 s	High	Periodic manual validation and updation	Deployed for serving other applications	> 1 million for each bot
Workflow	Structure and unstructured	Push incremental data in frequent batches	On-demand	< 3 min	High	Automated audit trail and periodic manual validation and updation	Deployed for serving other applications	> 1 million for each bot

(continued)

(continued)

Model type	Input data type	Input data pull/push frequency	Transformation execution frequency	Execution response	Accuracy or predictability of output	Validation methods	Output data delivery	Users
API for data and modelling process	Structure and unstructured	Pull or push data or transformation n real-time	On-demand	< 2 s	Very high	Automated audit trail Periodic manual validation and updation	Deployed for serving and consuming services from other applications	> 1 million for each API
Predictive engine	Structure and semi-structure	Push data + daily batch	Daily or pre-set frequency batches	> 1 day	Low	Periodic manual validation and updation	Deployed for serving other applications	> 1 million for each engine
Predictive engine with data pipelines	Structure and semi-structure	Pull data + push data + daily batch	Daily or pre-set frequency batches	> 1 day	Medium	Daily semi-automated validation and updation	Deployed for serving other applications	> 1 million for each engine
Predictive engine with ML feedback loop	Structure and semi-structure	Pull data + batch + push data + on demand	On-demand	< 3 min	Medium	Automated online ML-based validation and updation	Deployed for serving other applications	> 1 million for each engine
Monte Carlo simulation	Structure and semi-structure	Pull data in batch mode daily or frequently	Daily or pre-set frequency batches	> 1 day	Medium	Automated and manual reconciliation	< 10 for each model	< 10 for each model
Text extraction bot	Structure and unstructured document and text	Pull data in batch mode daily or frequently	On-demand	> 1 day	Medium	Automated audit trail manual validation	Deployed for serving other applications	> 1 million for each bot
Q&A bot	Structure and un structure	Incremental data in real time	On-demand	< 5 s	Medium	Periodic manual validation and updation	On smart devices and social networks—very limited questions are replied	> 1 million for each bot

12.5.4.6   Reusable Internal and External 50 Banking Datasets

The key determinant of the accuracy of AI models is data. Banks leverage public data and consolidated data about the customer internally to improve the accuracy of models.

With the availability of cloud infrastructure with inbuilt scalability, banks establish data lakes and use data virtualisation and semantic technology. It also means managing domain-wise datasets.

Based on the experience of the author, the following is an incomplete list of 50 datasets used by banks.

Financial data	Customer financial transactions	Customer daily transactions
Accounting data	Daily Financial Transaction	Daily Non-financial Transaction
Daily GL transaction	Daily Financial Transaction of Customer	Daily Product-wise and Channel-wise Customer Onboarded
Daily aggregated financial transaction	Daily Interest Income Transaction of Customer	Daily Non-financial Transaction of Customer
Financial transaction to be reconciled	Daily Non-interest Financial Income Transaction of Customer	Daily Prospect Onboarding Application Data
Financial metrics	Daily Financial Transaction of Product	Daily Credit Underwriting Application Data
Risk measures	Daily Financial Transaction at Channel	Daily Product-wise and Channel-wise Customer Complaint Data
Capital and risk measures	Daily Customer Account Balance and Limits	Daily Customer's Counterparty Reference Data
Credit risk measures	Daily Product-wise Non-financial Transaction of Customer	Daily Customer Communication with a Bank
Market risk measures	Daily Channel-wise Non-financial Transaction of Customer	Daily Defaulted Customer Recovery Transaction
Liquidity measures		Customer Communication to a Bank and on Social Media
		RM Feedback on NBP Offering

Customer financials	Reference data	External datasets
Customer financials	Bank reference data	External datasets

(continued)

(continued)

Customer financials	Reference data	External datasets
Customer financial Statements	Branch reference data of bank	Customer financial statements
Customer collateral and guarantee valuation	GL structure of bank	Customer registration and other reference data
Customer account in Collection balance	Relationship manager Reference data of bank	Prospect financial statement
Customer portfolio Transaction, balances, and collaterals	ATM and PoS reference data	Prospect registration and other reference data
Customer financial and non-financial metrics for approval	Legal entity and foreign branch of bank reference data	Charges registered
	Correspondent bank	Negative and default data
	Bank's partners and merchant reference data	Director's, manager's, investor's, owner's reference data
	Bank employee reference Data	Customer electricity consumption
		Industry and sector data and financials
		Social network funnel

12.6   Building Banking Knowledge Organisation and Representation

Build an approach for:

- Knowledge acquisition;
- Documenting expert knowledge—knowledge webs;
- Knowledge centres.

Knowledge representation:

- Machine processable knowledge;
- Expert/fact directories/libraries;
- Manually built, semantics, ontology, and vocabularies;
- Catalogue of services, models;
- Heuristics, decision rules.

Knowledge validation:

- Analytics;

- Text analytics;
- Model validation;
- F score for accuracy, recall, and precision.

Knowledge verification:

- Validate algorithms, models;
- Testing.
    Knowledge sources:
- Internal and external ontology and dictionaries;
- Internal and external sources.

Knowledge acquisition:

- Crowd sourcing;
- Documenting expert knowledge—knowledge webs;
- Knowledge centres;
- Analytics, extraction.

Knowledge representation:

- Catalogue of services, models;
- Heuristics, decision rules.

Knowledge verification:

- Frequency of verification;
- Cross-validation;
- Validate algorithms, models;
- Testing.

12.6.1   Establish Knowledge Architect and Knowledge Engineer

Knowledge Architect (KA), architect robotics, and cognitive system:

- Reimagine business process to leverage RPA and cognitive computing;
- Design automated, auditable, and learning systems;
- Design intelligent applications that can use machine-processable knowledge and logic and make a decision with the minimal human intervention;
- Defines collection criteria for the training data for intelligent automation application and cognitive agents.

Knowledge Engineer (KE):

- Capture domain knowledge in a machine-processable format. Identify objects and the relationship among objects.

- Ensure data quality, relevance, and accuracy of knowledge dictionary built/updated and test/verify that dictionary supports the bank's business policy.
- Define semantics and ontology and ensure it supports the bank's business policy.
- Identify contents for knowledge extraction. Knowledge extracted will be used for training the system only after accuracy and relevancy checks.
- Backtest and stress test intelligent automation models.

12.7   Case Study: Fintech AI Use Cases

Fintechs are ahead of banks in technology exploitation. AI is one such area where fintechs have been quite successful. Studying and learning from AI use cases may be helpful.

The differentiating mark of a successful fintech is that it builds the domain knowledge into the technology. Success is directly proportional to the quality and depth of the banking knowledge built into the solution.

Unless banks build subject matter depth, the adoption of technology like conversational UI will be limited. This includes banking terms, banking products, banking product computation, banking intents, and banking sentences. We need to keep in mind that the subject matter expertise of bots works both ways. Depth in expertise grows and shortfall reduces the adoption exponentially.

AI techniques	Retail banking	Mid-market and corporate banking	Treasury and market risk
Enhanced predictive using machine and deep learning	Enhanced credit scoring models	Enhanced mid-market credit underwriting models	Robo advisors complying with suitability
	Real-time retail fraud detection	Enhanced fraud analytics	Monitoring real-time trade fraud
	Hyper personalisation for marketing and services	Intraday liquidity risk management	Trade risk management
	Cyber fraud detection with deep learning	Hyper personalisation for marketing and services	Optimise risks in portfolio management
Machine perception based on graph analytics NLP, chatbots, CPA, RPA	KYC, Sanction, AML—investigation	KYC, Sanction, AML—investigation	NLP based wealth management advisors
	Facial and voice-based biometrics for individual digital ID	Facial and voice-based biometrics for corporate accounts	Sentiment analytics and financial forecasting

(continued)

(continued)

AI techniques	Retail banking	Mid-market and corporate banking	Treasury and market risk
	Customer chatbots for fraud investigation, AML, and customer servicing	Virtual assistance for real-time information	Virtual agents to provide real-time information
	Reconciliation of product ledgers	Data quality: machine learning	Reconciliation of trade ledger

12.7.1 Robo-Advice

Robo-advice is leveraged by the entire financial services industry: banking, asset management, private banking, retirement, and insurance firms.

Robo-advisors are automated platforms that provide algorithm-driven financial and investment management advice, starting from the information collected from individuals. Using a combination of different technologies, robo-advice suggests possible investment solutions tailored to the expectation and needs of an investor. Robo advice leverages:

- Cognitive computing;
- Natural language processing;
- Machine-learning supervised and reinforced;
- Expert system algorithms.

Investment advice has attracted a series of conduct risk regulation across the globe. Therefore, the advice algorithm and customer experience have to be regulatory compliant. Some financial services firms and investors feel robotic advice is the best way to comply with regulatory conduct risk requirements.

12.7.2 Customer Complaints

Based on the current regulatory framework, credit or financial institutions have to offer a service for customers to send their complaints to. The bank is also required to solve customer complaints/claims within a specific timeframe. If customers are not satisfied with the response given to their complaint by the financial institution, they can appeal to national competent authorities (NCAs). This creates a scale issue as a large volume of data has to be processed (in a specific timeframe) to reply to a claim or complaint.

By using AI technologies (notably natural language processing), banks can automatically classify large volumes of unstructured text documents and categorise hundreds of thousands of queries into types and ensure they are routed to the right team for resolution. This allows for faster resolution of complaints, benefitting the consumer who made the complaints, the financial institution, and the national competent authority (both in case a claim is dealt with quickly and appropriately and thus not escalated, and also as NCAs can rely on these processes). Besides, it will also help financial institutions to ensure consistency in response to the same type of complaint, as well as making the auditability of the process easier than with traditional manual classification processes.

12.7.3   Credit Scoring

Credit scoring is not a new application to use models or machine learning models. Credit scoring was one of the first applications of statistical modelling in the banking sector.

Today, to measure the creditworthiness of their clients, banks rely on gathering transactional data, statistical analysis, decision trees, and regression to better estimate the borrower's credit risk and assess whether the borrower will be able to repay the credit.

Improving Credit Scoring Predictability by Leveraging Additional Data Sets

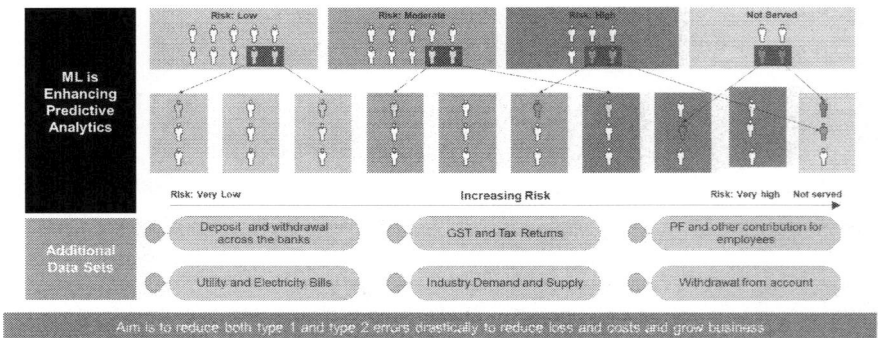

AI technology is used to enhance the accuracy of the credit scoring model and allows for improved access to credit by reducing the risks and the number of false positives and false negatives. Having a better credit scoring model (with better prediction) helps banks growing credit business by extending credit to borrowers who otherwise would have been refused.

It also helps for the better identification of potential defaults and thus refusing credit to those who otherwise would have extended their credit.

Better predictability is achieved by adding additional public datasets and internal datasets, including historical datasets for all rejection cases.

12.8 Conclusion: Banking AI as a Service is not a Technology Project

Embedding intelligence in a bank's technology should not be treated as a normal software project but should rather be treated like a business model disruption, the benefits of which are likely to accrue over a longer time horizon than a normal project horizon. AI should not be managed as a project but should be managed as a platform to get the necessary investment, effort, and attention. Building AI capability is an evolved process requiring strong domain knowledge coupled with cutting edge technology skills and associated skills like data science, modelling, and visualisation. Banks have experimented with different working models like partnerships with academic institutions, partnerships with fintechs, and getting talent from the academic world to build and run CoEs.

Making BAIaaS successful and commercially viable is a long journey since the technology industry has not invested in building banking intelligence into technology. Generic AI platforms provided by technology players need to be substantially upgraded and embedded with banking intelligence to get the business outcomes. A bank on a standalone basis or together with other banks needs to keep investing in AI for a long time. To provide 360-degree support to the AI initiative, banks are establishing AI CoEs.

Chapter 13
Fintech: The Innovation Benchmark

Fintechs are innovative companies that use new technology and have the potential to transform the business model of the financial sector. Fintechs hold the promise of spurring competition, providing sizeable efficiency gains and a larger and better choice for consumers, and enhancing financial inclusions. They have the potential to disrupt the business model of existing financial service firms.

Since 2013 or so, fintech has attempted to disrupt the financial services industry. Fintech is generally a point solution which within a short time disrupts the business and delivery model of a certain product market or a certain service or for a certain type of customer or in a certain market.

13.1 Fintech 1.0: Wakeup Call for the Banks (2014–2018)

Fintech disruption was more profound between 2014 and 2018. During this time, almost all banks had started their technology modernisation journey and were busy paying off their technology debt. During this period, some of the fintechs identified an opportunity or deficiencies in the offerings of established financial services firms and launched targeted product offerings in payment, retail credit, mortgage, and consumer offerings. Most of them either launched their products riding on the existing players or sought a suitable licence. All of them offered a point solution. Some of them have tasted success and have established themselves as a financial services firm.

13.1.1 Regulators Were in a Dilemma

Regulators in most jurisdiction were in a dilemma. Fintechs were offering financial inclusion, disruption in cost structures, and creating competition for the established players for the betterment of customers. However, regulators were in a dilemma as to

© Springer Nature Singapore Pte Ltd. 2022
M. Bhatia, *Banking 4.0*,
https://doi.org/10.1007/978-981-16-6069-6_13

how to deal with fintech. Regulators also were lacking the skills to engage fintech. To learn more about fintech modus operandi and to train its officers, leading regulators decided to engage fintech closely by establishing a sandbox.

13.2 Fintech 2.0: Challenger to the Banks (2016–2020)

By the time fintech wave 2 started in 2016, many banks advanced their digital journey, enhanced their technology infrastructure, upgraded their payment systems offerings, digitised customer engagement, established platform banking, and published APIs for integration with the marketplace. The real time or faster payment disruption in Europe and the USA, the mandate to comply with ISO 20022 requirements, the GDPR in Europe and the CCPA in the USA, and Brexit worked like additional catalysts to fasten the technology industrialisation journey at banks.

Financial firms have a regulatory licence, a large and loyal customer base, and a well-established distribution network: each of these is not easy to replicate by a technology fintech.

The net result is that the point solution which fintechs have has a lesser and lesser impact on the established financial services players.

In the second wave of fintech innovation, Fintech 2.0—a collaboration with banks—was the driver. Banks were themselves organising innovation and fintech conferences, providing early funding, conducting hackathons, and acquiring some of the fintech firms. Since AI and data science talent is scarce, with an AI-first strategy in every bank, banks had to promote, collaborate, and acquire AI and data science expert fintechs. A bank's approach also varies based on the idea and scarcity of skills:

- Innovation centres: inviting fintechs to collaborate and join banks;
- Setting up of AI CoEs by banks: some of them have done this by the acquisition of AI consulting firms;
- Fostering AI mentality.

13.2.1 Regulatory Sandbox: A Landmark Initiative Across the Jurisdiction

One of the landmark initiatives during this period was the creation of a regulatory sandbox by the UK's FCA in 2015. Since then, tens of regulators have started providing a regulatory sandbox. A regulatory sandbox for fintechs is a controlled testing environment in which they can try out their products on a limited set of customers under restricted authorisation; testing occurs under regulatory supervision. Fintechs receive advice to help them navigate through the complexities of regulation. Regulators also get opportunities to learn new technologies and business models.

13.2.2 Case Study: RBI Report of the Working Group on Fintech and Digital Banking

The Report was submitted in 2018. It aimed to get a deeper understanding of fintech products and their interaction with the financial sector. The Report identified three shades of regulation: (1) disclosures; (2) light touch regulation and supervision; (3) tight regulation and full-fledged supervision. It also tried to understand more about inherent risks in platform-based fintech business.

13.2.3 Digital Banks as an Extension of Fintechs to Regulated Banks

Digital banks are newly licensed banks in different regulatory jurisdictions to offer banking based on digital technologies, connectivity, and advanced data capabilities. Even if they are not fully on the Internet and mobiles, they have very few branches and no legacy IT systems. Digital banks are said to have a cost advantage over traditional banks. So, they have the technology of fintechs under the existing banking regulations. These are also called virtual-only or Internet-only banks or digital banks. In most jurisdictions, digital banks need to comply with ownership and control requirements and may be different from traditional banks.

Digital banks are subjected to very stringent technical requirements. Regulators have prescribed technology expertise for their boards and each bank has to obtain an independent third-party technical expert assessment for the adequacy and soundness of their IT governance and systems.

Every jurisdiction has prescribed a sound risk culture and risk governance framework, technology-related requirements, a fitness and proprietary test, and demonstrates a capability to meet customer obligations.

In some jurisdictions, they start with simplified regulation. On achievement of a certain asset size, banking regulations are applicable.

The regulator also considers internal control, frequency and type of compliance breaches, customer complaints, and sustainability of business performance.

13.3 Fintech 3.0: Partnering with Banks (2018–2022 Onwards)

In Chap. 8, we discussed the high cost to revenue ratio in low-interest-rate regimes. The interest rate has started moving downward even in Asian countries like China and India. The low-interest-rate regimen severely impacts the profitability of banks and financial services firms.

Besides, in every regulatory regime, financial assets are being severely impaired due to the economic slowdown caused by COVID lockdowns and the resulting moratoriums.

Amid severe stress on financial assets all around, to continue to maintain financial stability, the soft banking regulation for fintech is coming to an end in many of the regulatory regimes. Banking regulators are updating their regulatory frameworks to treat fintechs as regulated entities similar to existing financial services firms.

13.3.1   Fintechs as Technology Partners of Regulated Entities

This severely impacts on the flow of capital to the financial services industry. With scarce capital, the appetite to promote fintechs as financial services firms is going down. There may be a few success stories here and there of a fintech upgrading itself to become a financial services firm but, overall, fintechs are entering into business as a usual mode as technology partners of regulated entities.

13.3.2   Most of the Financial Services Firms Are Likely to Be a White Label in Their Offerings of Fintech Services and the Services of Other Financial Services Firms

The journey of Banking 4.0 is a long journey of investment and disruption. Not every bank has the requisite financial investment muscle and management bandwidth to travel alone on this journey. Considering the quantum of financial investment and management focus required for transforming a financial services firm into an industrialised entity, only 5–10% of financial services firms may be able to invest and transform on their own. The other 90–95% of financial services firms are likely to be at various stages of transformation during the next decade. Each will be at various stages of adoption and investment in digitisation. Their capabilities will vary widely across products and services, within a firm, across firms within the same jurisdiction, across the size of firms globally and different types within financial services regulation. To supplement and complement their offering, financial services firms are likely to use the services of fintechs and white label services of other financial services firms.

13.3.3   Provision of Business Outcome for Partner Banks Is Emerging as a Business Model for Technology Fintechs

The development of configurable and flexible technology infrastructure with APIs and microservices is opening up immense possibilities for the collaboration and outsourcing of parts of value chains, for a shorter time duration. In the white-labelled business model, fintechs and partner financial services firms are likely to partner and be compensated, based on business outcomes.

Going forward, fintechs need to build their value proposition beyond innovation and technology expertise. They have to enhance their offerings to the provision of business outcomes.

13.3.4   Fintechs Are Innovation Partners for Banks

COVID also had one unintentional positive impact on the journey towards industrialisation. Banks have greatly improved their delivery of a digital experience for their customers, partners, and employees. Banks have prioritised innovation, change, and investments in digital banking further. Therefore, fintechs seek partnership with banks as their innovative technology partners.

13.3.5   Disruptive Marketplaces Are Emerging as the Next Bed of Innovation

The primary source of disruption is promoting new and disruptive marketplaces. Players in the marketplace aim to grow stickiness for their services against the competition by promoting blockchain technology-based platforms, standardising contracts, providing and managing digital keys for the marketplace, and providing and managing digital identity for participants, though there may be some barriers to the competition. Fintech 3.0 is likely to disrupt the marketplace, blockchains, digital certificates and digital key and digital identify the area.

13.3.6   Banks Have a Shortage of AI Skills: AI Fintechs Are Likely to Get Better Traction

The entire financial services industry has an acute shortage of AI resources. AI fintech is likely to get better traction even from established financial services firms.

13.3.7   Case Study: Fintech Upgrading to Become a Financial Services Firm

- P2P fintechs, which started just as an information intermediary, have transformed themselves into lenders and wealth managers.
- Fintech lenders are also incurring huge credit loss in many markets, especially due to stress created by the COVID-led economic slowdown.
- Third-party payment fintechs expanded their services by providing investment services to online customers by offering a yield more than bank deposits and in the process greatly rattled banking deposits and asset management business. This was unregulated investment activity in any jurisdiction. Regulators are bringing investment services into the ambit of regulation.
- Regulators are discovering that digital lending fintech platforms have been over marketing loans and overdrafts and, when default occurs, they pursue coercive loan collection methods, causing social problems and unrest. This was possibly due to some scope of regulatory arbitrage for digital lending firms. Regulators in China and India are bringing digital lending platforms within the ambit of conduct risk, licensing, capital requirements, and disclosure.
- Data privacy is violated in many cases. Some of the fintech firms have used their customer data improperly. Regulators are of the view that some fintechs are improperly collecting, using, and have sold data without user consent and have seriously violated individual privacy.
- Many of the fintechs are not prepared for cybersecurity and cyber emergencies. Since they are closely integrated with the banking system, fintechs are exposing the entire financial system to cyber risk.
- Promotion of unfair market competition: with the advantage of data monopoly, big tech firms may be hindering fair competition. Regulators around the world have started consultations on regulating big tech data monopolies.
- Too big to fail has started appearing in the fintech market also. In most jurisdictions, and for most products, the market is dominated by a few fintechs. This attracts financial services regulations for too big to fail.
- Regulators in most jurisdictions have started consultations on establishing data rights. The lawful interest of all players is to be established and protected.
- Emerging regulation for cross-border data flow is becoming very important for fintechs since their cross-border operations are larger.

13.4 Fintech 4.0: Level Playing with the Industrialised Banks (2021–)

13.4.1 Fintechs Cannot Replace Banks, but They Will Make Banking Better

Banking runs on three pillars: capital, trust, and technology. Technology per se is not sufficient to run a banking business. Banks are the most trusted institutions in every economy: most trusted by their customers and regulators.

Fintechs excel in technology. To compete with banks, fintechs have to raise capital and earn trust. They also have to become regulated institutions with the requisite capital and trust of regulators. Some fintechs are likely to cross both barriers while most will end up as technology partners of banks. In either case, banking services will improve.

13.4.2 Developing AI/ML Models by Standalone Fintechs Will Be Challenging Going Forward

Banks have an advantage over fintechs in the development of AI/ML models, since they have access to their customer data. For fintechs, getting such data to build AI/ML models is very difficult, especially post-GDPR and similar privacy laws globally, laws on cross-border data transfer, and the emerging regulation of big tech firms.

13.4.3 Industrialised Banks Are Becoming Equipped to Compete with Fintechs Even at a Technology Level

Most of the established banks with asset sizes of USD50 billion and above have industrialisation on their technology roadmap. Some have started, some are at the midway.

Banks are investing to grow AI/ML adoption. Many have substantially reduced latency from their processes and have implemented real-time payments. Most have established innovation units and are seriously investing in paying off technical debt. In summary, established large and medium-size banks are not far off on innovation and capabilities compared to fintechs.

13.4.4   Regulators Are Establishing a Level Playing Field Between Traditional Financial Services Firms and Fintechs

Financial services regulators encourage innovation to meet the goals of consumer outcomes. To bring competition to the existing regulated financial services firms, and to bring down the cost of financial services for consumers, regulators have been encouraging and enabling fintech, regtech, and innovation.

To help fintechs to adopt innovative business models, regulators have established a sandbox where fintechs test their business model and get feedback from regulators. Getting feedback on the business model from a regulator is very different from complying with regulatory requirements for capital, conduct, licensing, and other compliance requirements.

A fintech converted to a financial services firm providing banking and payment services needs to comply with banking and payment regulations.

In every regulatory regime, at present, there are gaps in fintechs that have converted to financial services compliance requirements, especially for compliance with capital requirements, systemic risks, conduct risk, and data privacy.

Globally, a fintech regulatory framework has been adapted from the CFPB in the USA and the FCA in the UK. However, regulatory requirement realities are very different in the USA and the UK vs emerging economies. The USA and UK regulators have not included systemic risk, conduct, and privacy framework as a part of their fintech regulatory framework for the following reasons:

- In both these jurisdictions, pricing differentials for financially excluded consumers is very high. Therefore, regulators need to provide concessions and encouragement to fintechs.
- In both jurisdictions, there is a high prevalence of non-regulated players providing credit to consumers, therefore the unmet credit demand is not very high. Credit extended by fintechs are not so high as to create systemic risk for traditional financial services firms.
- In the UK and Europe, the payment system, privacy, and conduct risk regulatory framework is very strong. This framework applies to all non-financial entities. It is therefore applicable to fintech firms even without considering them as financial services firms.

However, in the rest of the world, regulators are waking up to the capital requirements, conduct risk, systemic risk requirements, and privacy requirements for fintech. This is likely to reshape the fintech business model, going forward.

13.4.5   Level Playing Regulation Case Study: Fintech Balance Sheet Lending

On the fintech firm side, regulators are seriously relooking at prescribing capital requirements, conduct rules, and consumer protection requirements for fintechs. This will create a more level playing field between established financial services firms and fintech firms.

A fintech balance sheet lender operates a digital and Internet platform for lending. There are five regulatory shades: (1) with a banking licence; (2) with a non-banking licence; (3) a money lender licence; (4) a non-banking financial intermediary; (5) an investment firm.

In some jurisdictions, fintechs can do lending business without any licence or registration. Regulators in some jurisdictions are establishing regulations very specific to fintech balance sheet lending.

13.4.6   Level Playing Regulation Case Study: Crowdfunding Platform

In all jurisdictions, crowdfunding requires registration and licence and/or authorisation. This licence comes with a mandate to manage conflict of interest and restrictions on investments. Crowdfunding platforms are also subjected to capital requirements. Regulators have also prescribed IT compliance requirements, consumer and investor protection, and disclosures to investors and borrowers. They are also restricted in dealing with certain activities.

Regulators are addressing fintech challenges and pain points. This will further fuel disruption.

Case studies from India and China are examples here.

13.4.7   Case Study: Emerging Regulatory Regimes in China for Fintechs in a Financial Service Business

The China Banking and Insurance Regulatory Commission and the People's Bank of China have established tighter rules for online microlenders, under which microloan companies are mandated to obtain an additional licence for an online micro-loan business to lend to borrowers online. The draft regulation also requires the CBIRC's approval for the companies to conduct online micro-loan business outside of the province in which they are registered. The draft regulation is also seen to reduce contagion risk by setting requirements on micro-loan companies' dealings with other institutions. Regulation has also prescribed capital requirements for the players so that only serious players are in business who can be held responsible and also manage contagion risk. Regulators have prescribed conduct rules very similar to banks.

13.4.8 Case Study: In India Digital Lending Is Being Brought Within the Ambit of Banking Regulation

Based on the various complaints received against digital lending in terms of excessive rates of interest and additional hidden charges, unacceptable recovery methods of recovery, data privacy, data selling, and misuse of KYC data, the Reserve Bank of India has set up a group to suggest changes in the regulation for digital lending fintechs and the digital lending activity of regulated entities. The focus of the group is to suggest changes in the regulation of digital lending, including through online application and mobile applications. This includes systemic risks posed by unregulated digital lending, measures to enhance consumer protection, data governance, data privacy, data security standards, and other regulatory parameters.

13.5 Conclusion: An Industrialised Bank Is Converging with Fintech

In the industrialisation journey, fintech started as a disrupter to the banking business model and competition to banks.

As banks started paying off technical debt and industrialising, fintechs' role is more matured and emerging as a partner, collaborator, and service provider.

Some fintechs have chosen to be financial services firms and are emerging as competition to banks. With the strengthening of regulatory regimes for fintechs as financial services firms, competition is on a level playing field with banks.

This level playing field is helping both banks and fintechs to mature and catalyse industrialisation at banks.

Further Reading Sources on the Web

Banks and Financial Services Firms

Analyst Reports, Annual Reports, CEO, and CTO interviews: 2015, 2016, 2017, 2018, 2019, 2020.

1. ANZ
2. Bank of America
3. Barclays
4. BBVA
5. Capital One Financial Corporation
6. Citigroup
7. Credit Suisse
8. DBS Group
9. HDFC Bank
10. HSBC
11. ICICI Bank
12. ING Group
13. JPMC
14. Lloyds Banking Group
15. Mashreq
16. National Australia Bank
17. Nedbank
18. OCBC Singapore
19. PNC Bank
20. Rabo Bank
21. Standard Chartered
22. State Bank of India
23. TD Bank
24. UBS Group AG
25. Wells Fargo.

© Springer Nature Singapore Pte Ltd. 2022
M. Bhatia, *Banking 4.0*,
https://doi.org/10.1007/978-981-16-6069-6

Fintechs, Digital Banks, Marketplace, APIs, and AI Firms

Analyst Reports, Annual Reports, CEO, and CTO interviews, Product Documentation, Blogs, Resources, Patents.

- https://kasisto.com/
- https://www.zeta.tech/in
- https://nubank.com.br/
- https://www.chainalysis.com/
- https://feedzai.com/
- https://databricks.com/
- https://www.celonis.com/
- https://paytm.com/
- https://www.rakuten-bank.co.jp/
- https://www.dbs.com.sg/personal/marketplace/
- https://www.sbiyono.sbi/index.html
- https://www.jpmorgan.com/onyx/liink
- https://www.coindesk.com/dbs-jpmorgan-and-temasek-to-create-blockchain-based-payments-joint-venture
- https://developer.rabobank.nl/api-documentation
- https://developer.nab.com.au/
- https://www.dbs.com/dbsdevelopers/index.html
- https://sandbox.developerhub.citi.com/us/home
- https://developer.jpmorgan.com/

Standards, Regulators, and Sandboxes

- https://www.bis.org/
- https://www.bian.org/
- https://www.iif.com/
- https://rbidocs.rbi.org.in/rdocs/PublicationReport/Pdfs/ENABLING79D8EBD31FED47A0BE21158C337123BF.PDF
- https://rbidocs.rbi.org.in/rdocs/PublicationReport/Pdfs/REGULATORYSANDBOX2333CA3224ED4B7991A2B55DBEFDA745.PDF
- https://rbidocs.rbi.org.in/rdocs/PublicationReport/Pdfs/ANALYSISQRCODED11971A9B9874EAFA1A61478F461E238.PDF
- https://rbidocs.rbi.org.in/rdocs/PublicationReport/Pdfs/CDDP03062019634B0EEF3F7144C3B65360B280E420AC.PDF
- https://rbidocs.rbi.org.in/rdocs/PublicationReport/Pdfs/WGFR68AA1890D7334D8F8F72CC2399A27F4A.PDF
- https://rbidocs.rbi.org.in/rdocs/PublicationReport/Pdfs/PCRRR09CF7539AC3E48C9B69112AF2A498EFD.PDF
- https://www.hkma.gov.hk/eng/key-functions/banking/banking-regulatory-and-supervisory-regime/virtual-banks/
- https://www.mas.gov.sg/development/fintech

- https://www.bnm.gov.my/-/launch-of-the-fintech-booster-programme
- https://www.eba.europa.eu/financial-innovation-and-fintech
- https://www.fca.org.uk/firms/innovation/regulatory-sandbox
- https://www.bankofengland.co.uk/research/fintech
- https://www.occ.treas.gov/topics/supervision-and-examination/responsible-innovation/index-responsible-innovation.html
- https://www.consumerfinance.gov/rules-policy/innovation/
- https://www.ecb.europa.eu/home/search/html/innovation.en.html
- https://www.eba.europa.eu/financial-innovation-and-consumer-protection
- https://www.rba.gov.au/publications/submissions/payments-system/financial-and-regulatory-technology/
- https://www.mas.gov.sg/development/fintech/regulatory-sandbox
- https://www.iso20022.org/

Bigtech and AI/ ML

- https://cloud.google.com/products/ai
- https://azure.microsoft.com/en-in/overview/ai-platform/
- https://aws.amazon.com/ai/
- https://www.ibm.com/in-en/it-infrastructure/solutions/ai?p1=Search&p4=43700052660399439&p5=b&gclid=EAIaIQobChMIpLvD8ZWA8QIVVDErCh0-bwAFEAAYASAAEgLWC_D_BwE&gclsrc=aw.ds
- https://www.lendacademy.com/wp-content/uploads/2019/02/Podcast-188-Zor-Gorelov.pdf
- https://www.pega.com/system/files/resources/2019-05/mit-cisr-digital-transformation-dbs.pdf
- https://www.idrbt.ac.in/assets/publications/Journals/Volume_02/No_02/Chapter_02.pdf
- https://newsroom.bankofamerica.com/print/pdf/node/9289
- https://docs.aws.amazon.com/lex/latest/dg/lex-dg.pdf
- https://www.fca.org.uk/news/speeches/robo-advice-fca-perspective
- https://www.fca.org.uk/firms/innovation/advice-unit-rules-guidance
- https://www.tableau.com/resources
- https://www.salesforce.com/in/resources/
- https://resources.snowflake.com/
- https://info.looker.com/analyst-reports
- https://www.h2o.ai/

Consulting

- https://www.mckinsey.com/industries/financial-services/our-insights/banking-matters
- https://www.weforum.org/agenda/archive/banking-and-capital-markets/
- https://www2.deloitte.com/in/en/pages/financial-services/topics/banking-capital-markets.html
- https://www.pwc.com/gx/en/industries/financial-services/banking-capital-markets.html

Printed in Great Britain
by Amazon

49765763R00192